NOBLE SUBJECTS

NOBLE SUBJECTS

THE RUSSIAN NOVEL

—— *and the* ——

GENTRY, 1762–1861

BELLA GRIGORYAN

STUDIES OF THE HARRIMAN INSTITUTE

NIU PRESS / DEKALB IL

Northern Illinois University Press, DeKalb 60115
© 2018 by Northern Illinois University Press
All rights reserved
Printed in the United States of America
27 26 25 24 23 22 21 20 19 18   1 2 3 4 5
978-0-87580-774-4 (paper)
978-1-60909-232-0 (e-book)
Book and cover design by Yuni Dorr

Library of Congress Cataloging-in-Publication Data is available online at http://catalog.loc.gov

Studies of the Harriman Institute
The Harriman Institute, Columbia University, sponsors the Studies of the Harriman Institute in
the belief that their publication contributes to scholarly research and public understanding. In this
way the Institute, while not necessarily endorsing their conclusions, is pleased to make available the
results of some of the research conducted under its auspices.

Publication of this work was made possible, in part, by a grant from the Harriman Institute,
Columbia University.

Contents

Acknowledgments

This book began as a doctoral dissertation in the Department of Slavic Languages at Columbia University, where I benefited enormously from the unflagging support and superb intellectual mentoring of Irina Reyfman. Robert Belknap, Eileen Gillooly, Cathy Popkin, and Richard Wortman provided exceedingly useful suggestions on my earliest mature draft.

A summer grant from the Department of Slavic Languages at Columbia enabled me to travel to Russia to conduct the first round of research. Junior fellowships at the Harriman Institute at Columbia supported the writing of the dissertation. Two grants for participation in the Summer Research Laboratory on Russia, Eastern Europe, and Eurasia at the University of Illinois at Urbana-Champaign provided a robustly administered setting for focused and efficient study of Russian imperial public discourse. A Yale University Morse Junior Faculty Fellowship supported additional research and writing.

My colleagues in the Department of Slavic Languages and Literatures at Yale—Vladimir Alexandrov, Marijeta Bozovic, Molly Brunson, Katerina Clark, Harvey Goldblatt, and John MacKay—were thoroughly encouraging and insightful interlocutors on every front; all of them have either read or heard (or both) a portion of this book, and each of them has shared ideas that have made a mark on the final product. Molly Brunson and Marijeta Bozovic deserve particular mention for always being at the ready to act as sounding boards, taskmasters, and so much more. As I was finishing revisions, Katherine Pickering Antonova, Marijeta Bozovic, Anne Lounsbery, and Ronald Meyer read portions of the manuscript and provided invaluable suggestions. Over the years this book has been shaped in ways big and small by conversations with Katherine Pickering Antonova, Julie Buckler, Paul Bushkovitch, Melissa Frazier, Hilde Hoogenboom, Valentina Izmirlieva, Liza Knapp, Anne Lounsbery, Catharine Theimer Nepomnyashchy, Thomas Newlin, Douglas Rogers, Nancy Ruttenburg, Sasha Senderovich, Vadim Shneyder, Susan Smith-Peter, Tatiana Smoliarova, Valeria Sobol,

Alan Timberlake, and William Mills Todd III. As I was completing the final stages of work on this project, Linda Gerstein, Timothy Harte, Marina Rojavin, Jesse Stavis, and Irina Walsh welcomed me warmly to the Department of Russian at Bryn Mawr College.

Each of the three anonymous manuscript reviewers engaged by the Harriman Institute and Northern Illinois University Press made excellent and perceptive suggestions, and Christine Worobec, the series editor at Northern Illinois University Press, shared some vitally useful comments at just the right moment—all four of them deserve my many thanks. I am grateful to everyone at Northern Illinois University Press; Amy Farranto's and Nathan Holmes's professionalism, expertise, and efficiency were a particular boon. I owe a great debt of gratitude to Ronald Meyer who, in his capacity as publications editor of the Studies of the Harriman Institute, provided a steady stream of sound guidance, perceptive critique, and encouragement at every stage.

Ingrid Nordgaard's superlative assistance with research accomplished something surprising: it warmed me to the use of spreadsheets. The graduate students in my courses on the Russian eighteenth century, on the bildungsroman, on romanticism, and on Pushkin and Gogol, have consistently enlivened my thinking with their observations and queries.

I am grateful to the Novoe Literaturnoe Obozrenie publishing house for granting permission to reproduce a substantially reworked version of an article that appeared in Russian as "'Figura blednaia, neiasnaia': Obraz pomeshchika v romanakh I. A. Goncharova" ("A pale, unclear figure": The representation of the landowner in the novels of I. A. Goncharov), in *Novoe literaturnoe obozrenie* 106 (December 2010): 117–29.

Note on Transliteration and Translation

When transliterating from Russian to English, I have used the Library of Congress system with occasional modifications when dealing with names of persons and places that will be familiar to Anglophone readers. Therefore, for example, I write Tolstoy instead of Tolstoi, Petersburg instead of Peterburg, and Ilya instead of Il'ia. Throughout the notes and bibliography, I have adhered strictly to the Library of Congress transliteration standards.

Unless indicated otherwise, all translations are mine.

NOBLE SUBJECTS

Noble Subjects and Citizens

I n March of 1847 a young Lev Tolstoy began to keep a journal while being treated for venereal disease at the Kazan University infirmary. As would remain his habit in the years to come, he documented his disappointment with his own behavior to date and hoped earnestly that he might learn to live better. The eighteen-year-old count, who would soon leave university due to lack of academic progress, had been assigned by his history professor a comparative study of Catherine II's *Instruction* (*Nakaz*)[1] to the Legislative Commission of 1767 and one of its sources, Montesquieu's *The Spirit of the Laws* (1748). In what now reads as a classically Tolstoyan attempt to live according to new rules of his own making, the young diarist records: "I was reading Catherine's *Instruction*, and since I gave myself the general rule that while reading any serious work I must reflect upon it and excerpt the remarkable ideas, I am writing here my opinion of the first six chapters of this remarkable work."[2] Thanks to his resolve to continue with the plan for self-improvement, Tolstoy produced an almost systematic commentary to the *Instruction*, summarizing what he took to be its most significant points and pausing periodically to express appreciation or disagreement. In Tolstoy's view, the *Instruction* did more to bring fame to its author than it did to transform Russian society. Addressed to the Legislative Commission that was called to but never did draft a coherent legal framework for her empire, Catherine's *Instruction* bears clear traces of its intellectual context (the Enlightenment) in its utopic articulation of the relations that might obtain between the polity and its subjects.

One set of such relations—those between the nobility and the state—underwent a dynamic transformation during the roughly one-hundred-year period that encompasses the entirety of Catherine II's reign (1762–1796) and ends with the ascension of Alexander II in 1855 and the Great Reforms of the 1860s. The century framed by 1762 and 1861 also saw the gradual appearance of a novelistic tradition that, by the early decades of the nineteenth century, tended to depict the Russian social worlds of its day.[3] To chart and interpret the rise of the Russian novel in relation to the political, legal, and cultural definitions that accrued to the nobility as a social estate (in Russian, *soslovie*) is the principal aim of this investigation.[4] The title of the introduction is intended to signal the interplay between subject and citizen as conceptual categories operative in the formation and successive iterations of the nobility. During much of the period covered by this study, Russian nobles had something approaching the rights of citizens expressed in legal discourse, but they remained subjects of an autocratic polity that systematically denied citizenship to *all* of its inhabitants. The culture and politics of the peculiar condition of subject-citizenship became novelized, were reflected in, and cohered into a nexus of both thematic and formal preoccupations that remained salient for the Russian novelistic canon throughout the first half of the nineteenth century. While I do not seek to identify a set of singular or exclusive cultural or formal origins of the genre,[5] in the chapters that follow I foreground the question of noble identity as a crucial preoccupation of the Russian novel. To this end, I begin by considering what I take to be a set of eighteenth-century pre-novelistic texts and devote the majority of the study to detailed readings of works by Alexander Pushkin, Faddei Bulgarin, Nikolai Gogol, Ivan Goncharov, Sergei Aksakov, and Lev Tolstoy.[6]

Despite his reputation as a notoriously poor university student, Tolstoy seems to have enjoyed his work with Catherine's *Instruction*. According to early biographers and Tolstoy's own recollections, he devoted so much energy to this project that he neglected the rest of his studies.[7] In his commentary Tolstoy sounds sympathetic to the republican spirit that permeates the empress's undertaking. However, he faults her for not going far enough, for falling short of a republican ideal and continuing to rule as an absolutist monarch. Throughout the *Instruction,* Tolstoy glimpses a pervasive contradiction in the empress's acknowledgment of the necessity (and eventual inevitability) of constitutional government and her uncurbed, "vain" desire to be the unrestricted autocrat of Russia (46:11). When in a discussion of Catherine's plans regarding a reform of legal procedures, he asks, "Can the security of citizens under the protection of laws exist in a place where not only court decisions but even the laws change according to the arbitrary actions of the autocrat?" Tolstoy acknowledges the condition of all Russian imperial subjects as persons whose rights depend almost wholly on the will of the current ruler (46:12). Nevertheless, the fact that what Tolstoy calls the "security of citizens under the protection of laws" warrants a good deal of discussion suggests the presence of a hybrid political culture of subject-citizenship, a circumstance that had a determinative role in framing the representation of the nobility in Russian public discourse both during and following Catherine's reign.

Tolstoy turns with particular (and unsurprising) verve to his own social estate: the nobility. He focuses on the insecurity of noble status and the instability of noble rights. Should one's status as a nobleman be inalienable or should those who commit crimes against the Crown be stripped of both title and property? Tolstoy agrees with Catherine's suggestion that no one should be able to "divest a nobleman of his nobility if he is worthy of that title" (46:22). However, just what the phrase "worthy of that title" might entail promises to complicate matters both for Tolstoy and for a host of other writers who considered the question. Whether nobility is an innate and immutable characteristic present at birth or a set of qualities to cultivate and to perform will inflect the representation of the Russian nobleman in public discourse throughout the period under study. In a discussion of noble rights, Tolstoy asks whether members of the gentry should engage in trade. The young student points out that

> If we had an Aristocracy that acted as a check on the Monarch, then indeed it [the aristocracy] would have a great deal to do even without trade. But we do not have one. Our Aristocracy of birth is disappearing and has already almost disappeared due to poverty; and this poverty resulted from nobles being ashamed to engage in trade. God grant that in our time the nobles understand their high purpose, which consists solely in their [the nobility] becoming stronger. (46:21)

The possibility that nobles might turn to commerce had begun to gain relevance in the Russian context with Denis Fonvizin's *The Trading Nobility* (*Torguiushchee dvorianstvo*, 1766),[8] a translation of Gabriel François Coyer's *La noblesse commerçante* (1756), and Johann Heinrich Gottlob von Justi's commentary to the same, texts produced in the course of a European debate about noble participation in commerce that took place at the start of the Seven Years' War.[9] In Russia the topic would gain increased urgency in the decades to come, especially after Catherine II outlined a set of noble rights to industrious enterprise in 1782, granting landowners extensive entrepreneurial control over nearly every aspect of their properties, especially natural resources. Taken in a cultural as opposed to a strictly legal or political key, the idea of nobles engaging in trade as true industrialists, however, would retain something of an air of impropriety for a long time.[10] Ambivalence about noble enterprise found ample expression in literature, including some of the texts treated in the pages and chapters to come. To give one example: as Tolstoy wrote these diary entries, Ivan Goncharov was in the process of publishing *A Common Story* (1847), a novel about Petersburg nobles who own, manage, and profit from a lucrative factory. And yet Goncharov's depiction of the Aduevs turns, at every step, upon the contrast between two conflicting and, in a sense, mutually supplementary, iterations of noble behavior: the active, industrious, almost bourgeois activities of the elder Aduev and the emphatic idleness of the noble dilettante embodied by his nephew. The contrast between the noble entrepreneur and the shiftless dilettante remains unresolved, much as, arguably, it animates Goncharov's entire novelistic oeuvre.

Tolstoy's endorsement of trade as a route to prosperity for members of any social estate would wane considerably as he began (quite early in his career) to advocate robustly for agriculture as the prime and perhaps only wholesome occupation for noble and peasant alike. However, his observations in 1847 encapsulate one of the central tensions in the late eighteenth- and nineteenth-century reconfiguration of noble identity as either a check on the political power of the monarchy or an estate of potential industrialists; the latter, should it develop, threatening to morph into an haute bourgeoisie. If the aristocracy could not act as a check against what would remain the unrestricted rule of an autocrat until the twentieth century, what shape should this part of the citizenry take? What rights or privileges and what duties should the empire's first citizens have vis-à-vis the state and in relation to their property, both human and immovable? Catherine II had answered these and similar questions in only a cursory manner in 1767; she would return to them later in her reign, in a more mature political document, the 1785 Charter to the Nobility, which will be discussed at some length in the pages below.

While reading the *Instruction*, Tolstoy reports the beginnings of a "passion for learning" (*strast' k naukam*), a growing taste for the life of the mind that prompted him to leave university in order to, as he explained it, devote his time more fully to intellectual pursuits (46:7). Once at his ancestral estate of Yasnaya Polyana, Tolstoy would also devote himself to another, more prosaic occupation, living as a country squire, and attempting to fulfill the obligations of his social estate and to reframe repeatedly and in various kinds of writing, both fictional and not, the multiple forms that noble privileges and obligations may take.[11] In the 1850s Tolstoy worked on two large-scale prose compositions, *Childhood, Boyhood, Youth* and what became the novelistic fragment *A Landowner's Morning*.[12] For a long time the latter work bore the title *Novel of the Russian Landowner* (*Roman russkogo pomeshchika*), a fitting description for a text centered around the young Prince Nekhliudov's efforts to become a good manager of his property and a source of assistance to his serfs. Tolstoy considered this text decidedly more important than his other attempts at fiction.[13] He describes his plans for this "novel with a purpose" as follows: "I shall give an account of the evil of [the Russian?] government and if I find it satisfactory, then I shall devote the remainder of my life to working out a plan for an aristocratic, electoral system of government joined with a monarchic system, on the basis of existing alternatives. Here is an aim for a virtuous life"[14] (46:137). As is frequently the case with personal diary records, Tolstoy's formulations here are rather vague and, as a result, the plan for an aristocratic electoral government linked to the autocracy is far from clearly expressed. I would highlight the interest in aristocratic participation in politics, not because it will remain an important feature of Tolstoy's artistic worldview (readers of *Anna Karenina* will recall the highly skeptical treatment of the noble assemblies, for example), but for its historical roots in Catherine's reshaping of the nobility as a political corporate body, a topic that will be treated in the pages to come. For the purposes of the present discussion, it may well be that the closest Tolstoy comes to articulating a political vision in *A Landowner's Morning* is to be found in Prince Nekhliudov's epistolary declaration, addressed to his aunt: "I have made a decision that will affect all the rest of my life. I am leaving the university so as to devote myself to life in the country. [...] Is it not my sacred and immediate duty to concern myself with the happiness of these seven hundred people [serfs] for whom I shall answer to God?" (4:123). By the early 1850s this idea—that the landlord has a sacred duty to his serfs—had an almost one-hundred-year pedigree, the outlines of which the rest of this study will trace. To historicize various aspects of Tolstoy's work, to explain them as not just "Tolstoyan" (read: protean, strange), but also as all but determined by Russian imperial cultural and political history is among the aims of this book.

So let us return to Tolstoy reading Catherine II at the hospital one last time. Concurrently with his commentary to the *Instruction,* the young man began to compile sets of his own instructions addressed to himself. This was the start of what looks like an exhaustingly systematic attempt to transform himself—his habits, behavior, and inclinations—through a rigorously detailed system for living, a discursive enterprise that Irina Paperno calls a "utopia of himself: his own personal *Instruction*."[15] Be it the desire to improve his abilities in such subjects as music, geometry, and English, or the drive to curb his gambling and limit the number of his trips to the brothel, Tolstoy's diaries and notebooks abound with plans and schedules, lists of tasks accomplished and not, catalogues of small successes and equally small (but still disheartening) failures, kinds of writing that seek to monitor and structure daily life in detail and hold the promise of a better future self. Arguably, such a mode of behavior—especially the faith in a rational system of self-improvement—belongs to the eighteenth century as much as, if not more than, it does to Tolstoy's own historical moment. More generally, Tolstoy's sensibilities as a young man in the 1840s (and, to some extent, beyond) share more with the late eighteenth century than they do with the romantics; as Boris Eikhenbaum put it, "it is as if Tolstoy has no connection with the previous generation—as if he decisively turns his back on the fathers and returns to the granddads."[16] I would add that this return to the eighteenth-century "granddads" is particularly palpable in Tolstoy's thinking about the nobleman as a social and political animal, a subject and a potential citizen who, in the novelist's artistic imagination, is shaped by the long aftermath of Catherine's large-scale and multivalent reorientation of noble identity, to an account of which I turn in the pages below.

This study draws on and endeavors to contribute to the growing body of work (the overwhelming majority of it produced by historians)[17] that has challenged the belief that autocratic Russia lacked a civil society. Contrary to the expectations that students of Western European polities may hold, in Russia the functioning of civil society tended not to endorse or presume an oppositional orientation vis-à-vis the polity. Instead, the institutional cores of Russian civil society—sites of sociability ranging from the press to the gentlemen's club—were more likely to be semiautonomous spheres of activity fostered by or working in concert with the state. By the last third of the eighteenth century, the Russian state under Catherine II's rule could be said to encourage actively, if cautiously, the formation of institutions and conditions analogous to those that enabled the rise of a politically powerful public sphere in some of the states west of Russia.[18] These institutions and conditions included an increasingly lively press and a growing readership,[19] the rise of voluntary associations, the prominence of cultural forms (for example, the newspaper and the novel) that enable and sustain the formation of modern political subjects, and, perhaps most important of all, the appearance of legal measures that promised to secure inalienable rights to specific groups within the empire. To be sure, all of these conditions were heavily, almost entirely, dependent on the wishes of the current monarch. In the absence of a constitution, nothing could be guaranteed when it came to the relationship between the state and its subjects.[20] Nevertheless, or perhaps precisely because of the volatile status of the subject-citizen endowed with rights, Russian literature of the period under study (1762–1861) processes quite actively such concepts as subject, citizen, public, privileges or rights, and obligations as they pertain to the nobility. I should make clear here that when I use such language as "civil society," "public," or "citizen," I do not aspire to make the claims of a historian, except in the limited sense of providing a historicized sociology of cultural forms, above all the novel.[21]

Ian Watt's classic account of the rise of the English novel posits the primacy of a middle class among other sociological conditions that precipitated the emergence of the genre.[22] Since Watt, the French and English novelistic traditions have been studied in relation to a sociopolitical reality marked by the ascendancy of the bourgeoisie or the middle class.[23] Russia lacked such a demographic category at least until the concluding decades of the nineteenth century.[24] More than any other Western cultural tradition contemporary to it, the Russian novelistic canon of the nineteenth century took the *gentry* as its prime object of representation and interest. I suggest that one way to account for the frequently avowed peculiarity of the Russian novel—a divergent strangeness discerned when it is placed in the company of Western European contemporaries—is to study the novelistic canon in relation to the history of the nobility in Russia.

Until the end of the imperial period, social estates retained a hold on the ways in which Russian society was organized in the legal and, to a considerable extent, the cultural sense.[25] From the state's point of view, the primary utility of estate designations had to do with differences in rights afforded to the nobility, clergy, merchants, townspeople, and peasants.[26] It was through the mediating system of estates that the polity granted privileges and imposed obligations. The historical scholarship on the constitution of Russian civil society—people who, for example, might act as correspondents with press organs both local and national, write and disseminate local histories, or take part in a voluntary association—continues to suggest a more diverse and complexly varied public than previously imagined.[27] In other words, people of various ranks, estates, and conditions—merchants, clergy, nobles, free peasants, townspersons—comprised the Russian public. However, the nobility occupies a position of especial interest as the estate with by far the most rights articulated in legal discourse; these were rights that were the nobility's both to have and to lose.[28]

Isabel de Madariaga begins her historical overview of what she calls "civil rights" in Russia with the Constitutional Crisis of 1730 that accompanied Anna Ioannovna's accession to the throne following the succession crisis that was precipitated by the sudden death of Peter II.[29] Anna had been selected by the Supreme Privy Council, a small body comprised primarily of the noble elite, which then "took the radical step of issuing a set of conditions under which the new empress would rule."[30] Among the limits that were to be placed on the autocrat were the curtailment of her right to declare war, impose new taxes, and deprive members of the nobility of their life, honor, and property without trial. As Valerie Kivelson puts it, "the conditions would have created a limited monarchy under the authority of the Supreme Privy Council."[31] However, because the conditions had been written up by a small group of men who belonged to the noble elite, other members of the nobility regarded the gesture as an attempt to establish an oligarchy. Thus, shortly after ascending the throne, the empress was urged to resume the exercise of absolute autocracy. Anna Ioannovna indicated her compliance by publicly ripping up a copy of the conditions. De Madariaga maintains that the ideas of 1730—the desire for inviolable rights to property and life, as well as immunity from corporal punishment and arrest without trial—survived in private transmission among the noble elite and were discussed at the Legislative Commission of 1754–1762, convened by the Empress Elizaveta Petrovna.[32] It is import-ant that both at these early moments and later in the eighteenth century, civil rights were conceived not as individual privileges but as something attached to the social estate as a whole.

Because the Russian Empire would not have a constitution until 1906 (although Alexander I came close to supplying one, he never did), it would not overstate matters to propose that a set of legal documents produced during Catherine II's reign was effectively the closest thing to a Russian constitution during the period under study. These documents would include her *Instruction*, which, according to Alexander Turgenev, fostered "a sincere respect for the freedom of the citizen, elevated feelings about his honor and defense, with the inviolable right of person and property," as well as the empress's subsequent legislative activity.[33] The Statute on Pro-vincial Administration of 1775, which the Catherinean statesman Jacob Johann Sievers called "the new constitution,"[34] created rural administrative units and promoted the development of such local institutions as a new judiciary and a new police, as well as bureaus of social welfare that were to establish provincial schools, hospitals, and poorhouses. Members of pro-vincial society were invited to participate in local administration, assum-ing roles that were understood to accord with their social estates. Nobles were given the right to choose local officials. The 1775 reform of the prov-inces paved the way for the Charters to the Nobility and the Towns of 1785, which gave fuller expression to the rights and obligations that Catherine's reign had been attempting to cultivate among the polity's subjects.

David Griffiths evaluates the 1785 Charters as a kind of constitution of the ancien régime. It should be noted that these documents did not guarantee rights in an absolute sense; at this time the term *constitution* meant "nothing more than the way in which something is established, organized or structured."[35] On the one hand, Catherine's Charter to the Nobility granted a broad range of legal privileges, including the right to trial by peers, freedom from corporal punishment, and various forms of control over property.[36] On the other hand, although the rights were to be possessed by the nobility permanently (*na vechnye vremena*), Catherine's son and successor, Paul I, essentially undid his mother's legislation. And although her grandson Alexander I restored much of what Paul I had undone, it is scarcely possible to speak about the rights articulated in the Charter as permanent or entirely inalienable.[37] Moreover, much as the Charter to the Nobility has been understood (aptly) as "one of the most consequential legislative acts in Russian history,"[38] in large part because it sought to secure the rights of a group of citizens, it should still be pointed out that as they were expressed in the language of the Charter, noble rights and noble status were understood as fundamentally *conditional*. As Brenda Meehan-Waters puts it,

> a careful reading of the Charter to the Nobility reveals a fundamental inse-
> curity of noble status in Russia. Few noblemen, if any, believed in the abso-
> lute inalienability of noble status. [. . .] Thus, nobility was as much a matter
> of achievement as of heredity, a matter of acting rather than of being. And
> for this reason [. . .] the idea persisted in the minds of nobles as well as
> the Sovereign, that nobles could lose their nobility for acts contrary to the
> dignity of a nobleman. The phenomenon of derogation was not, of course,
> limited to Russia, but what is noticeable in the Russian case, as expressed
> in Catherine's Charter to the Nobility, is the broad legal basis for loss of
> nobility.[39]

I cite Meehan-Waters's incisive commentary at some length, because the chapters that follow will trace the ways in which a broad range of texts both registered and responded to the insecurity of noble rights and noble status. The precarious character of legally sanctioned rights notwith-standing, Catherine's reign—and its legislative centerpiece, the Charters of 1785—radically reorganized the Russian imperial imaginary with the *possibility* of citizenship as the condition of having rights articulated in legal discourse. It is the main contention of this book that the nobleman, in his capacity as a landowner, came to embody both the aspirations and especially the anxieties associated with this shift in the empire's conceptual landscape. His right to own property would become the most active site for the evaluation of an incomplete, imperfect, and still inchoate *Rechtsstaat*, a polity defined, rather unstably, by the rule of law.[40]

The Russian nobility's control of property has a complicated history over which it is worth pausing for a moment here. In the words of Iurii Lotman, "the land had to serve" when it came to the Muscovite gentry's rights to occupy, not own, immovable property.[41] These pre-Petrine "conditional landowners" were a somewhat motley group of servitors who contributed to the state primarily in a military capacity.[42] In exchange for their service, the polity "placed" (*pomeshchali*) them on a piece of land; the family's right to use this land was contingent on having at least one male relative active in the armed forces.[43] The first emperor's attempts to reform what had been various kinds of *sluzhilye liudi*, or "people who serve," into a more organized corporate body amplified the link between male gentry identity and service.[44] Throughout this study I use the words "nobility" and "gentry" interchangeably, because when applied to Russia, these designations do not each refer to their own fixed, internally coherent or homogeneous populations.[45] Thus, there is no direct correspondence between such Russian terms as *shliakhtich* or *dvorianin* and the English "gentryman" or "nobleman." Both "gentry" and "nobility" provide an adequate if imperfect translation of the Russian *dvorianstvo*, the term used to refer to the emphatically new form the social estate took in the aftermath of Peter the Great's redefinition of it. The reformer tsar effectively collapsed the distinctions between previously varied elites into one heterogeneous estate. Members of this new state-generated aggregate upper class were united demographically by the shared requirement to serve the state in a civil or military capacity or at the imperial court. That the *dvorianstvo* could be entered through service was another Petrine innovation. The introduction of the Table of Ranks in 1722 made it possible for enterprising persons to attain noble status, thereby rendering the estate (*soslovie*) still more diffuse, inasmuch as its boundaries were legally defined as permeable.[46] The connection between gentry identity and state service persisted throughout the imperial period, following legal measures that granted the nobility freedom from obligatory state service and what came eventually to approach inalienable property rights. Moreover, due to cultural norms, for virtually the entire period covered by this study an adult man of noble birth could scarcely maintain respectability without ever serving the state at least for some years in some capacity.

On February 18, 1762, during his very short reign, Peter III issued a manifesto giving Russian noblemen the legal right to abstain from previously obligatory state service. The manifesto was not without precedent. Beginning in 1727, the state allowed some gentrymen to leave service in order to bring their domestic affairs into order. In 1736, one son per noble household gained the right not to serve in the army so that he might devote himself to estate administration. Retirement following twenty-five years of service became available in the same year. In 1746, the gentry gained a monopoly on the right to own populated land and serfs. The impact of the 1762 manifesto has been explained in many different ways. How broad was the phenomenon of noble retirement? How significant was the exodus to the countryside? How did retired noblemen pass their days? Historians differ on all of these points, but agree that private life in the eighteenth century remains understudied.[47] Both the origins and the aftermath of the manifesto have received multiple, at times conflicting, interpretations.[48] Was the manifesto the first sign of a large-scale mandate that permitted the nobility a private existence as permanent landowners increasingly secure in their control of property? Or, conversely, did the state, having cultivated a sufficiently large and capable workforce, abandon the nobles once they were no longer needed to carry out the empire's military and bureaucratic operations? These are far from mutually exclusive points of view. In fact, both the origins and the implementation of the 1762 manifesto are perhaps best understood to have issued from a complex network of factors.

The language of the manifesto itself is useful to consider, particularly as it gave expression to the fear that the newly liberated nobility might pass their time in "laziness and idleness" (*v lenosti i prazdnosti*). The royal decree had urged that such persons be shunned, "held in contempt and exterminated" (*prezirat' i unichtozhat'*).[49] Many, if not all, of the texts examined in this study may be viewed with some profit as responses to various iterations of this anxiety. In nineteenth-century historian Vasilii Kliuchevskii's seminal treatment of the subject, the so-called liberation of the gentry had resulted in an important imbalance. If previously, the "service nobility" (he uses the Petrine *sluzhilye liudi*) had compensated the polity for its privileges—including the right to own serfs—with considerable service obligations, the waning significance of such responsibilities during Catherine II's reign resulted in the decreasing legitimacy of the gentry's status, power, and lifestyle. In Kliuchevskii's account, the newly retired nobleman became, in essence, superfluous. The gentry had earned their privileges, including the right to profit from serf labor, through service; now they retained these rights without compensating the state for them.[50] Of these privileges, the non-serving nobleman's right to own serfs was the most problematic from a moral standpoint. Alexander Sumarokov's 1771 satire "On Nobility" ("O blagorodstve") phrased the problem thus: "Are we gentrymen so that the serfs work, / While we gobble up their labor due to our status?" suggesting that once service had ceased to be obligatory, noble extraction alone did not provide sufficient justification for the institution of serfdom.[51] Sumarokov's poem made a rather anxious and urgent case for the nobleman's learning, productivity, and service as a necessary condition to make palatable an otherwise flawed arrangement. The right to benefit from serf labor should, in the lyric subject's view, be earned through work, education, and, more generally, a lifelong rigorous cultivation of the self that, in its systematicity, begins to recall Tolstoy's "instructions" to himself. Sumarokov's poem is framed by references to the etymologically related concepts of noble "duty" (*dolg*) and "vocation" (*dolzhnost'*), the former of these containing the suggestion of debt. Repayment appears to come in being "a gentryman not in title, but in activity," as the lyric subject concludes that if he is "not fit for any vocation," then he is not a legitimate member of his estate: "My ancestor is a gentryman, but I am not a noble."[52] Thus, modulating Lotman's formulation that "the land had to serve," it would appear that beginning with the latter part of the eighteenth century, the Muscovite servitor's heir, the gentryman, "had to serve" or at least be of service to the larger polity, now more from a cultural imperative than from a basic need to maintain rights over property. Otherwise, he risked dropping out of his estate, as nobility became understood increasingly as something to cultivate and, eventually, to perform. The gentryman engaged "in activity," the much-emphasized work and process of *becoming* suggested by Sumarokov, would grow prominent in the decades to come as noble identity was negotiated through various textual regimes of mutual supervision and interpellation. Gradually, both in the immediate and in the long-range aftermath of the 1762 manifesto, the cultural anxieties about the nobleman who does not serve would become rerouted into a near-fixation on the landowner's domestic duties as a manager (whether a shrewd one or a wastrel) of an ancestral estate.

That Russian noblewomen exercised considerable control over property throughout the period under study certainly complicates matters. In particular, as Michelle Lamarche Marrese has shown, noblewomen not only owned immovable property but were frequently charged with the management of both their own estates and those of their male relations (for example, brothers and husbands).[53] As Katherine Pickering Antonova's recent microhistorical account of a reasonably average nineteenth-century provincial noble family suggests, the work of estate management may well have been viewed as a pursuit more appropriate for women than for men. Antonova proves that noblewomen's direct and extensive involvement in affairs of the estate was judged by contemporaries as scarcely worthy of notice, taken to be unremarkable and quite common.[54] What, then, does it mean that so many texts that evinced a preoccupation with noble property ownership in the aftermath of 1762 took the *male* noble as their primary and central figure? While the interplay between gender, noble identity, and property rights informs my readings in the chapters to come to varying degrees, I would like to offer here a provisional contention regarding the primacy of the male landowner in Russian public discourse. It seems productive to speculate that because the service obligation had been an attribute of the male and not the female nobility, the historically crucial tension between service and property ownership was of distinct and overwhelming significance for how the empire imagined its noblemen, but not its noblewomen.[55] This might go some way toward accounting for the preponderance of the male landowner in the Russian cultural imagination when it comes, specifically, to the questions surrounding the nobility's rights and obligations as owners of property, both immovable and human.[56]

In my selection of texts—works of fiction, journals and newspapers, domestic and farming advice literature, scientific treatises on agriculture, and occasionally legal documents—I do not aspire to an exhaustive treatment of an admittedly vast period. Instead, I focus on a handful of case studies. Placing works of literature in their broader media environment, for example, contextualizing novels in relation to farming manuals and the periodical press, shows that the rhetorical construction of the Russian landowner as a subject and a citizen took place in a multi-generic set of texts that cross-pollinated. As the print media grew more robust, the male landowner became a veritable fixture in the period's public discourse, an everyman who made frequent appearances as either a genuine or often fictitious contributor to the increasingly lively press. Ultimately, representations of the male landowner as an imperial subject and citizen came to

constitute a contested site of political, sociocultural, and affective investment in the Russian cultural imagination. Reading works of literature in
the context of the extra-literary spheres of Russian public discourse brings
to the fore the extent to which the modern novel developed as a carrier of a
gendered (complicatedly masculine) domestic ideology that contemplated
the nobleman as a landowner.

In chapter 1, I examine a multi-generic selection of texts produced by
such writers and entities as the Free Economic Society, Nikolai Novikov,
Andrei Bolotov, Nikolai Karamzin, and Fyodor Rostopchin. Whether literary, publicistic, or prescriptive, these texts register and narrate the evolution of the nobleman as a subject and a citizen in what may be regarded as
the long aftermath of the 1762 manifesto. It so happens that many of these
texts are purportedly letters addressed to a small group of familiars, then
printed for the public's consumption. Through the deployment of a double
addressivity (to both a small, specific group and a vast, anonymous audience, whose limits are, by definition, imprecise), the sense of a Russian
public develops. To a significant degree, male noble identity is constituted
through a twofold operation: (1) the rhetorical construction of a public
that includes members of various estates, male nobles very much among
them, and (2) the disciplining activities of this public upon the individual
subject-citizens who comprise it. The nobleman's relationship to his property, both his privileges and his obligations, proves crucial to the articulation of a masculine domestic ideology throughout the texts examined
in this chapter. Moreover, literary and prescriptive texts cross-pollinate to
produce important precursors to the formal and thematic preoccupations
of the nineteenth-century novel about the landowner.

In chapter 2, I maintain that looking squarely at a selection of texts
drawn from Pushkin's unfinished prose allows a glimpse at the novelization of male noble identity. I focus on three literary texts, which I contex-
tualize in relation to Pushkin's non-literary writings (for example, notes
and diaries) and to broad trends in the period's public discourse when it
comes, specifically, to the representation of the male gentry. I take *Novel
in Letters*—a text with clear meta-literary interests—to be a contemplation
of the cultural roots of male gentry identity in the eighteenth- and early
nineteenth-century ethos of epistolarity and the attendant intersubjec-
tive experience of selfhood described in chapter 1. I read the "History of
the Village of Goriukhino" in order to introduce another component to

its long-acknowledged generic ambidexterity: in addition to his creative reworking of historical writing, Pushkin also satirizes the popularity of various brands of quasi-scientific local or regional writing, for the production of which noblemen were then being enlisted by the press and, to some degree, by the state. I read the unfinished novel *Dubrovskii* with an eye to its considerable investment in underscoring the limits of noble privileges and obligations. I give noble rights to property particularly close attention in order to show *Dubrovskii* to be a novel that contemplates, on multiple fronts, the historically contingent nature and iterations of nobility. All of these texts taken together perform what may be called a novelization of noble identity in the sense that they subject noble masculinity to a novelistic (that is, inherently, unstably multiperspectival) investigation.

By the period covered in the next three chapters (1830s–1860s), the potential citizen of the eighteenth century had evolved into the nobleman-landowner and become something of a mainstay of the periodical press. In chapter 3, I read Faddei Bulgarin's multi-generic textual output with equal attention paid to his commercially successful novel, *Ivan Vyzhigin*, and to his works of advice literature on various aspects of domestic life, from agriculture to household chores. I suggest that all of Bulgarin's representations of the virtuous nobleman as a potential agriculturalist bear the marks of the period's shifting media environment, especially its turns toward something that began increasingly to resemble a very early and still inchoate iteration of print culture on a mass scale. Bulgarin's depictions of the landowner employ some of the discursive tools used in the agricultural literature of earlier periods (notably, Andrei Bolotov's writings), but fundamentally, they rely on a logic that issues from the decidedly modernizing market for printed fare that addressed a growing anonymous readership. Thus, Bulgarin's landowners become by turns stand-ins for a nebulously articulated sense of the public and, emphatically, products of public discourse in a commercial book market.

In chapter 4, I take up Nikolai Gogol's *Dead Souls* with a particular emphasis on the unfinished volume two of the novel. I suggest that various aspects of both volumes of the novel and, especially, the author's vocational crisis in the composition of the never-completed volume two may be explained through recourse to the period's media environment broadly and to the period's small but considerable boom in the production of advice literature aimed at the rural nobility more specifically. The characterization of some of the landowners in volume two of *Dead Souls* appears to have its origins in Bulgarin's multi-generic oeuvre. This makes for a rather high degree of cross-pollination between novelistic and pre-scriptive texts. As a result, volume two of *Dead Souls* evinces the sensibilities of a kind of borderline text, a novel that veers into advice literature. Ultimately, Gogol's drive to produce a virtuous landowner (in the figure of Kostanzhoglo, as well as in *Selected Passages from Correspondence with Friends* and elsewhere) registers the pervasiveness with which a normative masculine domestic and political ideology circulated in the period's public discourse.

The bildungsroman has long been understood as marginal to the nineteenth-century Russian novelistic tradition, much as it served a crucial, determinative role in the European novelistic modernity of the same period. Chapter 5 is devoted to a Russian writer whose novelistic oeuvre revolves around *Bildung*, or self-formation. I suggest that Ivan Goncharov's trilogy (*A Common Story*, *Oblomov*, *The Precipice*) contemplates noble masculinity as an idea and an identity suspended between two poles: the industrious, enterprising sensibility of the bourgeoisie and the provocative idleness of the nobleman, who appears sometimes as a *barin* (or master) of the pre-Petrine period, struggling to inhabit his social identity in the nineteenth century. Goncharov places his nobles manqués in what I show to be, formally, a middle-class vessel. It is possible to trace the presence of middlebrow (and, in some ways, distinctly middle-class) domestic advice literature throughout the trilogy, both in the narrative fabric and the compositional history of each novel. Thus, rather strikingly, both the discursive idiom and the textual history of Goncharov's trilogy have strong affinities with Western European "bourgeois" realism. In their meta-artistic self-consciousness, Goncharov's novels evince an awareness of the extent to which the literary representation of social identities involves the refracting influence of various cultural registers and generic modes.

In chapter 6, I turn to Sergei Aksakov's *Childhood Years of Bagrov the Grandson* for its mid-nineteenth-century wistful recollection of a late eighteenth-century childhood in order to reconsider some of the topics that animated the first chapter of this study. The central protagonist, young Sergei, comes to inhabit his social identity as a nobleman in large part through the experience of reading. Some of the texts in his library (notably, the children's periodical *Children's Reading for the Heart and Mind*

[*Detskoe chtenie dlia serdtsa i razuma*], treated in chapter 1) rehearse the mainstays of the Catherinean masculine domestic ideology aimed, as it turns out, at adults and children alike. By tracing and contextualizing the text's many references to the period's traffic in books, I suggest that in the representation of his young protagonist's reading habits, Aksakov narrates a story of modern subject formation. In sum, in chapters 3, 4, 5, and 6, moving from a picaresque (*Vyzhigin*) to an anti-picaresque novel (*Dead Souls*) to a trilogy of bildungs- and *Künstlerromane*[57] (*A Common Story, Oblomov, The Precipice*), then finally to a text that is eminently readable as a bildungsroman (*Childhood Years*), I consider how each of the novels thinks about nobility as a process that foregrounds the activities of becoming, practice, and performance.

The Great Reforms of the 1860s—above all but not only the emancipation of the serfs in 1861—altered considerably the discursive and political fabric of noble identity. In the conclusion, I turn to what may be the most widely known depiction of the nobleman-landowner in Russian literature: the representation of Levin in *Anna Karenina*, the novel Lev Tolstoy produced after the chronological endpoint of this book. I suggest that Tolstoy's preoccupations with agricultural labor, estate life, noble identity, and the period's media landscape issue from, echo, and rework the main thematic and formal attributes of the texts, both literary and not, considered in the course of this study. In general terms, then, *Noble Subjects* offers its readers a genealogy of the nobleman-landowner in Russian public discourse broadly conceived to include works of fiction, advice literature, and mainstream journalism, while foregrounding the formation of a modern Russian novelistic tradition and idiom.

Chapter One

The Century of the Letter

The Nobleman at the Plow

In 1806 Count Fyodor Rostopchin published a pamphlet called "The Plow and the Wooden Plow" or, somewhat less awkwardly in Russian, "Plug i sokha." The title refers to different varieties of the farming tool: the Slavic, native, wooden plow, or *sokha*, which Rostopchin endorsed heartily, and the European iron plow (in Russian, *plug*), which became emblematic of all agricultural practices that the author judged to be ill-advised imports from England. Like many men and some women of the time period Rostopchin was an avid if amateur agriculturalist, who conducted a variety of experiments with crops, cattle, and horse breeding. "The Plow and the Wooden Plow" was published as part of a broader polemic about English farming, which was fashionable at the time.[1] Rostopchin began his essay with two epigraphs, the second of which was a short piece of verse that the reader will find below:

> More than others I have gallivanted about the world,
> I have been busy with learning, people, and things.
> And because I have lived outside Russia for long,
> I've come to know how dear she is and to love her better.
> As a son I am devoted to her with my heart and soul,
> I've served in war, in governmental administration, and now I serve with the
> Wooden Plow [*teper' sluzhu s Sokhoi*].

I have always been a faithful advocate of public good,

I wish to assure you in that, and I rise in revolt against the Plow [*i vosstaiu na
   Plug*].[2]

Best known as military governor of Moscow in 1812, by the year of
the pamphlet's composition in 1806 Rostopchin had enjoyed a reasonably
lengthy career that had turned especially impressive during the reign of
Paul I (1796–1801) and that involved considerable travel and state service in both military and civil capacities, as well as at court. Following the
ascension to the throne of Tsar Alexander I, with whom he had a history of
difficult relations characterized by a degree of mutual animosity, Rostopchin spent the first years of the nineteenth century in retirement from service, mixing with other members of the noble opposition to Alexander in
Moscow and at his nearby estate.[3] The epigraph's line about service—"I've
served in war, in governmental administration, and now I serve with the
Wooden Plow"—could be read in an autobiographical key, referring to
Rostopchin as an accomplished state servitor, a grandee turned gentleman
farmer, were it not for the fact that the pamphlet was published anonymously, having issued purportedly from the pen of one Nobleman of
the Steppe (signed *Stepnoi dvorianin*). Thus, both the pamphlet's lengthy
defense of Russian farming practices and the epigraph's assertion of service "with the Wooden Plow" were to belong to a generic everyman-no-
bleman. This makes it all the more curious that Rostopchin's anonymous
pamphlet was misattributed by some readers to Princess Ekaterina Dashkova, who also had a penchant for fashionable agricultural experimenta-
tion.[4] The misattribution is interesting, because it suggests that Dashkova
would have been understood to be writing as the Nobleman of the Steppe,
an unquestionably male nom de plume. Why and in what context might
such a scenario, a noblewoman writing as a male landowner, appear logi-
cal? Russian noblewomen had extensive control over property.[5] However,
female and male landowners were represented differently in public discourse, in large part because of the divergent meanings that attached to
property ownership and management for male and female nobles.[6] The
relative prominence of male landowners in the period's collective imagination issued from the tendency to connect *domostroitel'stvo* (estate administration) closely with another highly significant topic at this time: state service. The misattributions of the pamphlet to Dashkova may well attest to

the prevalence in Russian public discourse of the male landowner, whose work at his estate is understood systematically to be commensurate with state service. Given this context, one would be hard pressed to imagine a noblewoman serving at her plow, because the link between land owner-ship and state service was a specifically male problem with a long history.

A confluence of factors made for the primacy and the prevalence of the nobleman-landowner in the Russian cultural imagination. The decades following the 1762 manifesto that granted noblemen the legal right to abstain from state service witnessed the appearance in Russia of various circumstances, including cultural institutions and legal measures, that enabled the growth of a peculiar brand of civil society. Encouraged by Catherine II, these social and textual formations sought to cultivate citizens in a new mold and to foster the practices and what may be called the performative *practicing* of civil society as a semiautonomous and pre- or quasi-political entity aligned with and always aware of being monitored by the state. Russia's first voluntary association, the Free Economic Society, was founded in 1765 for the betterment of agriculture. In 1769, under the empress's guidance and with her participation as a fellow journalist, Russian letters imported a lively satirical press modeled largely on the works of Joseph Addison and Richard Steele. The English Club, perhaps best known as the "temple of idleness" Tolstoy would describe in *Anna Karenina*, opened its doors in Moscow in the early 1770s. By 1775 the Statute on Provincial Administration had restructured governance in the country-side and provided new and unprecedented scripts for a positively viewed noble sociability and private life in the provinces.[7] Thanks to the Charters of 1785 nobles and townspeople became almost rights-bearing citizens, even if their privileges could (and, to a degree, would) be revoked by subsequent rulers. Like other European monarchies, Catherine's reign took a reactionary turn both in the immediate run-up to and certainly in the aftermath of the French Revolution of 1789. Nevertheless, the second half of the eighteenth century produced what may be regarded as a new social type in Russian public discourse: the gentleman farmer newly secure in his state-sanctioned return to his provincial properties, a nobleman who was *almost* a citizen in possession of certain inalienable rights, and, perhaps above all, a man ready as well as eager for interaction and community.

The narratives that comprise this chapter may serve as vignettes that illustrate the gradual constitution of the nobleman as subject and citizen during the second half of the eighteenth century and the first decade of the nineteenth from multiple, mutually illuminating, points of view. Not intended as an exhaustive survey of a long period, these moments coalesce and gain coherence due to a set of shared and recurring preoccupations. To begin with, some generic forms turn out to be more productive than others. In addition to pamphlets and ceremonial addresses to large groups, the discursive space of the letter—addressed simultaneously to social peers and the public at large—proves to be crucial for the articulation of a largely masculine domestic and political ideology. "No single text can create a public," writes Michael Warner, who identifies "the appearance of newsletters and other temporally structured forms oriented to their own circulation: not just controversial pamphlets, but [...] magazines, almanacs, annuals, and essay serials" as the "key development in the emergence of modern publics." Warner further points out that the "performative dimension of public discourse [...] is routinely misrecognized," because public speech must address its audience "as already existing real persons" and "cannot work by frankly declaring its subjunctive-creative project."[8] Many of the texts discussed below operate in this way. Throughout the period, communicative scenarios that involve a double orientation toward the addressee, figured at once as specific and finite (an individual, a small group) and imprecise in its vastness (provincials, the nation) are common. In part through the scenario of double addressivity, these texts create a sense of the public that will persist well into the first half of the nineteenth century. Letters loom large, because epistolarity enables a mechanism of subject formation through mutual interpellation and surveillance. These texts depict the evolution of male noble identity and its formation under the disciplining gaze of a public.

Products of the Russian variant of the Enlightenment, the texts and organizations discussed below operate didactically in order to reform and reformulate noble subjectivity through education, practice, and performance. The texts produced by such authors and entities as the Free Economic Society, Nikolai Novikov, Andrei Bolotov, Nikolai Karamzin, and Fyodor Rostopchin suggest that even when one is born a nobleman, it is still necessary to become one.[9] Many different iterations of an ethos of hard work and self-improvement permeate these narratives. Both the aspirations and the anxieties that attended the gradual formation of the gentleman farmer in public discourse find expression in a particular emphasis on the nobleman's role as a steward of property. In the texts examined in the pages below, the domestic life of the nobility becomes variously inscribed into the conceptual nexus of patriotism, duty, and service. A masculine domestic ideology takes shape. But, again, why masculine? As was mentioned above, a number of recent historical studies have shown that noblewomen took an active role in estate administration. To determine more fully the extent to which noble*men* were active as lords of their manors remains the task of historical scholarship of a sort the present study does not aspire to provide.[10] The materials examined in this chapter deal not in hard facts, but in representational mainstays of the long period between the years 1762 and 1806. These texts attempt to articulate a particular brand of male noble subjectivity after state service ceased to be compulsory in 1762. Repeatedly, the retired nobleman is imagined as a productive citizen who, in his capacity as a landowner (*pomeshchik*) and landlord (*khoziain*), is serving the state. What might have been the private life of the nobleman becomes legible primarily via reference either to the state or, somewhat more diffusely, to the public as beneficiary of a domesticity figured as work. At times, this tendency becomes rerouted into simply imagining a landowner who works the land himself—the nobleman at the plow, whose evolution this study will trace through a selection of texts that culminates in Tolstoy's *Anna Karenina*. Lastly, it should be pointed out at this juncture that the texts examined below will be shown to be pre-novelistic inasmuch as they prefigure in multiple ways the dominant thematic and formal preoccupations of the nineteenth-century Russian novel about the landowner. Said otherwise, these texts begin to "novelize" noble identity.

The Free Economic Society

At a December 1804 meeting of the Free Economic Society, the secretary, Stepan Dzhunkovskii, concluded a speech in which he urged landowners to become well versed in agricultural science with a question: "But would it not be degrading for a nobleman to do the work of a peasant?" Immediately, he supplied a reply, albeit one formulated as a rhetorical question, "But why is it that Heroes and Commanders, Senators, Legislators and Tsars, in ancient and in modern times, have not been ashamed to pick up

the wooden plow [*brat' v ruki sokhu*]?"[11] Dzhunkovskii went on to explain
that farming was a thoroughly aristocratic pursuit worthy even of royals.
At first glance, it may appear somewhat strange that some forty years after
the Free Economic Society's founding, its members should need to be
reminded of the nobility of their undertaking. The reference to picking up
a wooden plow also needs an explanation. Throughout the organization's
long existence (1765–1915), the addresses delivered at the Free Economic
Society tended to have a largely ritualistic dimension in that they reiterated the Society's goals and the characteristics as well as the aspirations of
its membership. In this context, Dzhunkovskii's emphasis on what constitutes properly noble behavior is to be expected. Likewise, Dzhunkovskii's
recourse to a scenario drawn partly from classical antiquity is entirely
unsurprising. It accords well with Iurii Lotman's seminal observations
regarding the pervasive theatricality of male noble behavior during this
period and the tendency to draw on historical, for example, specific Greek
or Roman, models in structuring lived experiences.[12] The reference to the
wooden plow in the hands of a noble warrior of antiquity or a highly positioned person of recent days is part of a larger set of rhetorical gestures for
framing agriculture as a suitable activity for nobles.

To convince nobles to take a more active part in estate administration
had been a decades-long undertaking. Plans to found an organization that
would oversee the administration of Russia's provinces go as far back as
the 1750s, when, as Joseph Bradley suggests, agricultural improvements
became connected to "an ethic of usefulness among the nobility," as well as
"a curtailment of the abuses of serfdom, and a more efficient and humane
economic and political system."[13] In the early 1760s three "institutional
strategies" were offered to the empress. One was to establish an agricultural division within the Academy of Sciences. Another was suggested
by the poet Mikhail Lomonosov who, in a document produced in 1763
and called "An Opinion about the Establishment of a State Collegium on
Rural Domestic Culture" (Mnenie o uchrezhdenii gosudarstvennoi kol-
legii zemskogo domostroistva), argued for the creation of a government
department, "a prototype of a 'ministry of agriculture,'" linked to the newspaper he had hoped since 1759 to start.[14] The poet opined that literate
provincials (including both nobles and, for example, merchants) could
act as correspondents, writing in with information about local conditions,
reporting on such topics as climate and harvests. Lomonosov had planned

to devote a special section of the newspaper to information about estate life and administration. Catherine rejected Lomonosov's plans and chose instead to pursue the idea, presented by Jacob Johann Sievers, to establish an agricultural society. Therefore, the agency that Catherine decided to support in 1765, the Free Economic Society, was not a governmental, but a nominally private organization. Very highly positioned Russian noblemen were joined by scientists and professional agriculturalists (for example, the court gardener) as founding members. Articles written or translated by the latter group filled the pages of the early issues of their quarterly periodical, the *Transactions of the Free Economic Society* (*Trudy vol'nogo ekonomicheskogo obshchestva*).

How did the founding members define the tasks of the Free Economic Society in 1765? How did they see their role in this enterprise? How did they imagine their audience? The inaugural issue of the *Transactions* contains a fairly protracted description of the project these men were about to undertake. Conceiving their work as a patriotic endeavor aimed at the betterment of the nation through scientific farming, the members directed their words chiefly at the landowning nobleman. But who may speak with authority on subjects pertaining to agriculture? The members sound anxious notes on this count. While "some might object" to their enterprise by pointing out that "very few of the Members have any experience in estate administration [*domostroitel'stvo*]," they submit that a person with knowledge of the natural sciences has a greater capacity for making "useful observations than he, who simply performs daily and with his own hands agricultural tasks, carrying them out like a machine," and they conclude that they "may comfort [themselves] with the hope that many of [their] members will toil in this venture with great utility, even though not one of them is capable of wielding the wooden plow [*sokhoi ne deistvuiut*]."[15] The founding members' reference to their inability to use the plow in 1765 may be understood as an early precursor to Dzhunkovskii's 1804 turn to imagine noblemen and other prominent persons who may be compelled to "pick up the wooden plow." (Of course, in neither case are their words to be taken literally.) In the years following 1765 the idea that noblemen might work the land, engaging directly in some aspect of farm work, gained considerable currency as more and more iterations of the nobleman at the plow appeared in various spheres of Russian public discourse and as the image came, eventually, to constitute a robust cultural myth.

In a more immediate historical context, inasmuch as the *Transactions of the Free Economic Society* created a forum for the public articulation of the duties and rights of the nobleman who does not serve the state and passes his days instead as a gentleman farmer, the organization and its periodical also contributed to an emergent, largely prepolitical public sphere.[16] Calling the Society "a radical departure from current practice in that the Russian government did not control it," Bradley argues that participation in the agricultural organization fostered "the creation of a new sense of identity, self-worth, and mission for the patriotic noble," while such voluntary associations came, with time, to form the core of nascent civil society.[17] In his study of the organization Colum Leckey highlights the absence of an independent public sphere in Russia as well as the Free Economic Society's failure to reach a reasonably numerous public and its very close ties to the empress. He sees the appearance of the figure of the "enlightened seigneur" in the Russian cultural imagination as one of the organization's chief accomplishments.[18] Virtually all historians who have written about the organization agree that especially during the initial decades of its existence, it did little to transform agriculture in the Russian Empire.[19] The Free Economic Society was as much a gentlemen's club as a group of scientists, perhaps more the former than the latter. It had a good degree of self-governance, understandably tempered by its close ties with the state and with the empress personally. Members met weekly, usually on Wednesday afternoons, over tea and coffee. For members at a greater geographic remove, the Society encouraged participation as correspondents.[20] At the inception of the *Transactions* readers of every rank and station were invited to take part in the periodical.[21] The inaugural issue included a lengthy questionnaire of sixty-five items. The authors requested that every knowledgeable person complete answers to all or any number of the questions posed and send responses to the group's address in St. Petersburg. And they received a number of replies, one set of which will be discussed in the pages below. Effectively, the Society launched an empire-wide project, a broad study of the provinces that would persist—both in the Society's and in other organizations' activities—well into the nineteenth century. Both in face-to-face meetings and through a print-generated zone of contact, the Free Economic Society attempted to provide sites of self-consciously useful, patriotically minded sociability. Thus, its failure to reach a large readership notwithstanding (and it should be remembered that in the second half of the eighteenth century, a reasonably "large" subscriber base could be counted in the few hundreds), the Free Economic Society used various rhetorical tactics—the public address, queries aimed at the readership, letters to the editor—to articulate a new role for the non-serving nobleman: that he, somewhat paradoxically, serve the state by fulfilling his duties as a landowner *and* by participating in the new media landscape by sharing his experiences with a community of like-minded nobles through publication.

Novikov's Nobles

The founding and the functioning of the Free Economic Society as, in part, an organization that enabled the formation of a prepolitical public sphere may be profitably viewed alongside another phenomenon of the 1760s: the development of Russian satirical journals. Catherine II initiated what may be regarded as the first considerably robust period in Russian journalism.[22] The self-styled grandmother of the press, Catherine's *All Sorts of Everything* (*Vsiakaia vsiachina*) was the first among a comparatively sizable group of periodicals that appeared in 1769 and that were modeled largely on the satirical journalism of Addison and Steele, particularly *The Tatler* and *The Spectator*.[23] Of course, the journal was not officially Catherine's. However, the empress's literary pursuits both as a journalist and a playwright, although carried out under nominal anonymity, were quite well known to the educated public. Her encouragement of the periodical press followed closely on the prematurely halted proceedings of the Legislative Commission, which were concerned primarily with Russia's social organization and included debates about the social estates in general, and the status of the nobility in particular. To a degree, the journals may be viewed as a surrogate for or the continuation of the debates held at the Commission's proceedings.[24] The journalist, publisher, and philanthropist Nikolai Novikov served as one of the four secretaries of the Legislative Commission.[25] His journalistic and, to a degree, even political sensibility agreed with and was probably encouraged by the early years of Catherine's reign, which appeared to endorse dialogue between the monarch and the cultural elite.

Between 1769 and 1775 Novikov edited a succession of satirical journals: *The Drone* (*Truten'*), *The Chatterbox* (*Pustomelia*), *The Painter*

(*Zhivopisets*), and *The Purse* (*Koshelek*). Throughout these ventures he tends to depict a vibrant public. The pages of his periodicals brim with talk, a quality likely underwritten by the relatively new ethos of useful and always at least potentially edifying social intercourse. Articles written as missives pepper the pages of both *The Drone* and Novikov's subsequent journals. Letters to the editor, texts that purport to be personal correspondence, reports of town rumors, anecdotes heard and recounted, compositions that catalog the dominant social types and habits of the period—these are the forms of discourse that dominate the journals and that create their virtual spaces of socialization, while a fictional editor acts as the ultimate arbiter of good taste and sound usefulness. By ventriloquizing a public of purported contributors, Novikov's journals construct normative scenarios for both private life and social intercourse by, for example, "correcting" a noblewoman's taste for luxury or a landowner's failure to acknowledge the humanity of his serfs. According to these periodicals, noble birth does not in itself yield a nobility of character. In other words, one may be born a noble, but one must work to become worthy of the social estate.

An interest in male noble identity is immediately palpable in the inaugural article of Novikov's first periodical, *The Drone*. The journal opens with the image of the lazy eponymous publisher, Mr. Drone. As the readers learn quickly, the would-be editor spends his time in utter inactivity. He enumerates every sphere of state service available to the Russian nobleman—military, civil, and at the court—only to reject each possibility as ill-suited to his particular proclivities. Having reiterated the paralyzing effects of his almost pathological idleness multiple times (he is so lazy that he cannot read, cannot make social visits, cannot engage in correspondence, cannot get dressed so as to leave the house), and having explained that he has been unable to choose a vocation, he exclaims: "How then may I be useful in society?"[26] Seeking to "perform at least the most trifling sort of service to [his] fatherland," Mr. Drone opines that although he cannot write the contents of the journal (since for this, too, he lacks the capacity), he may find a useful occupation in "the publication of other people's works," which may bring "profit to my compatriots" (*prinest' pol'zu sograzhdanam*).[27] Mr. Drone, then, becomes the passive center around which the textual universe of the journal accumulates. Produced only a few years after the 1762 manifesto that granted noblemen the right to abstain from state service, in its depiction of Mr. Drone's activities as useful and patriotic work, the journal may be responding to a cultural anxiety about the idleness in which the non-serving nobility may pass their time. In his capacity as a non-serving nobleman and yet a reasonably capable editor, Drone comes to model for the readership a relatively new iteration of male noble behavior. It is possible to be useful without serving the state, the journal's logic goes, so long as one engages in an activity that benefits the fatherland and the public. Taking a longer view, Mr. Drone may well be read as a reformed Superfluous Man avant la lettre, an early version of the familiar figure of the nobleman who seeks but cannot find useful activity in many a nineteenth-century novel.

More generally, in its representation of the nobility, much of Novikov's satirical journalism prefigures the directions that the nineteenth-century novel will take. A kind of "novelization" of noble identity takes place on multiple fronts. To begin with, the private life of the gentry occupies a position of considerable prominence in Novikov's satiric oeuvre. For example, the correspondence between a wastrel landowner and his village elder (*starosta*) published in *The Drone* has been seen as an intertext for the representation of the same sort of correspondence in Goncharov's *Oblomov*.[28] "A Historical Adventure" ("Istoricheskoe prikliuchenie," 1770), published in another of Novikov's journals, *The Chatterbox*, focuses on the tension between patriotism and private life. The text gives concrete shape to the inherited character of the problem of noble identity. In the representation of a virtuous noble family—the father Dobronrav (One of Good Character) and his son Dobroserd (One of Good Heart)—the text rehearses a good deal of what would become stock features of the nineteenth-century novel about the landowning gentry. Much of the story treats the young nobleman's departure from the country, his time in St. Petersburg, then his return to the family home in a way that anticipates the nineteenth-century novel's tendency to shuttle between city and country. Novikov's descriptions of young Dobroserd's difficulty becoming accustomed to the frivolous ways of the city, and especially the young man's trips to the theater, which are followed by an introspective search for personal shortcomings, read as a precursor to the psychologism of the next century's novel. Once back in the country,[29] Dobroserd reconnects with his sweetheart, Milovida (Good Looking). They become engaged; the young man proudly announces that he has found happiness with his betrothed. However, some time later, Dobroserd gets word that he must leave the countryside in order to fight in a war. Service obligations, which, the reader learns, he could have avoided since the family is well connected, pull him away from a personally fulfilling life. Ultimately, both Milovida and Dobroserd are presented as exemplary nobles for their willingness to sacrifice personal happiness for service to the monarch. Both understand this service as a condition that must be fulfilled in order for them to deserve personal happiness. The tension between obligations to the state and the right to a private life proves crucial to the entire account.

Novikov's depiction of the gentry gains complexity when his fictions participate in and respond to specific normative narratives about a virtuous nobility. In the June 9, 1769, issue of *The Drone*, Novikov published a fictitious letter from a landowner who had come to the country for the summer and found among his neighbors "many good-thinking and honest people, who are busy with estate administration [*uprazhniaiushchikhsia v domostroitel'stve*]."[30] The gentryman correspondent concludes his missive with what amounts to a kind of praise of country life. He writes, "in my opinion, when it comes to pleasantness, nothing can compare to life in the country," where people wake up early in order to "use the pleasant morning hours to tend to the administration of their estate [*prismatrivat' za svoim domostroitel'stvom*] and with their example encourage their servants to labor."[31] Published some four years after the founding of the Free Economic Society, the letter seems to echo the positive vision of a productive nobleman in the provinces promoted by the agency. The assertion that the nobleman's good example as a careful manager of his estate will compel the peasant farmer to work harder accords with the Free Economic Society's call that landowners take on a more active role in agriculture. Moreover, this correspondent promises to write to *The Drone* again, with more news about life in the country, as the affairs of the estate are deemed an interesting and important enough topic to warrant publication in a major journal. The correspondent's promise to write again, when viewed in the wider context of increased official interest in gentry domesticity, reads as a reflection of the cultural climate of the time. However, framed by these positive statements about the sort of life a nobleman might enjoy in the provinces is the main narrative of the missive: a pair of local landowners habitually appropriate the property of other nobles by cheating. They do this, it seems, by manipulating the law in various semi-criminal ways. Thus, while the letter both begins and ends with praise for country life, its central narrative registers the instability of noble property rights in the 1760s and the need to monitor the provinces so that the rule of law may prevail. Pushkin will deal with a similar topic in *Dubrovskii*; that is, the nobles' expectation that their rights to property should be inalienable and their disappointment with the instability of their claims to an estate.[32]

Still more interesting are texts in which Novikov's gentry correspondents attempt actively to make sense of their roles and obligations in the countryside. These instances are quite many and varied. The "Letters to Falalei," published in *The Painter* and long lauded by Soviet critics as a denunciation of serfdom, comprise perhaps the most famous example of landowners' correspondence in Novikov's journals. Overall, the letters offer *not* a critique of the institution of serfdom, but rather an illustration of virtuous nobility through a series of counterexamples. In other words, of prime concern here is not serfdom, but noble behavior. In these purportedly personal documents produced by fictional country nobles (the relations of the young man Falalei) and printed for public consumption, Novikov first shows an aging provincial landowner's attempt to make sense of his historical moment. Speaking for his entire estate, the virtuous Falalei's less than virtuous father, Trifon Pankrat'ich, judges that "nowadays our gentry living has become very bad."[33] "They say that the gentry have been given freedom: the devil knows what they're talking about, God forgive me, what sort of freedom? They gave us freedom, but there's not a thing one can do with it,"[34] Trifon continues, responding to and, in his own way, evaluating the 1762 manifesto and the rights that it granted in such areas as the freedom to travel abroad, for example. He reports that he is no longer able to "take away a neighbor's property" by force or distill spirits whenever he likes. In its many disappointments, Trifon's letter registers the alleged fulfillment of a *Rechtsstaat* (a polity defined by the rule of law) that both the Legislative Commission and, more broadly, Catherine's brand of enlightened autocracy had promised to deliver. Indeed, the pervasive new culture of the *Rechtsstaat* has even reached Falalei's sister who, aged fifteen, must now finally learn how to read in order to marry and to be able to read an ukase.

Trifon admits that his serfs are very poor and do not seem to grow any more productive no matter how one mistreats them. On the other hand, his neighbor, who happens to be Grigorii Orlov, has serfs who look as wealthy as gentrymen. An extremely influential statesman in the early

1770s, Catherine's favorite Grigorii Orlov was a founding member and occasional president of the Free Economic Society. In the first issue of the *Transactions*, his name is listed second, after Count Roman Vorontsov. Trifon's neighbor, then, is one of the most prominent participants in the construction of normative models for the nobles' behavior as stewards of provincial estates. Later in the correspondence, when in another missive Falalei's uncle, Ermolai, reports incredulously that "many say that it is possible, while living in the countryside, to become wealthy simply by means of estate administration [*domostroitel'stvo*] and the good cultivation of wheat; but I don't believe such liars,"[35] it begins to appear that the family have been reading the *Transactions of the Free Economic Society*, which encouraged rational agriculture as both a patriotic and profitable endeavor. That Ermolai and company know anything about the book culture of the metropolis is noteworthy in itself. Given the paltry size of the educated reading public likely to have access to such fare as Novikov's journal, it is striking that both Trifon and Ermolai are shown to be well aware of *The Painter*'s contents (thanks, as they report, to an acquaintance). Ultimately, there is something almost coercive about placing these crooked and, to all appearances, deeply provincial nobles so squarely in the context of some of the period's most explicit and most significant attempts to build a Russian Enlightenment and its attendant public and institutions. The potentially disciplining proximity of the Orlov estate has a formal resonance in the special conditions of addressivity enabled by the prominence of epistolary texts in the satirical journals. Trifon, Ermolai, and more generally the backward noble as a type are forced into participation in a public sphere that seeks to monitor and to mold (read: correct) their behavior. Virtuous nobility, again, is depicted as something to cultivate through practice and supervision, as Novikov's satirical journalism both in the "Letters to Falalei" and more generally becomes a kind of laboratory for the elaboration of male noble subjectivity under the disciplining gaze of a public.

Andrei Bolotov's Rural Resident

Historians of the Free Economic Society allude frequently to the response of one retired middling landowner to the first volumes of the society's proceedings. Andrei Bolotov recorded in his autobiographical work *Life*

and Adventures of Andrei Bolotov, Described by Himself for His Descendants
(*Zhizn' i prikliucheniia Andreia Bolotova, opisannye samim im dlia svoikh
potomkov*; hereafter, *Life and Adventures*) that he "nearly jumped with
joy" upon discovering the first tome of the *Transactions*, which he then
read cover to cover.[36] That such a publication should interest someone like
Bolotov can be explained by the fact that he, atypically for a member of
his generation, opted to retire from service early (as quickly as he could,
following the 1762 manifesto) and was actively interested in the cultivation of a variety of private pursuits, agriculture and estate life very prominent among them.[37] Bolotov's first contribution to the *Transactions* was
a lengthy reply to the 1765 query that had sought to collect information
about nearly every aspect of the Russian provinces. Sixty-five questions
had been posed treating a wide range of subjects: from fishing and the
cultivation of the potato crop to peasant health and local holidays. Easily
among the period's most avid consumers of periodicals, Bolotov attempted
to take full advantage of the available venues for communication with
like-minded men. While the *Transactions* provided the first medium for
Bolotov's attempts to connect with other landowners in a publicly circulated text, it was far from ideal. Finding that submitting his writings to
the Free Economic Society was too expensive (due to the cost of mail)
and too cumbersome (it took the editors too long to publish, and Bolotov
seems rather impatient in this regard), finding also that the *Transactions*
had a very low circulation rate, in 1778 Bolotov began publishing his own
periodical, the *Rural Resident* (*Sel'skii zhitel'*), a venture devoted entirely
to domestic culture.[38] After a relatively brief collaboration with another
publisher, Bolotov began working with Nikolai Novikov, who paid him
handsomely for his efforts. It would not overstate matters to claim that
Bolotov was a highly successful man of letters within his chosen area.[39]

   To a certain degree, Bolotov's editorship of the *Rural Resident* and the
Economic Magazine (*Ekonomicheskii magazin*), a continuation of his first
periodical, was prompted by the provincial nobleman's desire to commu-
nicate with an audience of like-minded peers. From the start, Bolotov's
activities as a self-styled private citizen and successful journalist positively
sparkle with enthusiasm for the new modes of sociability. But this is an
enthusiasm always tempered by the possibility that the community he
seeks will turn out to be little more than a spectral illusion, leaving him
in provincial isolation. In beginning to publish, the landowner turned

journalist seems to have been keenly aware of the vagaries of the trade he was entering. In the introductory article of the inaugural issue of the *Rural Resident*, Bolotov writes the following about an imagined audience's response to his undertaking:

> Whoever you may be, Mr. Author [*sochinitel'*], would it not be better for you to plow the earth [*pakhat' zemliu*] and to sit at home busy with your undertakings! Otherwise, you are getting involved in a business in which you have no place; it would be better for you to remain with your wooden plow [*sokha*] and your harrow [*borona*] and to practice working with them, not with the pen, and to leave us in peace.[40]

That the hostile audience Bolotov imagines prefers that he remain at his wooden plow (*sokha*) attests to the relative preponderance and growth of a cultural myth about the nobleman who works the land with his hands. The particular circumstances of his recourse to this figure—the nobleman at the plow—reveal that the purpose of Bolotov's periodical lay in articulating a scenario in which the nobleman-farmer becomes an emphatically public person, as much an agriculturalist as a man of letters. Rather like Rostopchin's Nobleman of the Steppe in 1806, Bolotov's editorial persona will perform a patriotic service by speaking about his experiences "at the plow."

It is for this reason that, rather strikingly, Bolotov contextualizes his new venture in relation to Russian letters more broadly. He writes,

> I do not doubt that many, seeing this first issue of my weekly compositions [. . .], will think the same thing that was said recently by a certain personage at a big gathering. [. . .] "What sort of weekly compositions are these!" he cried, "and will there ever be an end to these weekly compositions? There is not a single year in which the public isn't burdened by [periodicals], sometimes—when one doesn't seem to suffice—there are two or three of them. We have seen quite enough of these weekly compositions in the past few years!"[41]

Listing such Catherine-era journals as *All Sorts of Everything, Day-Labor (Podenshchina), This and That (I to i sio), Hell's Mail (Adskaia pochta), The Drone, The Painter, The Purse,* and "God knows what other sorts of publications," and noting that not one of them was able to survive for more than a year, "while some died in infancy," the hostile reader imagined by Bolotov marvels at the misplaced optimism of the new enterprise. He predicts that, in all likelihood, Bolotov's *Rural Resident* will "wilt in accordance with the example set by the others."[42] As soon as Bolotov imagines a readership, the public turns pessimistic about the state of 1770s print culture, and, consequently, the possibility of reaching his provincial[43] addressee is forestalled. Still, Bolotov's characteristically timid view of the public aside, noteworthy here is the way the author-editor effectively inserts his own periodical into the ranks of much more mainstream publications. Listing his *Rural Resident* alongside other journals was akin to laying claim to a place among the press establishment of the time. Although nearly ten years had passed since the beginning of the small boom, satirical journals bound into books still circulated among the reading public. Bolotov's gesture of contextualizing his periodical in relation to the satirical journals also meant that his work would take part in the public-building enterprise that was observed in relation to Novikov in the pages above.

In fact, Bolotov uses his own version of Novikov's journalistic tactics (which, of course, were borrowed by the Russian journalist from such writers as Samuel Johnson, Addison, and Steele) quite actively. As he introduces his periodical, Bolotov creates an audience for himself that includes an admiring reader, whom he calls his "defender" (*moi zashchititel'*). In the next issue, he prints a letter from this "defender." This fictitious reader begins with outsized praise: "Dear sir! Bravo! Mr. Rural Resident, bravo! Your leaflet [*listok*] is good, and I and many others like it."[44] In his response to the defender, Bolotov claims that he must stop writing his reply to the first letter, because he has just received another missive, which must also be printed. Bolotov later admitted that he had authored this and other similar letters himself.[45] In the subsequent issues of the journal, a near-encyclopedic treatment of every aspect of estate life is given in the form of personal letters exchanged between dear friends. Effectively, in *The Rural Resident* Bolotov fashions ex nihilo a lively, responsive audience of *very*, indeed, maximally, like-minded nobles. In his attempt to give rise discursively to a provincial reading public, Bolotov initially performs an operation that may be regarded either as a splitting or a multiplication of the self, populating a vast provincial landscape with correspondents who resemble him: concerned landowners who wish to participate in the newly robust print media and to use it as a vehicle for virtual community and sociability across a vast distance.[46]

Bolotov would repeat the same gesture in his next periodical, the *Economic Magazine*.[47] Hoping that this new venture will share some of the success of the previous one, he invites the new readership to correspond with him and "having gotten to know [him] better, to turn their acquaintance into friendship." Bolotov attempts to replicate exactly the communicative and discursive codes that governed the *Rural Resident*.[48] The *Economic Magazine* becomes a textually constituted meeting place for provincial landowners who appear in the publication under such names as Uedinen, Chistoserdtsov, Dobrozhelatelev, and Sostradatelev.[49] The names mean the following: Isolated, Sincere, Well-Wisher, Compassionate. Bolotov retains his old nom de plume: for those to whom his identity is unknown, he remains the Rural Resident. Even when Bolotov writes to no one in particular, as when composing a short note about a given subject (for example, an article about recognizing plants that contain blue dye), he often signs the piece as "Your friend, the Rural Resident," thus asserting friendly relations with the anonymous subscriber.

It is made clear throughout the *Rural Resident* and the early issues of the *Economic Magazine* that good gentry housekeeping is just as important as the friendliness of the exchanges and the purely communicative function of the periodical.[50] Bolotov and his correspondents are just as interested in rehearsing modes of private life in the provinces as they are in affirming the legitimacy of their undertaking as landowners by entering into conversation about the minutiae of estate administration. The civic dimension of this is perhaps most palpable at moments when the editor turns to a discussion of the periodical as an explicitly patriotic gesture. For example, Bolotov assures the general readership with great emphasis that he is to be trusted with the venture, because he is a compatriot (*sograzhdanin*) with whom they share an upbringing, and, by extension, a cultural background. The particular term for compatriot, *sograzhdanin*, can be translated more literally as "co-citizen," underscoring the emphasis on the shared experience of civic belonging and on perhaps the most important dimension of Bolotov's undertaking: the essentially horizontal terms of engagement and address that foster a conversation among peers and social equals in a reasonably autonomous sphere of discourse. Much like the satirical journalism of Novikov, Bolotov's agricultural periodicals represent virtuous nobility as something that must be cultivated under the gaze of a public whose judgments will discipline the participants as they articulate a shared masculine domestic and, to some degree, political ideology.[51]

Here a few last points should be noted. Be it the health effects of coffee and tobacco, methods for producing good fertilizer, the latest fashions in landscape architecture (a favorite topic), or ways of combating common vermin, Bolotov and company write at length. Their graphomania and the desire for communication from which it likely springs aid in the formation of a Russian prose idiom capable of rendering the very ordinary. This is to say that Bolotov's textual output is pre-novelistic not only in the sense that Thomas Newlin finds him to be the perfect *pomeshchik* as he would later be imagined by Pushkin, Gogol, and Tolstoy, but also because his remarkably copious, even prolix, writings on domestic culture likely made prosaic estate life more accessible to literary representation. If Novikov's texts contributed to the development of an artistically refracting prose idiom for the depiction of the rural nobility, Bolotov's prescriptive (as opposed to creative) prose develops the textual space and language for the same subject.

Furthermore, in his attempts to deal with low circulation figures, Bolotov borrows techniques developed at earlier stages of Russian periodical publishing by creating fictional and encouraging real provincials to participate in his journals as producers and consumers of agricultural advice. Karamzin's journalistic activity represents a subsequent stage in the formation of the nobleman-farmer as a public figure.

Karamzin's Gentle Readers

Nikolai Karamzin made his professional debut as one of Novikov's young collaborators, joining the Friendly Literary Society in Moscow in 1785. Soon thereafter Karamzin began to edit *Children's Reading for the Heart and Mind* (*Detskoe chtenie dlia serdtsa i razuma*), Russia's first children's periodical, which was appended to the *Moscow News* (*Moskovskie vedomosti*) contemporaneously with Bolotov's *Economic Magazine*.[52] *Children's Reading* had impressively varied contents, both original and translated: dramatic works, fables and fairy tales, treatises on the natural sciences written to be accessible to children, as well as a good deal in the way of edifying fiction (for example, conversations between a parent and child). In this last respect it may be said to have shared the sensibility of Novikov's earlier journalistic ventures in the emphasis on gentle didacticism and the cultivation of civic virtues.

Thus, for example, the journal published the fictional "Correspondence between a Father and Son about Country Life" ("Perepiska otsa s synom o derevenskoi zhizni"), a set of letters between an urban nobleman and the son whom he has sent to the countryside for a morally edifying experience. Once again, the dual addressivity of the letters both to father and son and to a broad public proves key. At an early stage in the correspondence, the not yet reformed youth reports incredulously that his male cousins "take their rakes and go to the vegetable garden," where "one plants beans, the other plants chickpeas, the third weeds the beds, while the fourth pulls out the weeds." [53] The country boys' education consists of such activities as lengthy discussions about the uses of the potato crop. To the considerable chagrin of the young correspondent, even their games amount to a useful activity related to life in the provinces: they play "cards" (*karty*) by taking local maps (*karty*) and reviewing information about provincial townships. Nearly every activity these young noblemen undertake at the estate seems a slightly refracted version of the Free Economic Society's vision of exemplary noble life in the provinces: from the emphasis on learning about the local geography, culture, and crops, to insisting that the educated landowner be a useful member of local society. Eventually, the young man who has been sent to the countryside is reformed and begins to work enthusiastically in the common garden. Once again, participation in manual labor is mentioned as constitutive of becoming good noble citizens and, as the final letter indicates, becoming "useful to your compatriots."[54] Karamzin's own subsequent writings about the role, duties, and life of the gentryman in the provinces show him to be an heir both to Novikov and one of his collaborators, Bolotov.

The most mature of Karamzin's periodical ventures, the *Messenger of Europe* (*Vestnik Evropy*) cultivates a sense of the public with great sophistication.[55] Russia's first private periodical permitted to print political news famously featured a good deal of European fare: translated literature, publicistic writings on historical and current topics, as well as much in the way of brief reports on the habits, novelties, and rumors that captured the European imagination. Printed in the "Miscellany" (Smes') section, these items were usually prefaced with some variation on the phrase "they say that . . ." so as to approximate a scene of virtual, textually generated sociability and polite conversation. Karamzin transferred the fashionable talk of the pan-European salon from the private drawing room to the pages of the journal. The cosmopolitanism of the journal's contents was tempered by the patriotism that dominated the publication. This feature was particularly pronounced in the many fictitious missives printed in the journal.

The inaugural issue opens with a letter to the editor authored by Karamzin himself. The gesture of announcing a new journal's goals and primary preoccupations in a fictive letter to the editor was fast becoming a very common practice. "I will tell you [*tebe*] in all sincerity that I became very glad to see that you intend to publish a journal for Russia," the correspondent begins, announcing hopefully what he perceives to be the recent growth of the reading public.[56] Karamzin deploys the discursive codes of intimacy and friendship that governed the cultural production of the preceding decades to forge warmly affective ties between a ventriloquized representative of an anonymous and distant public and the periodical's editor.[57] Writing from "the border with Asia," the correspondent reports that he regularly purchases reading material from itinerant vendors, colporteurs who, in his words, sell printed goods to "our country nobles" (*sel'skim nashim dvorianam*), whose families shorten long autumn evenings by reading novels.[58] The conflation of inhabiting a geographic periphery (the "border with Asia") and engaging actively in the empire's cultural life through reading recurs at multiple instances throughout the journal. Karamzin ventriloquizes his purported readers in such a fashion that they often write from a position of simultaneous alienation from and avid, participatory interest in the empire's public life. This scenario brings to mind the noblemen's correspondence in Bolotov's agricultural ventures. They, too, wrote from a position of simultaneous estrangement and engagement. As was mentioned above, Bolotov's agricultural advice amounted, among other things, to a kind of "novelization" of the life of the landowner. A similar dynamic is at play throughout Karamzin's journal. The provincial correspondent disparages such representatives of the eighteenth century's attempts at the genre of the novel as *Milord Georg*, which he calls a foolish book, and hopes that with encouragement, the current state of affairs ("we have so few Authors") may be improved.[59] Karamzin begins to populate the remote provinces with a gentry audience of avid readers in search of novels in which their own experiences may find reflection.[60]

As they are depicted on the pages of the journal, the experiences of the male nobility amount largely to a systematically articulated conservative and paternalistic masculine domestic ideology. Karamzin offers to reform wastrel noblemen by sending them to the countryside, where they may observe agricultural labor. In a very well-known article titled "The Pleasant Prospects, Hopes, and Wishes of the Current Period" ("Priiatnye vidy, nadezhdy i zhelaniia nyneshnego vremeni"), he advocates thrifty estate management and the betterment of the peasants' living conditions through the founding of schools and hospitals, and the introduction of better agricultural methods, calling all such activities a way to "leave for the fatherland monuments [that attest to the way you have lived] your life."[61] Good estate administration becomes a route toward the most lasting sort of self-creation and self-assertion for the nobility. The building of roads and bridges that will bear the names of the noblemen who financed the projects is encouraged in part because an individual landowner's name as a marker of self and identity will be inscribed onto the landscape, thus giving concrete expression to the fact that the nobleman was present at his estate, acting as a careful steward of his property. When Karamzin suggests that nobles become more responsible managers of their estates, he does so in terms that underscore that this will not only contribute to the betterment of the nation, but will also give permanent expression to both individual and corporate gentry identity. "The gentry is the soul and noble image of the entire nation" (*dvorianstvo est' dusha i blagorodnyi obraz vsego naroda*), and although "not all people can be warriors or judges ... everyone can serve the fatherland."[62] Karamzin concludes the article by enumerating various scenarios of virtuous nobility: "the hero destroys his enemies or keeps internal order, the judge rescues innocence, the father educates his children, the academician shares knowledge, the wealthy person creates monuments of his charity [*monumenty blagotvoreniia*], the master looks after his serfs, the landowner contributes to the successes of agriculture: all are equally useful to the state."[63] Said otherwise, the nobleman who does not serve the state can *serve the state* in his capacity as a good landowner.

In 1803 Karamzin would author a response to his own programmatic writings, a text written by one Luka Eremeev, a fictitious subscriber whose sensibilities have been shaped almost entirely by the journal.[64] In effect, Luka is Karamzin's perfect reader. In his "Letter from a Rural Resident"

("Pis'mo sel'skogo zhitelia"), Luka reports returning to his ancestral estate after a long absence to find it in complete disarray. Karamzin provides a long narrative about Luka's transformation as Eremeev himself understands it, using the rhetorical vehicle of the letter as a prime textual site for the contemplation of selfhood. Luka writes,

> You know that I once was ablaze with the zeal to have a vast sphere of activity, in my immodest reliance on my own love for goodness and humanity. But a lengthy education in the school of experience and hard knocks, this cruel master, has curbed my pride—curbed it to such an extent that I, having abandoned all further wishes for the lustrous lot of *glory seekers*, have taken up—the plow and the wooden plow [*vzialsia – za plug i sokhu*].[65]

Just what does it mean for this nobleman to have "taken up the plow"? Luka has become the model farmer, if not via direct participation in peasant work (this fantasy about the nobleman's manual labor would find its fullest expression in *Anna Karenina*) then by becoming "the most hardworking estate manager," taking an earnest interest in every aspect of estate life and work, from peasant huts and fertilizer to peasant schools and medicine. Still, Luka does describe how "with great pleasure, I dug up with my own hands a source of fresh water near the biggest road, I surrounded it with unpolished rocks, made a turf canapé, and now I often sit there and happily look at the passersby, who quench their thirst with *my* water."[66] The landowner here follows Karamzin's suggestion (articulated in the previous article discussed above) that a nobleman ought to mark the landscape by his work, alter it, and in a sense, make it all the more his own; hence the emphasis on both the land and the water being *his*. Property ownership and, to a significant extent, the very presence of the nobleman at his provincial estate, become once again expressed in part through a reference to manual labor, in a hypertrophied iteration of a cultural need to imagine retired noblemen who *work* by performing a service from which the community or the public may stand to benefit.

The letter ends with an affect-laden statement about the rights and obligations of the model landowner that encapsulates the masculine domestic ideology to which the concluding decades of the eighteenth century gave rise. Karamzin's Luka writes,

No, I cannot doubt their [the peasants'] love for me!

This certainty, dear friend, is pleasant for my soul; but much more pleasant, more sweet is the certainty that I am living in such a way that truly benefits the five hundred people who have been entrusted to me by fate. It is deplorable to live with people who do not wish to love us: but it is most intolerable to live a useless life. The main right of the Russian nobleman is to be a landowner, his main duty [*dolzhnost'*] is to be a kind landowner; he who fulfills it serves the fatherland as a faithful son, he serves the monarch as a faithful subject: because Alexander wishes the happiness of the peasants.[67]

The letter gives expression to the hierarchically imagined context for the modern experience of male gentry selfhood; being a good landowner is commensurate with serving the tsar. Luka here uses the space of the letter in order to articulate for himself and for his audience his own position as the steward of property and unfree labor in a way that both looks forward to the novelistic tradition of the nineteenth century and reads as a culmination of a long process. The title of Luka's letter repeats Bolotov's *Rural Resident*. The letter is addressed to a "dear friend" who "wishes to know all the details about my [Luka's] isolation" (*vse podrobnosti moego uedineniia*).[68] Both the friendly address and the reference to isolation (*uedinenie*) are Bolotovian, as are the prolix dimensions of Luka's prose about himself ("rural residents" like to speak at great length, he admits). To be clear, there is no need to insist on a direct intertextual link here, with Luka Eremeev as a kind of latter-day Bolotov. Karamzin's rural nobles appear as a particular stage within a longer cultural tradition that was replete with diachronically placed echoes. The subsequent chapters of this study provide ample evidence of this rural resident's longevity in the Russian literary and cultural imagination—particularly, though not exclusively, in the novelistic output.[69]

For the moment, it is equally useful to regard "Letter from a Rural Resident" in a narrower context, and to orient the missive, which appeared in September of 1803, in relation to Alexander I's legislation earlier during the same year, the Edict on the Free Farmers (promulgated in February), which gave landowners the right to grant freedom to peasants in exchange for compensation. This measure would subsequently be seen as an early step on the route to the emancipation of the serfs in 1861. Karamzin, like most conservatives of the period, did not support it. It may then be that the "Letter from a Rural Resident"—in its ardent endorsement of the landowner as the sole figure able to bring order and prosperity to the provinces—both expressed indirectly and assuaged potential anxieties about the erosion of the cultural and economic status quo that Alexander's legislation had begun to inspire. Certainly Rostopchin's 1806 pamphlet on agriculture with which this chapter began, as well as his immediately subsequent writings, some of them also from the point of view of fictive paternalistic everymen-landowners, may be regarded as at least partly motivated by concerns over peasant uprising.[70] As Alexander Martin puts it while considering Rostopchin's correspondence with Alexander I during this period (that is, when Russia had begun to engage in the War of the Fourth Coalition): "Rostopchin spoke for many nobles who feared peasant unrest."[71] There is a potential explanation here for the longevity of the nobleman at the plow in the period's public discourse. It is tempting to suggest that in the peculiar rhetorical constructions of both Karamzin and Rostopchin, the nobleman replaces or, better, supplants the peasant at the plow at moments when the institution of serfdom seemed to be in jeopardy. Writing in 1806 to a tsar during whose reign he had fallen into disfavor and retreated from public life, Rostopchin reiterates forcefully the nobility's position as "the sole pillar of the throne"—that is, the "sole pillar" vis-à-vis the members of other social estates, whom he regards implicitly to be more liable to revolt during wartime and, of course, to revolt "through the destruction of the nobility," who then come to embody political order at the national level.[72]

Although the gentry had not been an estate of state servitors in an obligatory sense for nearly a half century, it is unsurprising that at this moment an ethic of service and noble initiative in maintaining the status quo should gain force and even find refracted expression in such statements as the one with which this chapter began. Rostopchin's service "at the plow" has a particular resonance in 1806, much as it also has a long historical explanation. As was discussed in the introduction, until the manifesto of 1762 and Catherine II's subsequent legislation, noble landownership had been contingent on noblemen's active service to the polity. In reviewing the various iterations of the nobleman at the plow this chapter has offered, one might posit that these slippages into imagining noblemen working the land they own register tacitly the extent to which following the 1762 manifesto that made state service more a custom than a requirement, male noble land- and serf-ownership needed a new legitimizing narrative. In other words, the repeated appearances of the nobleman at the plow in Russian public discourse tell a story about the insecurity of noble rights and privileges prompted, in part, by the gradual waning of legally enforced noble obligations.[73]

As will be shown in the pages below, many novels produced in the nineteenth century turn upon the tension between noble privileges and obligations centered, in particular, around property ownership. "It is no accident that the eighteenth century became the century of the letter: through letter writing the individual unfolded himself in his subjectivity," writes Jürgen Habermas.[74] According to the German sociologist, from this epistolarity would emerge the West European novelistic tradition (for example, the literary works of Samuel Richardson or Jean-Jacques Rousseau), much of which tended to posit the primacy of middle-class experience and selfhood. In the preceding pages it was suggested that the cultural origins of the modern Russian novel are to be found, likewise, in "the century of the letter," but the "century" here described is comprised of texts that foreground noble identities. The concluding decades of the eighteenth century produced in Russia many of the cultural forms and institutions typically associated with the European Enlightenment. The nobleman as a subject and potential citizen occupied a prominent position in these texts' and institutions' ways of imagining civil society as a part of a hierarchically organized social world in which there exist the spaces for the experience of sociability along a demographic horizontality among one's equals and peers. With its suggestion of privacy (a letter that has a specific addressee), epistolarity delimited a semiautonomous sphere of discourse. At the same time, a letter may always be intercepted and even made available for public consumption. Inherent to this kind of writing is the possibility for the monitoring and surveillance of a potentially infinite number of intended and accidental readers. It was largely through this twofold effect of epistolarity, the illusion of autonomous privacy combined with the expectation of a vigilant, even critical audience, that the provincial landowner entered the Russian imperial imagination as a potential citizen. It so happens that the duality of this dynamic also maps onto the dominant literary movements of the period: Enlightenment satire's potential for didactic surveillance and the codes of friendship among equals that were so central to sentimentalism.

Chapter Two

Pushkin's Unfinished Nobles

In a set of notes produced in the 1830s, Pushkin asks: "*The Russian nobility*—what does it mean now?"[1] The question, although posed in pointed relation to the present moment, must have had a historical character inasmuch as potential answers would have indicated the contemporary consequences of a long process, the ways in which successive monarchs—Peter I and Catherine II, especially—had reimagined and reconfigured the nobility as a social estate. "By what means is a nobleman made?" Pushkin continues, "What follows from this. Deep disdain for this title. The nobleman landowner. His influence and importance—recruiting duty—rights. The nobleman in service—the nobleman in the countryside. The origins of the nobility. The nobleman at court" (12:206). Although schematic, these notes mark well the polarities that delimited noble identity in various contexts (for example, at court, in the countryside). That a nobleman could be "made" (*kakimi sposobami delaetsia dvorianin?*) refers in part to Pushkin's understanding of the Petrine creation of a service elite with permeable boundaries, the expansion of the estate, and the consequent shifts in the fortunes of the old gentry. Evident throughout these and other sets of Pushkin's notes is a keen interest in the historical origins of the nobility, as well as the estate's roles, its privileges, and its obligations in relation to the state and in the context of different reigns and their attendant shifting political cultures. Pushkin's unfinished prose—texts that may be categorized as literary, scholarly, or personal—registers robustly the meanings of gentry identity and status in the modern Russian culture of the poet's own day. Pushkin tends to treat the subject as an inherited problem that promises to (but does not necessarily) gain clarity through historical investigation.

The texts examined in the pages that follow range in completeness from schematic and sketchy notes never intended for publication to quite polished prose fiction (notably, *Dubrovskii*). Perhaps because the overwhelming majority of Pushkin's prose works remain unfinished, specialists have tended to treat this relatively large and diverse body of texts as deserving of close scrutiny nonetheless. The very boundary between completeness and incompleteness has tended to be obscured in such investigations. The selection of this particular sampling of the poet's prose has been motivated by a few factors.[2] First, these texts tend to evince the familiar Pushkinian fascination with the Petrine recalibration of the Russian elites. Second, and more germane to this study, these texts also, either overtly or tacitly, evaluate the condition of the nobility in the long aftermath of the 1762 manifesto that freed the male gentry from obligatory state service and that was followed by the rearticulation of noble obligations and privileges during Catherine II's reign. Third, these texts, be they fictional or not, may be understood as variously pre- or quasi-novelistic. This is not to reiterate a mainstay of literary histories: that from Pushkin's drafts sprang the great Russian realist novelistic giants. (Sometimes this was indeed the case, as will be discussed briefly in this study's concluding comments regarding *Anna Karenina*.) It should be highlighted from the start that each of the texts treated in this chapter entertains some aspect of what would become the chief preoccupations of both the novelistic and the broadly multi-generic public discourse about the Russian landowner. Of prime interest is what may be called the "novelization" of noble identity that these unfinished texts all but place on display for the critic. This novelization involves the subjection of nobility as a concept to a worldview that highlights the following points: the contingency or slipperiness of noble status in the poet's own historical moment, the idea that different, sometimes conflicting, iterations of nobility are emphatically products of historical epochs and transformations, and finally the tension between definitions of nobility as an innate characteristic and a set of qualities that may be acquired, learned and cultivated, or performed.[3]

The specific readings elaborated upon in greater detail below are as follows. Pushkin's unfinished *Novel in Letters* wears its eighteenth-century pedigree on nearly every page and sounds notes that will be familiar to readers of this study's first chapter. Modern gentry selfhood is constituted through epistolary correspondence with other, like-minded peers, the novel's logic goes. A retired nobleman may serve the state by taking good care of his property. This sensibility, although developed in the course of the last decades of the eighteenth century, will become a commonplace in the nineteenth-century multi-generic (that is, both novelistic and non-literary) discourse about the landowner and the masculine domestic ideology to which it gave rise. Pushkin's "History of the Village of Goriukhino" paints its central character, Belkin, as an awkward heir to the likes of Andrei Bolotov, the long-winded and self-consciously provincial nobleman-who-writes par excellence. How Pushkin's text will evaluate the lot of the retired nobleman in the new media environment that encourages, nay, invites, his participation as a chronicler of the exceedingly local, is quite another matter. Finally, the novel *Dubrovskii* is concerned squarely with the nobility's complicated, disconcertingly far from inalienable rights to property and what turns out to be the related question of noble identity and privileges as products of historical transformation. Taken together, the texts (not all of them literary) examined in the pages below betray an ambivalence about the modern condition of the nobility as a social estate. The premodern, medieval elites surface as potential, if tentatively entertained, alternatives to the current arrangement. The conceptual pairing of new and old nobles and the resultant acknowledgment of different iterations of nobility being contingent on historical circumstances animate much of Pushkin's prose.

Why the medieval upper classes should have interested Pushkin deserves an explanation. In a lengthy set of notes structured as a dialogue with himself, Pushkin conducts a broad comparative and historical overview of the nobility both as an abstract (and here perhaps implicitly European) and a specifically Russian social formation. He asks,

> What is the gentry? The highest hereditary estate of the nation, that is, endowed with great privileges in relation to property and individual freedom. By whom? By the people [*narod*] or by its representatives [*predstaviteliami*]. With what purpose? With the purpose of having powerful defenders or immediate advocates who are close to the government. [...] Is a preparatory education necessary for the gentry? It is. What might the gentry be taught? Independence, courage, nobility (honor in general). Are these

qualities not innate? They are, but a way of life may develop, amplify, or stifle them. Are they needed among the people, in the same way that, for example, diligence is needed? They are, for they are the bulwark [*la sauve garde*] of the diligent class [*klass*], which has no time to develop these qualities.

Who comprises the gentry in republics? Wealthy persons, who feed the people.

And in states? Military persons, who comprise the guards or the monarch's army.

What will the gentry in republics *lead to*? Aristocratic rule. And in states [*gosudarstvakh*]? The enserfment of the people, a = b.

What comprised the ancient aristocracy in Russia? The *variagi*,[4] wealthy military Slavs and warlike foreigners. What were their rights? Equal to princely, for they were minor princes, had their own retinues, and went from one monarch to the next. Why does Mr. Polevoi say that they were equal to the *smerds*?[5] I do not know. But the very silence of the chroniclers about their rights shows that their rights were not limited by anything. What was the time of our boyars' *power*? The time of the *udels*,[6] the *udel* princes who became boyars. When did the boyars fall? During the Ioanns, who only left *mestnichestvo*[7] untouched. Were there gentry charters [*gramoty*]? ... (Minin.) Was *mestnichestvo* wrong? Is it natural? Did it exist everywhere? Why was it destroyed? And was it really destroyed? PETER. The destruction of the gentry with ranks. Primogeniture and entailed estates [*maioratstva*]— destroyed by Anna Ivanovna's knavishness. The gradual decline of the gentry; what follows from it? The ascension of Catherine II, December 14, and so on. (12:205–6)

Part research plans, part diary, and quite possibly a draft of a reply to Nikolai Polevoi's *History of the Russian People* (*Istoriia russkogo naroda*), these notes register the perception—for Pushkin both scholarly and personal—that the decline of the old nobility all but determined the course of Russian history, culminating in Catherine II's coup in 1762 and the Decembrist uprising of 1825. The decline of the nobility is understood to have issued in large part from the practice of partible inheritance, which Peter I abolished, but which Anna Ioannovna reinstated, at the nobility's urging. The splintering of estates resulted in the impoverishment and the disempowerment of the old nobility. As an alternative to the current state of the gentry, Pushkin imagines a pre-Petrine elite who, (he maintains), if one examines the sufficiently remote past, had considerable autonomy from the premodern princely state. These are minor princes whose power is identical in quality to that of the royals. Moreover, nobility rests conceptually and definitionally on the endowment of the elite with "great privileges in relation to property and individual freedom." It is debatable whether any subject of the Russian Empire of Pushkin's day would have understood himself to have had such privileges and such freedom, which is perhaps why Pushkin relegates these rights to the boyar past. For Pushkin, as for his contemporaries, the medieval elite's purported liberty (and it is useful to bear in mind that the poet is dealing here not with hard facts but with a wistfully imagined past) would have contrasted sharply with both the then-current Nikolaevan and the preceding reigns. In particular, Paul I's short reign proved probably the most corrosive to any illusions nobles might have had about their autonomy and dignity. Yet it is Catherine's transformative reign, during which the nobles gained something akin to rights but lost political power in the process, that receives a particularly complex evaluation from Pushkin. In the 1830s, her reign appears all but inevitable to the poet. In the younger Pushkin's view, the Russian "Tartuffe in a skirt" appears villainous for having weakened the nobility both in its corporate self-consciousness as well as in more tangible ways by redistributing estates among a new elite to a still greater degree than had been the practice of her predecessors. "While reading her hypocritical *Instruction* it is impossible to curb one's righteous indignation," writes Pushkin, for whom the promise of a Catherinean civil society defined by the rule of law had gone unfulfilled from the start (11:17). But much as the contents of Catherine's reforms may have inspired an at best ambivalent response in Pushkin, his prose nevertheless registers the transformative character of her reign in various ways that have to do as much with the politics of noble rights and privileges as with the discursive vessels, the very rhetorical situations, in which these ideas may be explored and expressed.

Consider *Novel in Letters*, a text that foregrounds the eighteenth-century roots of modern noble self-fashioning and self-understanding. The unfinished epistolary novel reads as a lively contemplation of the past and potential future of the Russian novelistic tradition placed in a selectively European context. The text offers the personal letter as a medium for the discursive exploration of selfhood and epistolary intersubjectivity as a means of gentry self-fashioning. Structured around a juxtaposition of city and country, the novel presents a series of epistolary exchanges between four young nobles: two men and two women. One in each pair—Liza and Vladimir—has returned to the country, while Liza's female friend Sasha and Vladimir's unnamed correspondent remain in the capital. Replete with discussions about the nature of literary production, the text displays an active interest in juxtaposing the outdated with the current, in addressing meta-literary concerns with an emphasis on literary evolution, all in a search for an aesthetically sophisticated prose idiom that will depict the Russian social world of the moment.[8] *Novel in Letters*, then, is at least partly about the business of writing a novel about the Russian gentry. Young Liza, who admits that she "reads a very great deal," muses about the depiction of men and women in the novels she has been reading (Samuel Richardson's *Clarissa*, Benjamin Constant's *Adolphe*), placing an emphasis on aspects of novelistic representation that become outdated with time (8:51). In the Russian context of his own time, Pushkin's choice of the epistolary mode in 1829 may well have created a readerly expectation for a society novel. But his reference to Samuel Richardson's *Clarissa; or the History of a Young Lady* (1747–1748) might prompt an association with the eighteenth-century English and more broadly European cultural heritage. Richardson's oeuvre generally and *Clarissa* particularly have long been regarded as part of a broad transformation in European culture, one that saw the rise of cultural forms that are often studied for their discursive cultivation of scenarios for experiencing modern selfhood.[9] An aggregate sense of these issues—put simply, the notion that social and political identities are formed through reading and while writing texts addressed to one's social peers—takes center stage in *Novel in Letters*.

Pushkin works quite actively with Richardson's text, at times rewriting the eighteenth-century English classic. Much of Clarissa's turmoil comes as the result of her wealthy family's desire to advance socially, to gain aristocratic status. Pushkin reverses this situation: his heroine, Liza, comes from the old but impoverished gentry and is in love with Vladimir, a wealthy but upstart nobleman. Liza's statement regarding the difference in backgrounds between herself and the young man comes in the form of another reference to novelistic representation, as she hastens "to note proudly, like a real heroine of a novel, that [she] comes from the most ancient Russian nobility" (8:49). As Liza and her friend

Sasha discuss the former's fears about the romantic dalliance she worries will come to no good end because of the difference in wealth and social standing, Sasha jokingly remarks: "Have you become some sort of provincial heroine [of a novel] [*Uzh ne sdelalas' li ty uezdnoi geroinei*]" (8:52). It is when Liza writes pointedly about her social identity that she is likened to a novelistic heroine. Both women's statements attest to a keen if, characteristically for Pushkin, lighthearted awareness of literature as a vehicle for the performative cultivation of social identities through a kind of verbal play.[10]

Pushkin explores various possibilities for plot development. For example, there is Liza's early forecast of her plotline: "If I should ever get married, then I will choose here some forty-year-old landowner [*kakogo-nibud' sorokaletnego pomeshchika*]. He will be busy with his sugar factory, I with the housekeeping—and I will be happy" (8:49). The mature nobleman who would make such an end possible never appears. It is quite clear that Liza, accustomed as she is to Petersburg society culture, would find such a mate less than agreeable. Why, then, does the novel suggest him? Why does Pushkin's text approach without ever achieving the representation of a prosaic country domesticity: the older, practically minded landowner, young Liza turned into a provincial lady of the house?[11]

Novel in Letters offers, if not a "finished," then a suggestively potential landowner. Upon spending two weeks in the country, Liza's genuine love interest, the young Vladimir, reports that, having grown tired of life in St. Petersburg, he enjoys village life a great deal. In a letter addressed to his friend, Vladimir writes at length about the meanings that accrue to male noble identity as he understands it:

> To not love the country is forgivable for a young girl, a Smolny graduate, who has been recently let out of her cage, or an eighteen-year-old *kammerjunker*.[12] Petersburg is our foyer, Moscow our maids' room, whereas the country is our study. A decent man passes through the foyer as it is necessary and rarely goes into the maids' room; he spends most of his time in the study. And this is just how I will end up. I will retire from service, get married and go off to my Saratov village. The title of landowner [*pomeshchik*] is the same service as any other. To be busy with the administration of three thousand serfs, whose entire well-being is completely dependent on us, is more important than leading a platoon or copying diplomatic dispatches . . .

The state of neglect in which we leave our peasants is inexcusable. The
more rights we have over them, the greater our obligations toward them.
(8:52–53)

Vladimir explains what he takes to be the lamentable decline of the old
nobility in economic terms and muses further, "when I speak in favor of
the aristocracy, I do not contort myself into some awkward English lord;
my own pedigree, although I am not ashamed of it, does not give me any
right to do so" (8:54). The correspondence showcases a young nobleman
in the process of attempting actively to understand the broad spectrum
of cultural, economic, and political choices available to a person of his
social estate. Using the language of rights (*prava*) and obligations, Vladimir outlines what will become a mainstay of the nineteenth-century novelistic tradition: the nobleman's assertion that to retire to the countryside
and mind his property constitutes service to the polity. Vladimir admits
that he "has been doing all of this thinking" while living in the provinces,
observing the estate life of small-time landowners for whom "the times
of Fonvizin have not yet passed. Among them still flourish Prostakovs
and Skotinins!" (8:53).[13] Having placed his Vladimir among the country
squires of neoclassical comedy, Pushkin all but invites his reader to look
to the preceding cultural tradition. Vladimir has been treated by critics as
little more than Pushkin's *raisonneur*. While it is true that the impoverishment and general disenfranchisement of the old aristocracy occupied
Pushkin as a political thinker, his Vladimir is an heir to a long tradition. As
discussed in chapter 1, a variety of eighteenth- and early nineteenth-century texts produced by such entities and individuals as the Free Economic
Society, Nikolai Novikov, Andrei Bolotov, Nikolai Karamzin, and Fyodor
Rostopchin contributed to the formation of the figure Vladimir wishes
to become: the retired nobleman who serves the state by performing his
duties as a landowner in the countryside. In the concluding decades of the
eighteenth century, the discursive space for the expression of the landowner's domestic ideology was constituted by texts that frequently purported to be personal documents, most often letters circulated for public
consumption. Thus, both Vladimir's assertions regarding the life of the
landowner and the rhetorical scenario in which his statements appear—
an epistolary novel—have their roots in the Catherinean refashioning of

noble culture and self-understanding, the Russian "century of the letter," as it was described in chapter 1. In other words, while the direction of Vladimir's thinking about the nobility is, undoubtedly, Pushkin's own, the novelistic rhetorical vessel for the articulation of his ideas appears strikingly Catherinean.

If *Novel in Letters* gives relatively optimistic expression to the inherited character of noble identity in the figure of Vladimir, the "History of the Village of Goriukhino" offers a more caustic appraisal. In the representation of the landowner-turned-writer Belkin, the text subjects the avenues through which a relatively unremarkable country squire might hope to participate in the public life of the empire to pithy comic ridicule. Like a number of other characters in Pushkin's poetic and prose works concerned with social status, Belkin comes from an old and, of late, quite impoverished noble family. Goriukhino is the sole remaining village of their once considerable properties. Belkin's very composition of the history is underwritten by a question that may be expressed as follows: how is a thoroughly middling nobleman like Belkin to engage with the social world he inhabits? The first and initial answer seems to be: by writing. But by writing what sort of text? Like another of Pushkin's naïve noblemen-narrators, Grinev of *The Captain's Daughter*, Belkin begins his writerly pursuits with poetry. He attempts an epic poem, then moves downward on the neoclassical generic system to arrive, at last, at humble prose.[14] Also like Grinev, Belkin ultimately writes a historical text that is composed using a highly stylized, provincial idiom that all but flaunts the landowner-writer's lack of sophistication. But just what sort of text does Belkin end up producing? Surely, the answers are many. Pushkin's use of Belkin's less than competent narrative to comment on the state of Russian historical writing has inspired robust commentary. In particular, it has been established that Nikolai Polevoi's *History of the Russian People* is among Pushkin's prime targets, and that even Nikolai Karamzin's *History of the Russian State* (*Istoriia gosudarstva rossiiskogo*) becomes the object of (far lighter) satire. The reading offered below adds another dimension to the text's long-acknowledged satirical ambidexterity. Certain, relatively underexplored aspects of Belkin's writings become particularly prominent in the context of this study. For example, under what generic rubric might one file such episodes from Belkin's history as the ones that follow below?

From ancient times Goriukhino has been renowned for the fecundity of its land and for its healthful climate. Rye, oats, barley, and buckwheat grow on its fertile fields. A birch wood and a fir forest supply its inhabitants with timber and firewood for the construction and heating of their dwellings. There is no shortage of nuts, cranberries, cowberries, and bilberries. Mushrooms grow in unusual quantities; broiled with sour cream they make a tasty, albeit unhealthy, dish. The pond is full of carp, and the Sivka River teams with pike and burbot.

[...]

The inhabitants of Goriukhino have since ancient times carried on an abundant trade in phloem fiber, baskets, and bast shoes. This is facilitated by the Sivka River, which they cross in boats in the spring, like the ancient Scandinavians, and ford in other seasons of the year, with their trousers rolled up to their knees.

[...]

The Goriukhinian men's attire consisted of a shirt worn over the trousers, a distinctive feature that revealed their Slavic origin. In the winter they wore sheepskin coats, but more for adornment than out of real need, since they would fling the coat over one shoulder only and would throw it off altogether for the slightest job that required physical exertion. (8:135–36)[15]

Belkin's review of local crops, his description of peasant trades and lifestyle, even his discussion of fishing, provide an artistically refracted version of a type of writing that flourished in both the short and especially the very long aftermath of 1762. Much of Belkin's discussion quoted above resembles such kinds of writing as the replies to the 1765 questionnaire published by the Free Economic Society. Readers of chapter 1 will recall the Society's publication of a lengthy questionnaire with the request that every willing literate person in the provinces reply with information about their local conditions. Despite some initial hurdles, the Free Economic Society's long-ranging investigation of Russia's provinces and the imperial strategy of which it was but one product had a long afterlife. Both the *Transactions of the Free Economic Society* and various other publications (for example, the *Farming Gazette* [*Zemledel'cheskaia gazeta*]) continued to print reports about local, provincial conditions. The landowning nobility were the much hoped-for and oft-solicited contributors to major agricultural journals and especially to the local periodicals that were encouraged by the Nikolaevan state beginning in the 1830s.[16] In this context, Belkin appears eminently readable as a nobleman engaged in the fashionable business of local writing.

That Belkin's appreciation for literary pursuits and his aspirations to the life of a writer should issue in part from a chance meeting with one litterateur B., a thinly veiled reference to one of the period's most successful journalists, Faddei Bulgarin, only amplifies Pushkin's lampooning of various kinds of local writing. As will be discussed in greater detail in the next chapter, Bulgarin was an exceedingly prolific and prominent writer especially when it comes to topics pertaining to the provincial middling nobility. Small-time landowners like the fictional Belkin counted in large numbers among the journalist's audience. Moreover, in his writings, Bulgarin cultivated various scenarios (in some respects not unlike those treated in chapter 1) for textually constituted peer-to-peer interactions among his noble provincial subscribers. When read in the context of a cultural and media environment that invited noblemen to participate in the period's developing public sphere through the popular vehicle of local writing, the "History of the Village of Goriukhino" appears to register considerable ambivalence about the available modes of noble sociability and belonging. Again, this reading is offered not to supplant the text's other preoccupations—notably, its engagement with historical writing—but rather to bring out a largely unexamined dimension of the text.

A number of critics have made the observation that the novel *Dubrovskii* picks up where Belkin would appear to leave the narrative about Goriukhino: with the possibility of peasant unrest.[17] Moreover, Sam Driver suggests that when the political dimension of a given work of fiction became pronounced, Pushkin tended to abandon it, leaving it incomplete.[18] Perhaps more than any other work by Pushkin, the unfinished (but quite polished) novel *Dubrovskii* revolves explicitly around noble rights, their limits as expressed in legal discourse, and the potential for their violation. Pushkin describes a dispute between two landowners. Both Dubrovskii and Troekurov are said to come from noble families, although it is likely that only Dubrovskii's nobility is genuinely ancient.[19] Whereas the fortunes of the Dubrovskii family have declined, Troekurov has risen in rank and become rather affluent: he owns three thousand serfs to Dubrovskii's mere seventy. During a visit to the wealthy landowner's dog kennel, Dubrovskii is insulted by his friend's serf, who says that some nobles might like to live like Troekurov's dogs. Dubrovskii demands that the offender be handed over to him for punishment; Troekurov refuses to comply, and the dispute escalates. At the crux of this part of the narrative is Troekurov's announcement that he intends to take away Dubrovskii's estate "without any right" (*bezo vsiakogo prava*) to do so (8:166). The estate once belonged to the Troekurov family; because the Dubrovskii family's papers have been lost in a fire, Troekurov succeeds in obtaining rights to the estate, using technically legal but obviously circuitous channels. Dubrovskii-père falls ill and dies as a consequence of this takeover. Dubrovskii-fils leads their peasants in vagabondage that has its generic origins in the heavily allusive fabric of this part of the text, and its reliance in particular on the genre of the *Räuberroman*.[20]

The concern with noble rights is focused largely on property. The narrator's position becomes quite clearly aligned with the perspective of the disenfranchised nobility when the readers are offered a full transcript of the court's decision regarding the Troekurov-Dubrovskii conflict,[21] because "it will be pleasant for all to see one of the means by which in Russia we may lose an estate to the ownership of which we have an incontestable right" (8:167). Noble landholding patterns receive ample attention in both the plotline and the conceptual vocabulary of the novel. Throughout *Dubrovskii* nobles are shown not to have old, lasting ties to specific locations in the countryside. Kistenevka,[22] the Dubrovskii estate, has gone through three sets of hands in about as many generations. The aging, worldly prince Vereiskii visits his estate for the first time in his nearly fifty years. Dubrovskii-fils comes home to a place that is only a little familiar, since he has spent his youth away from the estate, first at the Cadet Corps, then in an infantry regiment, based, for a time, in St. Petersburg. However, there is the suggestion that the Dubrovskii clan may be understood to be connected to a particular place. Their name has etymological links with the words oak (*dub*) and oak wood or simply a wood (*dubrava*). The latter of these associations proves operative in the story's spatial organization.[23]

Following the Dubrovskiis' loss of property, and after the young son burns down the family home, the estate—or, at any rate, a part of it—is transplanted into the woods. The peasants prove remarkably loyal; they remain with their young master even when he has ceased to occupy that position legally. In a sense, they assert his status as their lord and owner at a time when the state no longer recognizes it. By chapter 19 of the text, it becomes apparent that the house serfs and craftsmen have essentially transported the estate (in the sense of *usad'ba*, meaning the manorial holdings) from the house to dirt dwellings built in the deep, dark woods. (Ultimately, the group disbands when the government sends troops to the forest.) The association of the Dubrovskiis with the woods is illuminated by Jane Costlow's observation that the forest may be understood as a repository of Russian historical memory.[24] From a perspective that would foreground relatively recent history, Dubrovskii's gang may be understood to refer obliquely to the Pugachev rebellion, about which Pushkin wrote both a novel, *Captain's Daughter*, and a historical treatise. From another perspective, it may be (and this is offered as a more distant possibility) that Dubrovskii—in his extralegal occupation of the forest as master— becomes briefly a figure akin to the representatives of Russia's old, pre-Petrine elite, for example, the medieval princes (*udel'nye kniaz'ia*) who, especially as Pushkin imagined them, had only tenuous obligations to the tsar and weak, largely voluntary (as opposed to compulsory) connections to a larger polity. Dubrovskii's retreat to the woods is, at base, an assertion of noble independence from the Crown and state. This is how the novel registers disappointment with the failures of the Catherinean *Rechtsstaat*: forced out of the family's last remaining village, Dubrovskii-fils literalizes the seigneurial associations of his name (Dubrovskii can mean "of the wood") and, for a time, insists on inhabiting the forest as both Romantic robber and, from the serfs' perspective, an old-style *barin*.

But in what sense is the failed *Rechtsstaat* depicted in *Dubrovskii* Catherinean? It is clear that the events of the novel transpire some time after the 1790s, thus after Catherine II's reign. But beyond this point, it proves very difficult to date the events of the text with any sort of regularity and precision. It has been possible to read *Dubrovskii* as either a historical novel or a work of fiction about Pushkin's own period. However, in either case, it quickly becomes difficult to account mathematically for the various dates indicated. Troekurov's repeated whistling of "Sound, Thunder of Victory" ("Grom pobedy, razdavaisia"), the panegyric to Catherine II written in 1791 by the poet Gavriil Derzhavin to mark the Russian victory at Izmail during the Second Russo-Turkish War, marks him as a Catherinean man. A draft comment that the Troekurov family's fortunes went up specifically in the aftermath of the 1762 coup seals this highly significant association (Troekurov is a Catherinean upstart), much as the inclusion of 1762 would further confuse the dating of the events. Even working only with the dates suggested by the final extant version of the novel, it remains difficult to compile a chronology that would include the fact that Dubrovskii-fils's parents corresponded about little Vladimir's well-being during the Turkish campaign of 1787–1791, the fact that Vladimir is said to be about twenty-three years old when the main action transpires, and the reference to an 1818 piece of legislation. Even if he were somehow born in 1791 (the latest possible date for his parents' correspondence about him), he would be twenty-three sometime around 1814, and quite a bit older by the time the events of the novel transpire, after 1818. Of course, the text is unfinished, and some irregularities in its temporal structures are to be expected.

The coexistence of such relatively distant and disparate moments in modern Russian history as the 1762 of the Troekurovs' precipitous rise and the 1797 of Dubrovskii-père's last uniform suggests that the compositional history of the text shows the main events of the narrative hovering about some of the most important milestones in the history of the nobility. The origins of the instability of noble property rights are, therefore, more complex than can be accounted for by a single reign; however, the legibility of this instability may well be made possible by the expectations for the rule of law that Catherine's policies generated. When it comes to the specific dates mentioned by Pushkin, the relevance of 1762 will be obvious: it suggests Catherine's coup as a vehicle for the promotion of new nobles. The 1797 uniform surely refers to Paul I's sartorial reform, used here as an emblem for the many ways in which his reign was processed as insulting to the nobility, who lost many of their privileges at this time. All of this is to say that rather than attempting to date the text in some precise historical moment, it seems preferable to consider it as a contemplation of the very *historicity* of noble identity, its status, in other words, as a product of recent historical transformations.

The nobles of *Dubrovskii* are depicted, to a startling extent, as stock figures and pointedly as products of both imperial and their own personal clan histories. Thus, the upstart Troekurov must be consistently a boorish man who does not exhibit the honorable behavior of a true nobleman. Conversely, Dubrovskii-fils, who comes from an ancient noble family, even when he is disguised as the Frenchman Deforges, cannot help but act as an honnête homme of a recognizably old-style Russian, bear-killing variety. Thus, the noble politics of *Dubrovskii* are unsurprisingly conservative, in the sense that nobility of person turns out to be innate and not, as so many of the texts treated in the previous chapter suggested, the product chiefly of practice and cultivation.[25] The novel, of course, turns upon this tension between the innate nobility of the ancient upper classes and the uncultivated uncouthness of the newly ascendant elite.

Dubrovskii is not the only prose text in which Pushkin's examination of noble identity results in the introduction of multiple, rather distant, historical epochs into the narrative's fabric. In an unfinished prose piece anthologized as "Fragment," dated 1829, and concerned with the interactions of a celebrity poet with a motley and unsophisticated public that cannot appreciate him, Pushkin describes the poet's genealogy and potential future prospects. He writes,

> My friend issued from one of our most ancient noble clans, in which fact he took pride with all possible good-naturedness. He held dear the three lines of the chronicler, in which his ancestor was mentioned, as much as a fashionable *kammerjunker* holds dear the three stars of his uncle once removed. Poor, like almost all of our old nobility, he stuck up his nose as he asserted that he would never marry or else marry a princess of Riurik blood, specifically one of the princesses Eletskii, whose fathers and brothers, as is well known, now till the soil themselves, and when they encounter one another on their furrows [*borozda*], they shake clean their plows [*sokhi*] and say, "God help, prince Antip [Kuzmich], how much has your princely health plowed today?" "Thank you, prince Erema Avdeevich." (8:410)

The princes who plow come from pre-Romanov Riurik dynasties. Their names (Erema, Antip) suggest the medieval period. Their startlingly active farming might recall for the reader the currency of the nobleman at the plow as a rhetorical figure discussed in the previous chapter. However, these princes' plowing has a distinctly different set of associations here. Whereas the eighteenth- and early nineteenth-century nobles plowed in a rhetorical flourish that expressed their allegiance to the reforming polity that had invited them to become active landlords of their estates, Pushkin's Antip and Erema appear, at first, to be estranged from all modern cultural life. These are not, in other words, Catherinean nobles who engage in farm work (and, more often, in discussions of farm work) as a surrogate for state service. Rather, these are nobles who have become so impoverished that they perform the work of peasants. What historical time period might they inhabit? Immediately following this passage, readers are informed that the young poet's little "weakness," his considerable pride in his own genealogy, has been acquired in imitation of Lord Byron, "who also sold his poetry very successfully" (8:411). As moderns who live in the nineteenth century, the princes who plow are spectacularly bizarre; their characterization registers a disappointment with the contemporary condition of the old nobility in part through an implicit recourse to the pre-Petrine, indeed, pre-Romanov period, offered as an alternative to the present moment. Pushkin's princes plow to express the opposite of an allegiance to the reforming polity. For them, farming becomes a vehicle for the expression of a noble independence understood as an attribute of their clan histories.

The fortunes of the old nobility occupied Pushkin a great deal during the 1830s. The account provided in this chapter is far from exhaustive. It is meant, simply, to indicate some of the ways in which the tension between the old and new nobility animated both Pushkin's creative, novelistic imagination and his politics. Thus, in a diary entry made toward the end of 1834, the poet records, "imagine what a foolish thing they have printed in the *Northern Bee* [*Severnaia pchela*]" (12:334). He is recounting a conversation he had had with the Archduke Mikhail. The two men had shared their indignation at the fact that the newspaper had insisted repeatedly that the emperor had "bowed *low* (low!) to the people" when he appeared before the public during a visit to Moscow. "Don't forget that shopkeepers read this," the archduke had added (12:334). "The Archduke is correct, and the journalist is, of course, foolish," Pushkin concludes, before moving on to the rest of their conversation:

> Then we talked about the nobility. [...] I remarked that either the nobility is not needed by the state, or else it should be protected [*ograzhdeno*] and closed to entry except by the tsar's express will. If it is to be possible to enter the nobility from other estates, as one moves from one rank to another, and not according to the exclusive will of the tsar, but rather according to the order of service, then soon the nobility will not exist or (which is the same thing) everyone will be noble. As for the third estate [*tiers état*], what meaning is there to our ancient nobility with its estates [*imeniia*], destroyed by endless splitting, with its education, with its hatred for the aristocracy

and with all its pretensions to power and wealth? Even in Europe, there is no such terrifying mutinous element. Who was on the [Senate] square on December 14? Only nobles. How many of them will there be at the first new disturbance? I don't know, but I think many. Speaking about the old nobility, I said: "Nous, qui sommes aussi bons gentilshommes que l'empereur et vous ... etc."[26] The archduke was very gracious and open. "Vous êtes bien de votre famille; tous les Romanofs sont révolutionnaires et niveleurs."[27] "Thanks; so you have made me into a Jacobin! Thank you, voilà une reputation qui me manquait."[28] [...] I managed to tell him a great deal. God grant that my words may have yielded at least a drop of good! (12:334–35)

As this record of his conversation with the archduke attests, by the mid-1830s Pushkin had become interested in the so-called protection of the nobility (in Russian, *ograzhdenie dvorianstva*), a measure that would effectively close the estate to the vast majority of the newcomers who, ever since the introduction of the Table of Ranks, could enter it by advancing in service. The shifting role of the nobility in relation to the polity—the estate's privileges and obligations, its permeability—figures prominently in Pushkin's writing. In particular, the situation of the old nobility to which Pushkin himself belonged permeates much of his political thinking. The waning of the old, pre-Petrine elite, its impoverishment and weakness by the early decades of the nineteenth century, take center stage in Pushkin's political and, likewise, his novelistic imagination. Whether the nobility is "not needed by the state" is a question contemplated in many of Pushkin's personal, political, and literary writings. The relationship between the polity and its first citizens can take many forms. Under the best of circumstances, the nobility was to act as a necessary check on otherwise unlimited autocratic power in a manner that recalls Tolstoy's university musings about the Catherinean reformulation of noble privileges and obligations in her *Instruction*.[29] But such reciprocal relations between the elite and the state were more a wished-for scenario than a reality. Ultimately, disappointment with the old nobility's fortunes under the shifting political regimes of the day comes to be registered in Pushkin's writings partly in the recognition implicit in the texts discussed in this chapter of the multivalent, shifting, and historically conditioned character of noble identity.

CHAPTER THREE

Bulgarin's Landowners and the Public

In 1825 the poet Petr Viazemskii disagreed with Faddei Bulgarin's recent critical overview of Russian literature in general and with his appraisal of Vasilii Zhukovskii, Pushkin, and the fabulist Ivan Krylov in particular. Responding to Bulgarin's admittedly awkward comment that in Krylov's older fables the critic had sensed the authentic national character of "the Russian chicken, the Russian crow, the bear, the nightingale [...], the animals that inhabit my ancestral estate [*votchina*],"[1] Viazemskii published the following in a retort:

> Our sincere congratulations to our Aristarchus-landowner [*Aristarkh-pomeshchik*] regarding his ancestral estate [*votchina*]; it is not every scholar who can boast of such property; our congratulations once more regarding the fact that at the estate he has chickens and nightingales, pleasant sustenance for the stomach and the ears, although we regret vicariously that *bears inhabit* the estate [*votchina*], for country walks may result in unpleasant encounters for the landlord [*khoziain*].[2]

To be sure, in its general outlines Viazemskii's quarrel with Bulgarin was chiefly about the development of Russian poetic forms and had relatively little to do with the particular rhetorical vessel into which Bulgarin had packaged his comments.[3] Still, Bulgarin's easy donning of the mask of a patriotically minded Russian nobleman, and clearly a provincial one at that, seemed to add insult to injury, if Viazemskii's tone is any indication.

The amusement and outrage were not Viazemskii's alone. In a letter written about a month after the rebuttal was published, Pushkin advised his brother Lev that he should warn Viazemskii to be careful and not show the poet's newest works to anyone, "or else I will get robbed again—and I do not have an ancestral village [*derevnia*] with nightingales and bears" (13:158). In warning that he may "get robbed again," Pushkin was referring to the unauthorized republication of his works by Evstafii Oldekop, who had printed a German-language translation with the Russian original on facing pages. The tongue-in-cheek quipping about the ancestral village with nightingales and bears indicated at least two things. First, Pushkin was likely alluding to the fact that whereas Bulgarin was fast becoming a major force in the Russian book market of the period as a professional journalist, Pushkin and his associates retained an air of the gentryman dilettante about them. And, second, there was the fact that Bulgarin, as a Polish nobleman who had settled in Russia after the War of 1812, could have no claim to a *Russian* ancestral estate (*votchina*), as both Pushkin and Viazemskii before him surely meant to stress. And yet it will be the chief contention of this chapter that Bulgarin succeeded marvelously in writing *as* a Russian nobleman-landowner, a figure he treated almost wholly as a product of the period's quickly shifting media landscape and culture. In other words, as represented by Bulgarin, the landowner was a man created by the public discourse of the epoch. As the pages that follow will illustrate, the landowner was Bulgarin's public in more senses than one.

Easily among the most commercially successful men of letters during the second quarter of the nineteenth century, Faddei Bulgarin was known to contemporaries by many different names. Most notoriously of all, the so-called literary aristocracy had dubbed him Vidocq Figliarin.[4] The first name referred to Eugène-François Vidocq, former criminal and eventual founder and first chief of the French National Police (then, La Sûreté Nationale). In the Russian context, the name Vidocq reflected primarily the literati's awareness of Bulgarin's collaboration with the Third Section, Nicholas I's secret police. The surname issued from the word *figliar*, meaning a circus acrobat and, by extension in Bulgarin's case, someone willing to contort himself in order to please the public. Although meant as an unequivocal insult, the characterization of Bulgarin as a writer-journalist whose acrobatics both lured and, to a considerable degree, created the Russian purchasing public is not off the mark. In collaboration with

Nikolai Grech, Bulgarin edited the period's most widely distributed private newspaper, the *Northern Bee*, and stood at the helm of a number of other popular periodical ventures.

Throughout his career Bulgarin cultivated a kind of aggregate image of the Russian reading public on the pages of the periodicals he edited. Writing about the state of Russian public opinion approximately between 1825 and 1835, Abram Reitblat points out that periodicals, Bulgarin's very much chief among these, simulated on their pages the existence of public opinion about a range of permissible topics.[5] One of the most striking ways in which they did this was through the use of everymen-personae from whose points of view various items—for example, book reviews, observations about current mores and manners, travel notes—might be narrated. Bulgarin used this device with great skill. His newspaper, the *Northern Bee,* and his various other ventures tended to include articles written purportedly by non-professional representatives of the public. For Bulgarin the persona of an everyman-provincial landowner was a favorite beginning as early as the first issues of the *Northern Bee* in 1825; these featured, among other things, tales about and from the point of view of a rather comically hapless provincial in St. Petersburg.[6] Best known among such works is Bulgarin's journalistic reportage from the point of view of one Finnic landowner (*Chukhonskii pomeshchik*), largely because these articles were reworked by Gogol in the episode in "Diary of a Madman" ("Zapiski sumasshedshego") when Poprishchin remarks that Kursk landowners write well.

However, the public for which Bulgarin wrote and the public that he imagined on the pages of his periodicals, while it certainly included the nobility, would be best described as middling (in the parlance of the period, *srednee sostoianie*), rather than exclusively noble. Throughout the 1820s and 1830s, the so-called literary aristocrats would continue to find it difficult to establish their own periodicals. This is both because the state deemed many of them politically unreliable and because during the 1820s and 1830s they were not yet willing to deploy the tactics of the middlebrow press that catered to the tastes of middling readers who found Bulgarin's awkward fictive landowner's musings pleasing. Incidentally, Bulgarin's noms de plume were not meant to hide his identity. The journalist had an excellent ear for the middling, even mediocre public's tastes; the Finnic landowner and his likes appear to have been what the readers wanted.

Just what was the composition of the public and how might one describe the journalistic and literary public sphere during the second quarter of the nineteenth century? If chapter 1 presented a relatively optimistic view of the limits and potentials of civil society in Catherinean Russia as it was expressed by the cultural producers who came of age during her reign, the pages to come treat texts that suggest a grimmer picture, acknowledging that the promise of enlightened monarchy central to the early decades of the empress's rule went largely unfulfilled. And if it is not customary to speak of any such promise as a central tenet of Nicholas I's reign (although its legendarily repressive dimension has become both a popular and a scholarly mainstay that sometimes does more to obscure than to explain the period), it will nevertheless be the case that a parallel sort of simultaneous encouragement and curbing of autonomous public activity is to be glimpsed at this time. During the second quarter of the nineteenth century, despite the tacit discouragement of the privately owned periodical press, the reading public grew steadily. If in the 1800s the subscribership of a successful journal could be counted in the several hundreds, by the 1830s a handful of private periodicals had between three and ten thousand regular readers. That both the period's most successful private newspaper, the *Northern Bee,* and its most widely distributed private journal, the *Library for Reading* (*Biblioteka dlia chteniia*), were, to varying degrees, aligned with the state has, perhaps, been overemphasized. During this period it would have been scarcely possible to stand at the helm of a periodical without at least some collaboration with the state and, more specifically, with the Third Section.[7] In a situation broadly analogous to the one observed during the first two decades of Catherine's reign, there existed a not quite political and not entirely autonomous public sphere constituted, for our purposes here, above all by the press. The professionalization of writing, both literary and journalistic, proceeded concurrently with this development.

The growth of the institutions that enabled increasingly robust public discourse yielded the greater prominence of advice literature aimed at a variety of readers, the male nobility among them.[8] The inaugural issue of the *Farming Journal* (*Zemledel'cheskii zhurnal*, founded in 1821) described improvements in agriculture as the "holy duty" of Russia's landlords.[9] Founded in 1834, the *Farming Gazette* sounded similar notes, as did a growing number of both specialist and less than expert persons for whom writing about agriculture became something it had not been in the previous decades: profitable. Just who were the writers charged with for-mulating the gentryman's domestic ideology? Some were knowledgeable, serious scientists; others were actual landowners wishing to share their experience and findings. Still others, to paraphrase Vladimir Burnashev, an exceedingly prolific author of domestic advice literature aimed at the rural gentry, had little real knowledge of the matter.[10] During the second quarter of the nineteenth century, the task of writing about the duties of the nobleman in the provinces could potentially be undertaken by writers as different from each other as Alexander Pushkin, whose notes on the subject were treated in the previous chapter, and Vladimir Burnashev, whose poor command of the Russian language was lampooned in the periodical press of his time.

Between the late 1820s and early 1850s, a good number of authors of domestic advice literature had close ties to such leading figures in the commercially minded, middlebrow institutions of Russian print culture as Faddei Bulgarin, Nikolai Grech, Osip Senkovskii, and Nikolai Polevoi.[11] Bulgarin wrote instructional literature himself. He also had professional connections with Burnashev. Nikolai Polevoi's brother Ksenofont helped their sister Ekaterina Avdeeva (née Polevaia) to become one of the period's most popular authors of instructional nonfiction on a variety of subjects, from cooking to establishing farms. Burnashev and Avdeeva were some of the most prolific authors on their subjects during these years. Osip Senkovskii's *Library for Reading* catered to the provincial reader's tastes by publishing a good deal of information about gentry domestic culture. Senkovskii's journal had a famously high circulation rate. Although claiming that these writers had a monopoly on gentry domestic ideology would push the point too far, it certainly would not be an exaggeration to suggest that a strong contingent of the Russian how-to book market during the 1830s and 1840s was held by these representatives of the middlebrow institutions of Russian print culture. As writers and cultural producers more broadly gained the fiscal stability of professionals, a veritable industry developed around writing for and, as it turns out, often *as* rural landlords. Arbiter of good taste, avid reader, country simpleton, voice of reason, and patriot, the rural landlord wore many hats and all but dominated the public dis-course of the middle decades of the nineteenth century. So frequent were the appearances of the local *pomeshchik* (a contributor identified only as a landowner of a specific region) that this figure threatened to morph into

the public itself as a kind of stand-in or surrogate for the newly anonymous and distant readership of the emergent media culture.

Bulgarin's multi-generic output as a novelist and a journalist essentially
capitalizes on as well as showcases some of the chief preoccupations of
the phenomenon described above, the transformation of the Russian book
market and print media more broadly during the second quarter of the
nineteenth century. Bulgarin's novel *Ivan Vyzhigin* (1829), a transposition
of Alain René Lesage's early eighteenth-century picaresque *Gil Blas de San-
tillane* (1715–1735), may have accorded with the public's tastes and expectations for long prose fiction that would depict familiar, Russian life.[12] It
appears to have sold exceedingly well. Specific figures tend to be given at
approximately seven thousand copies in 1829 alone, with the first print
run selling out within weeks of publication, a considerable achievement
for the period. The novel's commercial success is to be attributed as much
to the middling tastes of its readers as to the veritable advertising campaign that preceded and accompanied its publication and was carried out
on the pages of the periodicals edited by Bulgarin, Grech, and their other
associates.

Moreover, the novel's structure and plot—an episodic treatment of the
titular picaro Vyzhigin's peregrinations—have an aesthetic simplicity that
asks for little from the reader familiar with Lesage's original, which had
been popular in Russia until as late as the 1810s.[13] Like its source text,
Vyzhigin has a didactic dimension expressed in what sophisticated contemporaries would have considered a stale, long-outdated tendency to
split characters into positive and negative versions of a given concept or
idea. For example, Bulgarin presents his novel's model landowner in a
chapter titled "A Landowner of Whose Sort May God Grant More to Russia. As Goes the Clergyman, So the Parish." The title of this chapter as well
as the landowner's name, Rossiianinov, combine to frame this figure as
more universal than particular; an all-Russian *pomeshchik* who embodies
the domestic ideology put forth by the novel. Likely in order to amplify
the edifying effect of the exemplary gentryman-farmer, Rossiianinov is
followed in the text by the landlord Glazdurin, a squanderer, who serves
as didactic counterexample. (Both names "speak" in the manner befitting
neoclassical comedy.) The Rossiianinov chapter is a protracted description of the provincial landowner's exemplary domesticity, punctuated
occasionally by the visitors' admiring commentary. As soon as the titular

hero Vyzhigin and his companions approach Rossiianinov's property, the reader is provided a view of the landscape: canals, properly tilled and fertilized fields, neat and well-tended meadows, tree-lined roads, well-maintained bridges, the peasants' excellent dwellings; these are followed by such attempts at rational modernization as an almshouse, a hospital, a smithy, a village supply store, and even a schoolhouse.[14] Everything proves worthy of mention, from the simple but tasty dinner of four dishes accompanied by a limited but first-rate selection of beverages to the superior cattle, harnesses, and agricultural instruments used by the serfs. Even the serfs' footwear deserves a digression on the practical benefits of wearing bast shoes—*lapti*, or *shmony*, as Bulgarin opted to render the term, using a regional dialect and thus introducing an ethnographic dimension to the novel. As if the succession of perfectly crafted elements of an estate were not enough to direct the reader's response, the visitors make such comments as: "Do you notice, [...] that we have arrived at the property of a decent person?"; "This is what all of Russia can and ought to be like!"; and "This Mr. Rossiianinov certainly is good at what he does."[15] The landlord himself is asked to speak about his activities and tells his audience about becoming disenchanted with service, retiring and following the advice of his father's old friend "to be useful to the tsar and the fatherland" by devoting himself to the "happiness" of his "five hundred peasant souls."[16] Bulgarin novelizes very straightforwardly what was fast becoming a cliché of Nikolaevan agricultural literature: that the nobleman may serve the state in his capacity as a good steward of property.

Much about the novel's representation of the model nobleman may be interpreted in relation to the period's shifting media culture. In particular, Rossiianinov is depicted as an all-Russian landlord both in the sense of being exemplary and (it is hoped, one day) representative and as all-Russian in another key. In the strong suggestion about the extent to which Mr. Rossiianinov ought to serve as an example to follow, there lurks the possibility that his characterization is the product of a media landscape that is beginning (very slowly and very unevenly) to approximate something approaching a mass culture sensibility. Rossiianinov, after all, inhabits a novel that is itself replicable inasmuch as it is an adaptation, a novel of the *Gil Blas* type, of which there were many and could always be more. Thus, both Bulgarin's model landowner and his novel are, to a considerable degree, products of a media environment that foregrounds reproduction

and reproducibility. The title hero Vyzhigin's lengthy peregrinations cul-
minate in retirement at his own country estate, where, at novel's end, he
and his family "work in their fields"; the reformed picaro becomes a figure
akin to Rossianinov.[17] Thus, the shape and structure of the novel as a whole
rearticulate and affirm ideas about the reproducibility of the virtuous
nobleman. It may well be that Bulgarin's interest in and relative ease with
producing a normative discourse about gentry life has to do with a broader
investment in the capacity of literature to transform the reader, in other
words, the edifying effects of fiction.[18] Inasmuch as this is the case, Bulgarin's fiction would seem to approach the sensibility of advice literature.

A little more than a decade after the publication of *Vyzhigin*, Bulgarin
would add advice literature to the multiple genres in which he worked
throughout his highly prolific career. "Now that is enough, Faddei, stop
beating a dead horse. You've talked everyone's ears off with your agronomy, about which you can reason about as well as a pig about oranges,"
writes Vladimir Burnashev while recounting a conversation in another set
of recollections, this one about how Bulgarin founded *Ekonom, a Univer-
sally Useful Domestic Library* (*Ekonom, khoziaistvennaia obshchepoleznaia
biblioteka*), a venture in which the two would come to collaborate.[19] The
weekly how-to periodical contained information on a wide range of subjects. Topics under regular discussion included estate administration (animal husbandry, crop cultivation, and sales), as well as housekeeping on a
smaller scale (recipes, interior decoration, cleaning).[20] Initially, Bulgarin's
presence all but dominated the journal. In order to inspire trust among
Ekonom's readership, the author alluded to the fact that the subscribers
"[had] known the Editor for over twenty years."[21] In the early 1840s, Bulgarin often contributed two or three long articles to each issue. He wrote
on such varied subjects as growing potatoes and popularizing this crop
and the need to establish trade relations between Russia and the Middle
East in order to sell domestic products. Alison K. Smith suggests that the
editor of the *Northern Bee* likely had a hand in the gastronomical section
of the periodical, contributing relatively highbrow recipes and what might
now be called food writing.[22]

One of the chief tasks undertaken by Bulgarin on the pages of *Ekonom*
was to offer a program for the proper administration of the country estate.
He treated the endeavor explicitly as a business venture, and the estate
as a space that presented ample opportunities for profit. In the inaugural

issue of *Ekonom* (January 1841), Bulgarin promised to make estate-keeping a more lucrative enterprise, alluding explicitly to higher revenues for his landowning readers. In "A Practical Home Course on Agriculture for Beginning Landowners" ("Prakticheskii domashnii kurs sel'skogo khoziaistva, dlia nachinaiushchikh khoziainichat'"), Bulgarin refers to agricultural enterprises undertaken at his estate of Karlovo near Dorpat, which he purchased in April 1828.[23] Much like in chapter 20 of *Vyzhigin*, he provides a detailed and lengthy account of the model estate. However, the estate life in question is no longer fictional, no longer novelistic: it is instead on the one hand abstractly exemplary and, on the other hand, purportedly the author's own. Bulgarin becomes a figure akin to his novelistic creation—the model landowner, Rossiianinov—rendered in a genre with a still higher capacity for detail as a formal feature of narrative. He writes for pages about choosing the right sort of cattle in accordance with the quality of pastures; he offers meticulous recipes and charts related to cattle feed; he discusses at length when and in what order he planted specific crops. It would be difficult to determine the extent to which Bulgarin's claims were grounded in real experiences. It is known that he lived on his estate from 1831 to 1837, leaving it occasionally for visits to St. Petersburg.[24] There is at least one piece of epistolary evidence (from Nikolai Grech) that the Dorpat landowner admitted that he had a bad harvest in 1832.[25] Of course, quite regardless of the rootedness of Bulgarin's formulations in any sort of documentary reality (something that would be interesting to determine so as to understand better the circumstances of his very public performance as an all-Russian landowner), what remains readily discernible is the degree to which Bulgarin cultivates for himself the persona of an exemplary *pomeshchik* and an authoritative voice in the growing market of how-to literature about home life. The editor's name became nearly synonymous with *Ekonom*, in part because he reported that upon meeting him at a bookshop, a representative provincial reader, "a clever landowner" on a visit to the city to purchase books, addressed him as "Mr. Ekonom."[26] This image encapsulates perfectly the situation: Bulgarin's discursive projection of an interminable series of "clever landowners" and the cultivation of himself as a universal landlord *and* king of the book market, or the King of Gostiny Dvor, as Nicholas I reputedly called him, referring to his considerable commercial success among a less than refined readership.

The very close association between Bulgarin and his weekly soon turned problematic. Between 1841 and 1846, *Notes of the Fatherland* (*Otechestvennye zapiski*) published a series of exceedingly negative reviews of Bulgarin's latest project. The attack was part of the long-standing rivalry between Andrei Kraevskii's journal and Bulgarin's and Grech's periodical enterprises. The particular shape that the polemics took reveals another dimension of the degree to which the landowner was becoming a surrogate for the reading public. The first review of *Ekonom* published in *Notes of the Fatherland* begins with some biting commentary from an anonymous critic, who then introduces a notebook appended to a letter received by the editors from "one very learned and experienced Russian landowner, who seems to have been offended by the agronomical heresies published in *Ekonom* and the *Northern Bee*."[27] The rest of the reviews are also from this and other clever landowners. Since works of instructional literature were usually reviewed by critics (sometimes as famous as Vissarion Belinsky and Vladimir Odoevsky), it is entirely possible and even likely that the provincial authors of the letters to the editor are an invention of Kraevskii and company, who frequently criticized the *Northern Bee* and Bulgarin.[28]

The offended provincial had become what Melissa Frazier calls "a well-known trope" in Russian periodicals by the mid-1830s.[29] George Gutsche explains one of the most famous examples of writing pseudonymously from the point of view of a provincial reader: Pushkin's 1836 letter to the editor of the *Contemporary* (*Sovremennik*) (himself) in response to Gogol's article "On the Movement of Journalistic Literature in 1834 and 1835" ("O dvizhenii zhurnal'noi literatury v 1834 i 1835 godu").[30] In Gutsche's view, "obviously someone from the provinces would be an ideal defender of the taste and judgment of provincials and, as a persona, he could serve polemical purposes relating to Pushkin's taste as well. These purposes included openly criticizing the infamous Bulgarin, and laying before the public reasonable views about language."[31] Pushkin's A. B. is an avid and knowledgeable consumer of periodicals. The provincial landowners who wrote to *Notes of the Fatherland* "subscribe to every periodical about domestic advice literature" and show an analogous interest in this part of Russian print culture. Their first two letters (published in 1841) are sent in by a person who is identified only as "a Tver province landowner." Pushkin's 1836 A. B. had also hailed from Tver, as did Osip Senkovskii's 1837 fictional trio of Tver province landowners, whose missive the editor both authored and published in his *Library for Reading*. Here is how Senkovskii characterizes Tver province while writing from the point of view of his three landowners: "When we say—Tver province, we mean by that all intelligent provinces, all of Russia."[32] Frazier explains that "as the landowners themselves acknowledge, their quintessentially average address suggests that Tver may be nothing more than an abstraction, the imaginary home of a Russian Everyman who does not really exist."[33] Moreover, as the province that served as the setting for Catherine II's 1775 provincial reforms, Tver retained a special status as both a generic province (the province as abstraction or conceptual category) and a place emblematic of modernization.[34] As Mary Cavender has shown, much as by the 1830s the Tver provincial nobility had considerable local ties, when they were invited to contribute to the provincial periodical press, the majority of them chose not to. Her observation lends further support to the case for Kraevskii and his associates masquerading as average provincials.

In response to Bulgarin's investment in the cultivation of his own persona as a model landowner whose efforts are appreciated by provincial subscribers, the reviewers of *Notes of the Fatherland* employ their own exemplary *pomeshchik*, a well-informed and, to a degree, representative reader. The reviews criticize *Ekonom* for faulty advice about specific agricultural undertakings, incompetence in the natural sciences, poor command of the Russian language, and rampant plagiarism from such comparatively venerable publications as the *Farming Gazette* and the *Transactions of the Free Economic Society*.[35] Whatever is not "borrowed" by *Ekonom* is judged to be lacking in quality and substance, with the potential to bring financial ruin upon the gullible provincial landlord. In response to the first negative reviews, the editor of the *Northern Bee* penned a lengthy retort. Taking the reviews to have issued from the pens of Kraevskii's editorial staff and not genuine provincials, Bulgarin himself plays the part of the landlord again and bitterly invites the journalists to come see "how well [his] grains are growing, how good [his] potato harvest is."[36] Ultimately, the broader quarrel between Bulgarin and Kraevskii, much as it had an aesthetic and ideological dimension, was in some part about being unable to share a purchasing reading public. The crude exchanges about *Ekonom* that took the form of a debate between clever and experienced landowners lay bare the device. Given that in the press of the period the landlord has become the public's surrogate, it makes sense that both parties would try to lay claim to his authoritative position.

By 1844 Bulgarin passed on the editorship of *Ekonom* to Burnashev, then asked (publicly on the pages of the *Northern Bee*) that all inquiries about *Ekonom* be directed to the new editor.[37] *Notes of the Fatherland* published another review, this time taking on Burnashev as well to suggest that having published a plagiarized translation of a book entitled *A Complete Practical Guide to Bovine Husbandry*, the indeed very prolific Burnashev might now go on to supplement this work with such titles as "*Complete Bull Husbandry, Complete Ox Husbandry, Complete Calf Husbandry, Complete Heifer Husbandry*, and so on with various other husbandries."[38] The joke expressed a growing concern, evident to any reader of the period's reviews of advice literature, that the available works appeared to all but replicate one another and that the market was becoming flooded with agricultural titles, not a few of them of poor quality.

Perhaps the best illustration of the perception about the overproduction of works about estate administration comes in the handful of articles published by Vladimir Odoevsky as Dr. Puf, his gastronomically fixated alter ego, who wrote erudite and lighthearted sketches about cooking and shopping for food, his "Notes for Landlords" ("Zapiski dlia khoziaev"), which were appended to the *Literary Gazette* (*Literaturnaia gazeta*) during the early 1840s and in which Alison K. Smith has glimpsed a potential parody of Faddei Bulgarin's food writing.[39] Published in the normally rather somber Domestic Advice (*Domovodstvo*) section of Kraevskii's journal, a section devoted to serious, scientific treatments of subjects pertaining mostly to farming, Odoevsky's articles bear such strange titles as "A Conversation about the Mining of Industry and the Tilling of Factory Ventures in General, and about Pickled Cucumbers in Particular" ("Razgovor ob izyskanii promyshlennostei i vozdelyvanii fabrichnostei voobshche, i o solenykh ogurtsakh v-osobennosti").[40] Puf's first article begins with a title that takes up an entire page. The heading "Estate Management and Home Economics" (*Domostroitel'stvo i domovodstvo*) grows increasingly tautological in the subtitle "Theory of Estate Management from the Ethical, Physical, Speculative, and Practical Points of View," which, it is announced, has been "expounded by Dr. Puf, professor of all sciences and many others."[41] The title page continues with a "Book One: Estate Management in General," then "Part One: Estate Management as Such," "Chapter One:

Estate Management on Its Own," "Section One: Estate Management as It Is," "Subdivision One: Estate Management as a Science," the list concluded finally by "Subsection One: About Estate Management from a Philological Point of View."[42] Odoevsky's copious footnotes refer to fictitious titles given in a funny mixture of Russian and Latin. For instance, the third note directs the reader to *Concerning the Serving of Mustard after Lunch: Fourteen Books with Commentary*, while the fourth refers to volume three of a book about sausage and salami production. The other footnotes have such titles as *Concerning the Art of Making Money in a Greedy and Appropriate Way*, as well as *The Art of Cheating Honestly in Society*.[43]

Puf writes: "I am a most honest and truthful person—my rules are well known, and I can say, as says the well-known writer Mr. Bulgarin: 'I am the brother of every honest, noble, and gifted person!'"[44] Even without the mention of Bulgarin, the very title of Odoevsky's undertaking, in its entirely unsubtle critique of farming literature as too specialized and as produced in order to prey on gullible readers, would have recalled Mr. Ekonom. The reader soon learns that like Bulgarin, Dr. Puf has been attacked by the editors of *Notes of the Fatherland*. In retaliation, he has decided to revise the terms of his contract and to fill his pages however he pleases. But had it not been for the attack, Puf claims that he would have published "entire treatises regarding Potology, Spoonology, Casserolism, Chandelierism, Lamposophy, Stainology, Carpetology, Parquetism, Table Management and Chair Management, Bedology, Cellar Studies, Sideboardosophy" (*tselye traktaty otnositel'no Gorshkologii, Lozhkologii, Kastriulizma, Shandalizma, Lampomudriia, Piatnosloviia, Kovrologii, Parketisma, Stolovodstva i Stulovodstva, Posteleslovia, Pogreboznaniia, Bufetomudriia*).[45] Puf's assertion that all of these "dissertations" would have contained ample references "not only to the European literatures, but also to the Sanskrit, Chinese, and Persepolitan and so on and so forth literatures" is a hyperbolic rendition of Bulgarin's oft-articulated promise to his readership that *Ekonom* is the first among domestic instructional periodicals because the editors consult a formidable body of foreign-language works on the subject.[46] On the whole, Dr. Puf's performance targeted Bulgarin and Burnashev on multiple counts. More generally, Odoevsky's creative "review" of Bulgarin's enterprise gave hypertrophied expression to the perception that the market for advice literature had taken on absurdly large dimensions characterized above all by the tendency to multiply its subjects and titles. Odoevsky's lengthy joke was as much about advice literature as it was about the relatively new conditions of the increasingly robust media environment and the increasing reproducibility of its contents.

Despite the attacks on *Ekonom*, Bulgarin's hiatus from the journal did not last very long. In 1849 Vladimir Burnashev left *Ekonom* to concentrate on editing the more reputable *Transactions of the Free Economic Society*. Bulgarin resumed his editorial duties.[47] An announcement for the upcoming year's installment was printed; Bulgarin's name appeared in large letters likely to attract the provincial reader. What sort of editorial persona did Bulgarin project to his readership upon his return in 1850, following the merciless lampooning he had received a few years ago? Bulgarin greets his reader with a passage that in some ways calls to mind Andrei Bolotov's agricultural writing (although in many ways the two men could not be more different in disposition): "Two mountains will not come together, but a man will meet another man again. I did not think that I would ever converse with the gracious readers of *Ekonom*, and yet fate has united us again!"[48] Bulgarin manages once again to forge a familiar, casual rapport with his provincial reader, casting the periodical as the textual space that fosters a friendly intimacy between himself and the subscriber. The familiar relations with the readership grow closer in the next sentence as Bulgarin predicts enthusiastically,

> Again, we will walk around the fields and the forests, look after the gardens and the vegetables, tend to the orangeries and the greenhouses, [tend to] cattle husbandry and stud farming, working to fill up the granaries and the pantry with various supplies, [working toward] the establishment of rural crafts and manufacturing, we will be building and rebuilding, and finally, we will begin to dine together, since neither a landlord nor a non-landlord can do without that.[49]

Inviting the readership to join him on an excursion across a markedly provincial landscape (comparable to the table of contents of his periodical), Bulgarin writes from the position of a well-wishing neighbor and fellow landowner. The owner of Karlovo proudly reports that, while his neighbors have suffered from poor harvests and epidemics of cattle disease, Bulgarin's own estate has fared better: the granaries remain full of provisions, and the cattle have been healthy for the last twenty years.[50] He adds that he will "always have enemies for publishing *Ekonom*" precisely because he will continue to "insist on the same points."[51] Once again, he alludes to the *Northern Bee*, this time to remind readers that even during his absence from *Ekonom*, he has been publishing articles on the topic of rural domestic affairs in his newspaper. The abstract all-Russian *pomeshchik* and the extremely well-known journalist Bulgarin become one as the Aristarchus-landowner of 1825 readies to end what was, from a commercial and sociological point of view, a dizzyingly successful career, with an assurance that *Ekonom* will be a periodical of excellent quality thanks to the "many years' experience of your humble servant *Faddei Bulgarin*" (emphasis in the original).[52]

Bulgarin's influence waned in the 1850s. It is possible that he returned to edit *Ekonom* in some part because much of his most enthusiastic and naïve audience appears to have been located in the provinces. Katherine Antonova's microhistorical study of a middling gentry family in Vladimir province reveals that the paterfamilias, Andrei Ivanovich Chikhachev, continued to admire Bulgarin despite the fact that as an avid consumer of the Russian press he subscribed to and read *Notes of the Fatherland*, among other publications.[53] Calling the *Northern Bee* his "little bee" (*pchelka*) and by various other diminutives, Chikhachev recorded enthusiastically that Bulgarin for him was "such a joy! Such a little berry!"[54] As Antonova explains, the newspaper's political orientation appealed to Chikhachev's own sensibilities, and it appears to have also opened for him additional zones of contact with like-minded men. Like Bolotov, Bulgarin cultivated a rapport of equals between his editorial persona and his readers through a kind of multiplication of the self that invited identification. He appears to have been so successful in this regard that Chikhachev, inspired by Bulgarin's example, decided to take up the pen. He then contributed a great deal in the way of articles about his native region (Vladimir) to various local and central periodicals devoted to agriculture and other kinds of local writing. Also like Bolotov, Chikhachev (who, unlike Bulgarin, resembled his elder compatriot in disposition and sensibility in many respects) made his private concerns as a provincial landowner and father a matter of public interest. He saw his work as patriotic and as akin to service to the polity. Antonova suggests that there are few reasons (possibly excepting his graphomania, in which he is also the descendant of Bolotov) not to count Chikhachev an average, middling nobleman of the time. The pursuits Chikhachev was inspired to take up by Bulgarin—in sum, various kinds of local writing—enabled him to participate in some of the period's most active sites of sociability for the male nobility. Thus, in this case, there is a set of documentary evidence to suggest that Bulgarin's prodigious activities as a journalist made the emergent Russian quasi-political public sphere more inviting to potential participants.

CHAPTER FOUR

Dead Souls in Its Media Environment

On July 24, 1829, Nikolai Gogol wrote the following in a letter to his mother:

> It would be different if a man groveled somewhere where not a single minute of life was lost in futility, where every minute was a storing of rich experience and knowledge; but to fritter away one's entire existence in a place where absolutely nothing looms ahead, where years and years are spent in petty occupations, this would resound in one's soul as a very heavy indictment—this would be death. What happiness is there in attaining at fifty, say, the position of a State Counsellor [*sic*] with wages hardly sufficient for a decent living and without the power to bring mankind a pennyworth of good? The young people of St. Petersburg seem to me very absurd: they keep on shouting that they serve not for the sake of grades, not in order to be rewarded by their superiors—but ask them why they serve at all, and they will not be able to answer; the only apparent reason is that otherwise they would remain at home and twirl their thumbs. Sillier still are those who leave the remote provinces where they own land and where they might have become excellent farmers—instead of the useless people they are. *Why, if a person of gentle birth must serve the state, let him serve it in his own manor*; but what he does is dilly-dally in the capital, where not only does he not find an office but squanders an incredible amount of money that he gets from home.[1]

A few paragraphs later in the same letter Gogol would apologize for having kept for himself the money sent by his mother and meant to be paid to the Custody Board. As compensation for his transgression, the young writer offered that his mother become "the lawful and absolute owner" of his patrimony.[2] Vladimir Nabokov, who calls Gogol's correspondence "dreary reading" but quotes the above letter in full, writes that "the part about the futility or even sinfulness of striving to become a pen-scratching official in an abstract town instead of cultivating the 'real' land given by God to the Russian gentry, foretells the ideas Gogol later expounded in his *Selected Passages from Letters to Friends*; that he himself was quite eager to dispose of that land in any fashion also explains some of their contradictions."[3] It is worth emphasizing Nabokov's point about this early glimpse of what would become one of Gogol's chief preoccupations in the concluding years of his career: the domestic duties of the Russian provincial landowner. The pages that follow will be devoted to some of the texts in which Gogol tackles this topic—notably, the novel *Dead Souls*.

First, a closer look at Nabokov's translation of the 1829 missive is in order. Where his English text reads, "Why, if a person of gentle birth must serve the state, let him serve it in his own manor," Gogol had written, "esli uzhe dvorianinu nepremenno nuzhno posluzhit', sluzhili by v svoikh provintsiiakh" (10:146). Nabokov's choice of "serve in his own manor" clarifies and, to a degree, interprets the Russian original, because to "serve in their own provinces" (a more literal translation) could also mean taking a civil service position in the local provincial town, potentially still leaving one's "manor" nearly as mismanaged as it would have been had the owner taken up residence in the capital.[4] Which does Gogol mean: province or manor, state service or estate administration? This seemingly trivial potential for a dual translation of *provintsii* points to a topic that surpasses the simple matter of what the young author meant to convey to his mother. By the time at which Gogol made the rather impatient formulation (*esli uzhe dvorianinu nepremenno nuzhno posluzhit'*), the nobility had been freed from obligatory service for some sixty-seven years. But the very definition of state service had expanded considerably. In her study of food and agriculture in tsarist Russia, Alison K. Smith writes that "during the 1820s, in particular, agricultural writers developed the idea that Russia's nobles had *a duty to the state* and to its citizens to pursue an active role in improving local agriculture—to become authorities on the subject, and authoritative on their estates" (emphasis added).[5] Increasingly, a nobleman's estate administration took on the characteristics of an important contribution to the nation, a vocation akin to state service. As Smith shows, this was due both to Nicholas-era economic conditions and a long-standing view (dating back at least to the 1760s) that Russian agricultural practices lagged decades behind their Western counterparts and were in urgent need of active reconsideration and improvement. Following the previous century's attempt to articulate a masculine domestic ideology for the nobleman-landowner, the perception gradually arose in public discourse that the rural landlord may well be among the most virtuous servants of the state. To a degree, Nabokov's translation conveys this idea: working in one's "manor," becoming "a good farmer," *is* service to the state.

As was suggested in the previous chapter, Bulgarin's multi-generic oeuvre is replete with multiple iterations of the virtuous nobleman-landowner as he appeared in Russian public discourse. Publishing chiefly during the second quarter of the nineteenth century, both Bulgarin and Gogol wrote at a time characterized by the transformation of the Russian literary establishment and the gradual appearance of a newly distant and anonymous readership. For a good deal of this time, Bulgarin and Gogol were "perceived by much of the reading public as genuine literary rivals," to borrow Anne Lounsbery's formulation. [6] Abram Reitblat has long suggested that considering relatively understudied aspects of Bulgarin's prolific and multi-generic career could yield considerable insights when it comes to understanding the process of literary production during this time, noting particularly the need for more studies that juxtapose Bulgarin with Gogol.[7] It would be fair to say that readers, rendered as competing iterations of the public, figure extensively in the literary polemics between the two writers. In some cases, the examples are very well known. Famously, Gogol's madman Poprishchin reports reading the *Northern Bee*, whereas Major Kovalyov of "The Nose" visits the offices of a newspaper that closely resembles it. As suggested in the previous chapter, in "Diary of a Madman" Gogol's thinly veiled reference to Bulgarin's writings from the point of view of a Finnic landowner (in Poprishchin's naïve admiration of Kursk landowners who write well) begins to register the extent to which the mainstream media environment of the period is populated by fictitious landowners who threaten to become a stand-in for both writer and public.

It is among the main contentions of this chapter that *Dead Souls*—both the completed first volume and especially the unfinished second volume—bears remarkable traces of the meanings that had begun to accrue to the rural landowner as a kind of media mainstay and cultural fantasy produced by the growing book market of the period, particularly by advice literature. Much especially in the second, unfinished volume appears all but overdetermined by the period's media environment.[8] Gogol reworks what is essentially an artifact of middlebrow culture when he produces his novel through active engagement with, almost a rewriting of, Bulgarin's *Vyzhigin* in both volumes.[9] Moving by turns toward, against, and away from the picaresque, Gogol ultimately all but arrives at the bildungsroman. In part as a result of the generic orientation of *Dead Souls* toward *Bildung* and in part due to the novel's incorporation of the figure of the provincial nobleman as represented in contemporary public discourse, in both volumes the acquisition of the attributes of a virtuous landowner is understood as a process of becoming, but one with no quantifiable, clear end in sight. Relatedly and just as crucially, Gogol's writerly activity, especially his practice of rewriting, turns out to be its own interminable process of becoming, a process conditioned by the period's multifaceted investment in the figure of the nobleman-landowner.

Dead Souls opens with the infamously middling (*gospodin srednei ruki*) not quite picaro, not quite protagonist Chichikov, an emphatically average man (neither good-looking, nor bad; neither too fat, nor too thin; neither old, nor young) who seems to embody the age of reproducibility enabled by the growing media environment. If the journals and newspapers of the time are filled with both named and nameless landlords, one difficult to distinguish from the next, Chichikov represents another, but related, iteration of this mid-century media man. The novel's flirtation with Chichikov becoming a real landowner gives further illustration of this. If in *Vyzhigin* the edifying capacities of estate work find their ultimate embodiment in the titular picaro's transformation into a model landowner, both volumes of *Dead Souls* promise such an end without delivering it. In *Dead Souls* proper, the ending a naïve audience accustomed to reading picaresque novels might have expected comes in the form of the ruse that Chichikov will move his peasants (all of them dead, of course) to Kherson province. The gullible local nobility utter mirthful toasts to the health of their "Kherson province landlord," his peasants' well-being, their safe journey to the new home, and the health of the landowner's lovely wife (nonexistent), and continue in this manner until Chichikov takes on the role and begins to discuss the three-field crop rotation system (6:152). In a move that all but literalizes the idea that a nobleman can be *made* by the public's desiring and disciplining gaze and the performance that it inspires, by evening's end Chichikov falls asleep "decidedly a Kherson province landowner" (6:152). Incantatory talk (or, a brand of interpellation on a very small scale) turns out to make the man and to endow Gogol's famously chameleon-like creation with a new social identity that he inhabits, if only for a brief time. Of course, *Dead Souls* proper ends with Chichikov careening away from the scene of his exploits, with no indication that he will ever live the life of a Kherson landowner.

It is remarkable that in volume two Gogol comes much closer to making an almost honest landowner out of Chichikov. But volume two is closer in sensibility to Bulgarin's *Vyzhigin*. Here, as Chichikov is in the process of purchasing an estate, he "feels pleased, pleased, because he had now become a landowner—not a fantastic, but a real landowner, who now even had lands, territories, and peasants. Not dreamed-up peasants who reside in his imagination, but real ones" (7:89). Still, the enterprising hero soon considers selling the best parts of the property, then mortgaging the rest along with his dead souls. Here he threatens to become a nobleman-entrepreneur taken to an extreme, in the sense that the complete sale of the property would make the new landowner Chichikov no longer technically a landowner. The plotline of a picaro turned *pomeshchik* eludes Gogol once again. This "failure" to make a good landowner out of Chichikov turns out to be an artistic and compositional difficulty[10] that grows more prominent as well as more complex if one takes into account that volume two includes various reworkings of Bulgarin's model landowner Rossiianinov, as well as references to and echoes of other aspects of the successful journalist's prodigiously productive career.

There are several ways in which the characters of volume two function as different iterations of the virtuous landowner of Russian public discourse, frequently in pages of the novel that incorporate references to Bulgarin. The first landowner whom Chichikov meets in volume two, Tentetnikov, describes his decision to retire to the countryside in a way that replays what should be by now a *very* familiar formulation:

I have another job [*sluzhba*]: three hundred peasant souls, an estate that is in disarray, an overseer who is an idiot. . . . I—what do you think?—am a landowner <this title is also not a trifling matter>. If I attend to the keeping, the preservation, and the betterment of the lot of the people who have been entrusted to me and if I present to the nation three hundred of the most sound, sober, hardworking peasants—in what way will my job [*sluzhba*] be worse than the job [*sluzhba*] of some head of division, Lenitsyn? (7:18)[11]

The idea that being a good landowner is a form of state service grows at the expense of Tentetnikov's understanding of other kinds of work, which he now imagines as a "paper, fantastic management of provinces situated thousands of versts away, where I have never set foot and where I can only do many inane and preposterous things!" as contrasted with the "real management" of his estate (7:19). By the 1840s, the notion that being a good steward of property may be analogous or even superior to service had become ossified into a commonplace in texts to which Tentetnikov has access. Before returning to his estate, he procures "the newest books on the subject of rural domestic culture," texts that seek as much to transform the country estate as to create a particular kind of nobleman (7:18). But why does Tentetnikov fail? After all, he seems to be following Gogol's advice to the "Russian Landowner" ("Russkii pomeshchik") from *Selected Passages from Correspondence with Friends*, a work that Catriona Kelly shows to embody an extreme version of trends that are to be observed in the period's advice literature.[12] Like Gogol's model nobleman in *Selected Passages*, Tentetnikov goes out to the fields, supervises the various agricultural enterprises, even gives the peasants a shot of vodka for their hard work. Yet in the novel, the set of behaviors prescribed in Gogol's own brand of advice literature (direct participation in or at least observation of serf labor) still leaves the hero with a disorderly piece of property.

To a degree, Chichikov is welcomed by Tentetnikov with the hope that the latter may learn something useful (even possibly something relevant to running an estate) from him. Upon first seeing Chichikov, Tentetnikov anxiously takes him for a government official who has come on unpleasant business regarding the latter's brief participation in a politically subversive circle. The country landlord's fears dissipate when Chichikov introduces himself and explains, in what appears at first to be a classic Gogolian near non sequitur, that "he has been traveling around Russia for a long time, compelled both by needs and curiosity; that our nation is rich in remarkable items, not to speak of the plethora of crafts and the diversity of soils" (7:27). To the reader of agricultural treatises and periodicals from this time period, it becomes clear that Gogol's con man is masquerading as a scientist who travels around the empire gathering information, in large part because such a mask will foster the sorts of quick friendships that have enabled his ruse throughout volume one. Reports from itinerant correspondents were printed in such mainstream periodicals as *Notes of the Fatherland* and such subject-specific agricultural journals as the *Transactions of the Free Economic Society*. And this is more or less the conclusion Tentetnikov reaches as he judges that Chichikov "must be some sort of inquisitive learned professor, who travels around Russia, perhaps, in order to collect some sort of plants, or perhaps, minerals" (7:27). Tentetnikov immediately warms to Chichikov-the-professor. He suggests that his guest make himself at home, and invites him to have a seat in the Voltaire armchair as he gets ready for a lecture about "natural sciences" (7:27). Chichikov's ruse works perfectly, as it turns out that the two men have much in common. After becoming disenchanted with the business of running his estate, Tentetnikov himself has embarked on the composition of a book that would "embrace Russia from all points of view—civic, political, religious, philosophical," the description very likely to be Gogol's jab at Bulgarin's *Russia from a Historical, Statistical, Geographic, and Literary Perspective* (*Rossiia v istoricheskom, statisticheskom, geograficheskom i literaturnom otnosheniiakh*) (7:11). As in the episode with Tentetnikov so throughout volume two, Chichikov's feigned interest in estate life and administration, agriculture and the natural sciences, becomes his chief means of forging connections with the local nobility, a tendency particularly prominent in portions of volume two that are the most closely entangled with *Vyzhigin*.

Notably and perhaps predictably enough, Chichikov's visit to the estate of the excellent master landowner Kostanzhoglo parallels the analogous portions of Bulgarin's novel.[13] However, in Gogol's novel Rossiianinov has been split into two characters: Kostanzhoglo and another landowner, Koshkarev. In both versions of the surviving chapters of volume two, Chichikov's visit to Kostanzhoglo's estate is interrupted by a day trip to see Koshkarev, whom readers of volume two may recall for the excessive bureaucracy that is the dominant feature of his estate. Koshkarev is a parody of Rossiianinov: Gogol satirizes the modern and useful institutions

of Rossiianinov's estate (the drugstore, almshouse, general store, village
school) in Koshkarev's Depot for Agricultural Equipment, Main Bureau of
Audits, Committee on Rural Affairs, and School for the Normal Education
of Villagers.

Yet the veritable lampooning of Bulgarin's modern landlord goes
further, quite possibly reaching as far as the journalist's tenure as Mr.
Ekonom, an author of agricultural advice. Instructional literature has a
prominent place in Koshkarev's library, a "huge hall, filled from top to bot-
tom with books" (7:65). Whereas Rossiianinov's study had new journals
and newspapers, as well as books in Latin, Greek, French, English, Italian,
and finally Russian, the first mention of the contents of Koshkarev's library
reads as follows, "books on all subjects—on the subject of forestry, animal
husbandry, swine husbandry, gardening, thousands of various journals,
containing the latest developments and improvements in stud farming and
the natural sciences. There were also such titles as *Swine Husbandry as a
Science*" (7:195).[14] Since these are the first books Chichikov discovers in
the library, the list creates the initial and temporary impression that Koshkarev is reading exclusively domestic advice literature. Gogol's treatment
of this subject recalls the tactics of *Notes of the Fatherland*'s criticism of
Bulgarin's *Ekonom*, which was discussed in detail in the previous chapter. The title *Swine Husbandry as a Science*, arguably more absurd than
Odoevsky's *Housekeeping as a Science*, signals the novel's awareness of
the tendency to produce purportedly scientific accounts of animal husbandry, a tendency also satirized in the reviews of *Ekonom*. The list of
such subjects as forestry, cattle breeding, swine breeding, and gardening
(*lesovodstvo, skotovodstvo, svinovodstvo, sadovodstvo*) evinces a sensibility about the overproduction of instructional literature that again recalls
the tactics of both Odoevsky, whose Dr. Puf offered dissertations on a list
of topics derived via a similar manipulation of language characteristic of
instructional publications, and the reviewers of *Ekonom*, who suggested
that Burnashev author a series of animal husbandry books on exceedingly
specific topics. From another perspective, since *Ekonom* was marketed as
a "generally useful domestic library" (*khoziaistvennaia obshchepoleznaia
biblioteka*), the contents of this part of Koshkarev's library can be taken to
be analogous to Bulgarin's periodical publication. Interesting here is the
otherwise rather odd juxtaposition of "horse breeding" and the natural
sciences. Bulgarin, whose incompetence in the natural sciences *Notes of*

the Fatherland ridiculed repeatedly, was a member of a special commission on horse breeding from 1844 to 1857. Furthermore, the fear of the *Notes of the Fatherland* reviewers that relying on untrustworthy publications may bring a landowner to financial ruin is materialized in the figure of Koshkarev, whose serfs have "not only been mortgaged, but even remortgaged for the second time" (7:66). The verbosity characteristic of every pursuit undertaken at Koshkarev's estate is mirrored suggestively in the contents of the library. The bureaucratic chaos that has engulfed Koshkarev's property may have an explanation here. Readers of volume two will likely recall that at Koshkarev's, Chichikov's standard request for dead souls results in a long paper trail, portions of which are reproduced as Gogol ridicules the awkward style of the landowner's scribe. Koshkarev's statement that Chichikov gave him the opportunity to "see the course of the bureaucratic process" reveals that paperwork is the main thing produced by Koshkarev's serfs (7:197). The worst tendencies of the market for instructional literature find a hyperbolized representation on Koshkarev's estate. If the how-to book market is too prolific, too verbose, Koshkarev's estate is a direct representation of this trend, itself producing little more than a great deal of paper. Koshkarev, then, is another, albeit somewhat grotesque, permutation of the virtuous nobleman-landowner of the period's increasingly robust public discourse, ruined by his zeal for the growing traffic in books.

While Koshkarev can be read as a representation of the worst trends in contemporary constructions of model domestic culture, Kostanzhoglo would seem to offer a didactic counterexample. Chichikov's first words upon meeting him are a plea for help, a request ("teach me, teach me") for "wisdom about the difficult task of standing at the helm of rural housekeeping, the wisdom to derive profits, to acquire property that is not fantastic, but real, thereby fulfilling one's obligation as a citizen, and gaining the respect of one's countrymen" (7:62). The partly feigned interest in estate administration, the almost ritualistic recitation of the landowner's and the citizen's obligations, come from a script that helps Chichikov establish his own identity as, once again, almost a landowner and hence a potential equal, peer, and friend. Kostanzhoglo's wisdom comes in the form of various pronouncements about the current trends in the discourse about the model landowner. For example, Kostanzhoglo is likely referring to the growing popularity of public courses on estate administration offered to the aspiring landowner beginning in the 1830s when he complains that "they're a good bunch, these political economists! One idiot sits upon another and drives him on. He cannot see further than his own stupid nose. Never mind that he's an ass, he'll get up to the podium, put on his glasses . . . Idiots!" (7:69). It is even possible that Kostanzhoglo here alludes to Mr. Ekonom himself, since *Notes of the Fatherland*, tongue planted firmly in cheek, called Bulgarin a well-known political economist. But to what extent does the representation of Kostanzhoglo himself offer an alternative to the all-Russian model landowner described by the likes of Bulgarin?

To begin with, Kostanzhoglo is "not exactly Russian." He does not know much about his own background, and it is reported that the model landowner finds his ancestry irrelevant, because it has no application in agriculture (7:61). Just as Gogol's text comes close to representing an exemplary Russian nobleman, it turns out that the expert landlord is neither Russian, nor verifiably noble. The perfect Russian *pomeshchik* eludes Gogol again. But why? Many readers have remarked that Kostanzhoglo is not quite what he should be: convincing, believable, a properly "positive" hero. In a rare instance of producing a statement with which few would disagree today, Valerian Pereverzev calls Kostanzhoglo "the most unsuccessful and lifeless" character in all of Gogol's art.[15] Robert Maguire considers the landowner "a caricature," and "an unlikely role model."[16] What makes Kostanzhoglo elicit such a response? To put the matter simply, Kostanzhoglo is Gogol's most overt reworking of contemporary advice literature. As Kostanzhoglo's brother-in-law Platonov and Chichikov approach his grounds, Platonov's comment that "when everyone else has a bad harvest," Kostanzhoglo is unaffected sounds similar to Bulgarin's self-fashioning as a landowner immune from even climatically caused hardship (7:58). The first issue of *Ekonom* had opened with the promise that the reader's income, estimated at 20,000, would grow to 40,000 if he followed the advice of the periodical.[17] The review in *Notes of the Fatherland* treats this assurance with skepticism. Gogol's Kostanzhoglo has turned his 20,000 (or, in another version, 30,000) into 200,000. Finally, Kostanzhoglo's famous "poem in prose" about the virtues of the landowner's domestic pursuits—the long speech he delivers, himself becoming as enraptured as his audience, while he lists the order in which agricultural projects are to be carried out in the course of the calendar year—is largely derived from Gogol's notes about agriculture, some of which come directly from scientific advice literature (about which more below). This makes for an amplified level of contact between a novelistic text and instructional literature. In fact, as will be suggested below, the expanded Bulgarin intertext of volume two may be emblematic of a veritable vocational shift in Gogol's work.

In the 1840s and early 1850s, while working on volume two of *Dead Souls*, Gogol attempted what Edyta Bojanowska has called "an epistolary course on Russia," asking several of his correspondents for information about the Russian provinces: descriptions of local provincial types, peasants' crafts, and trades.[18] While abroad, Gogol requested a number of books on related subjects. Among these books were such titles as Bulgarin's *Russia from a Historical, Statistical, Geographic, and Literary Perspective*,[19] *Domestic Botany*, as well as the 1844 and 1846 issues of *Notes of the Fatherland*. Gogol's notebooks contain observations and book titles related to estate life and agriculture. A particular set of Gogol's notes that are usually dated (with some difficulty) at 1849 and considered to have been preparation for volume two of *Dead Souls* reveals still more about what the author may have been reading during this decade. Gogol writes on such subjects as the relationship between types of soil, climate, and crops appropriate for a given region. The specific details of these notes, as well as references to agriculturalists, show that by the late 1840s, Gogol had become quite familiar with instructional nonfiction about the country estate. At times, it is possible to identify Gogol's sources. For instance, in his notes "About Black Earth" ("O chernozeme"), he refers to the findings of one *penzenskii pomeshchik* (a Penza landowner), Ivan Saburov, whose long treatises were published serially in the domestic culture section of *Notes of the Fatherland* in 1842 and 1843 under the title "Notes of a Penza Agriculturalist about the Theory and Practice of Rural Home Economics."[20] Gogol records that "black earth, in the opinion of the Penza landowner, is not humus, but is rather soil with a high concentration of clay" (9:437). The Penza landowner Saburov begins one of his articles by asking that the readership forgive him for pausing to explain the difference between black earth and humus, but that such an explanation is necessary because the agricultural writers employed by the *Library for Reading* have been mixing up the two.[21] In this article, he goes on to present his views couched in a critique of the articles in Senkovskii's journal on the subject of estate administration and agriculture, offering his own experience as an authentic landowner and not one of "our armchair agronomists" (*kabinetnye nashi agronomy*).[22]

In this and other articles, Saburov continually dismisses the utility of the "theory" put forth by professional agriculturalists, offering instead the "practice" of the "thinking landlord" (*mysliashchii khoziain*). In his notes about the fertility of black earth, Gogol repeats Saburov's formulations, calling the particular qualities of this soil a "fact known to all experienced and thinking landlords" (Gogol uses an inflected form of *mysliashchii khoziain*) (9:437). The Russian original is given here to show that Gogol appears to be quoting directly from Saburov. Gogol's notes "About Soil" ("O pochve") restate verbatim Saburov's views in still another of his *Notes of the Fatherland* articles.[23] Finally, a section of Gogol's notes published under the heading "About Peasant Dwellings" ("O krest'ianskom zhilish-che") (9:434–35) contains what should perhaps be considered a separate entry, because the final paragraph that deals with the inutility of "theory" in obtaining a proper understanding of agriculture repeats word for word much of a passage from Saburov's inaugural article, where he had begun his critique of agricultural advice literature.[24]

Was it Gogol's attempt to prepare for the composition of volume two that prompted this turn to scientific literature about farming? In the new preface that introduced the 1846 republication of *Dead Souls*, Gogol famously invited the reading public to send him suggestions on how to improve the novel: members of every estate and vocation were asked to advise the author, to "correct" his rendering of Russia. What looks like a genuine desire for information of this sort is also discernible in both *Selected Passages* and his personal correspondence. Considering the preface as a text created by a writer of fiction, Donald Fanger has called this "bizarre document" an "eloquent testimony to Gogol's creative crisis," finding that the introduction reveals a writer's "drama that is vocational and literary."[25] It may be added that insofar as the drama is vocational, it may even mark a departure from the purely literary. For authors of advice literature, the invitation that readers aid them in the enterprise is so common it is possible to call it a feature of the genre. Such authors very often asked their audience to help improve the volume for its subsequent printing; they often incorporated the new material and even thanked the readership for their help. And since there could be factual errors in a book about, say, bovine husbandry, the collaboration between author and reader made sense. Vladimir Burnashev's 1843–1844 *Attempt at a Termi-nological Dictionary of Rural Domestic Culture, Manufacturing, Crafts, and*

Peasant Lifeways (*Opyt terminologicheskogo slovaria sel'skogo khoziaistva, fabrichnosti, promyslov i byta narodnogo*) provides a good illustration of how such writers worked. Contemporaries saw *Attempt* as an excellent reference tool for landowners. The rather hefty encyclopedia had a practical purpose quite close to that of advice literature. The final product includes information on nearly every topic of relevance to the provinces imaginable: hunting, botany, architecture, peasants' habits, and much more. By definition, such a survey of provincial life continues to aspire to, without ever claiming, absolute completeness and accuracy. Recognizing this even prior to publishing the book, Burnashev offered the readership some forty-three entries as samples, which he published in *Notes of the Fatherland*, where he also asked for the public's appraisal of and assistance in his work. He thanked a long list of specific contributors in the introduction to his book. Both in his introduction and in various editorial reviews, Burnashev and the periodical press continued to encourage the readership's participation in the enterprise.[26]

To the reader of Burnashev's *Attempt at a Terminological Dictionary*, parts of Gogol's notebooks from the 1840s (his records regarding local habits as well as his definitions of farming tools, for example) bear a marked resemblance to the former's published text. That these notes are preparation for volume two makes all the more interesting the juxtaposition of Gogol's concern that the first part of his book contains "a great number of various mistakes and blunders" with similar formulations made by Burnashev and other writers in his genre (6:587).[27] Gogol's drive to document the provinces as part of his work on volume two of *Dead Souls*, when read against the period's media environment, begins to appear as an internalization of the perceived necessity to learn about the countryside before describing and then, perhaps even, transforming it. The purpose here is not to counter or challenge the long-standing contention that Gogol did not really know Russia. It is, in a sense, irrelevant whether Gogol's information was accurate, although there are good reasons to believe that Gogol did not have a good understanding of agricultural science.[28] What remains rather striking is the drive to gather information and to incorporate it into the sequel to *Dead Souls*, especially inasmuch as the compositional history of volume two recalls the methods employed by authors of advice literature about the estate. Gogol's 1846 invitation that his readers help him, then, signals a shift toward a new kind of writing. If volume two was to function as art that, in Susanne Fusso's formulation, can "present an accessible, unambiguous, and unmistakable message to the greatest possible number of people," then this art is approaching the sensibility of the domestic or farming manual.[29] One might then posit another sort of relationship between volumes one and two: not one of continuation, but a rewriting. Volume two seeks to "correct" the blunders of volume one, and Gogol seeks to become a producer of better, more edifying, and almost no longer novelistic figures, the model nobleman and expert landowner chief among these.

Gogol's apparent internalization of the period's enthusiasm for the figure of the virtuous nobleman-landowner went well beyond his novel. In letters written while he summered at his ancestral estate of Vasil'evka in 1848, Gogol relates a host of complaints: a near-epidemic of cholera, his own ever-failing health and the resulting difficulty of work, the unbearable heat and the rather grim expectations for a bad harvest. While in the country, largely unable to work on volume two of *Dead Souls*, Gogol authored another document, one he likely never intended for publication: "The Distribution of Garden Works for the Autumn of 1848 and the Spring of 1849" ("Raspredelenie sadovykh rabot na osen' 1848 goda i vesnu 1849"), a set of instructions to be carried out by his mother and sisters. These notes begin:

AUTUMN WORKS.
September.
  Start of September; digging of trenches and garden-beds, beginning with the last days of August and until September 10th.
  Middle of September: collection of acorns and seeds in the forest.
  End of September: sowing of seeds, sending for trees from Iareski.
October.
  Continuation of sowing and planting of trees in all such places where trenches and small trenches have been made.
Digging.
  On this side, a trench for the planting of poplars, through the cabbage beds [upon the harvesting of cabbage] past the apiary to the cherry trees that have been marked.
  On the other side, small trenches at the marked places.

A trench along that side in the direction of the pond to the brick factory, for the planting of poplars.

Small garden-beds for the planting of acorns in a row, along the edges of the soil that has been plowed for the vegetable gardens: on this side—along the big alley, on that—behind the Sumakov grove, behind the small trenches for the birch grove, along both sides of the alley along the garden-beds. In the event that there is time, see article: "Subsequent Works."[30]

Written in a familiar, conversational tone, these instructions assume the reader's familiarity with the landscape. Meant for a very small audience, this is a decidedly private, domestic kind of text that will only be fully understood by someone who knows well the spatial organization of the estate, as well as the markings made by the author prior to his departure. By the time of its composition, Gogol had already retracted his most recent book: in epistolary correspondence, he had admitted that the publication of *Selected Passages* may have been premature, judging that he had spoken too soon and with an authority he now found misplaced. Nor would Gogol be able to finish another text (volume two of *Dead Souls*) in which he set out to describe the provincial nobleman's domestic pursuits. Here, he turned to manage Vasil'evka—if from a distance. At the risk of trying the reader's patience, this lengthy passage is quoted in full so as to illustrate that in this most private of his attempts at a text about estate administration, Gogol's attention to detail is remarkable. Be it dates, locations, or methods, Gogol's instructions address every aspect of the undertaking at hand. In the months that followed (after the author had left Vasil'evka), the family's correspondence contains brief snippets about this project, harvests, and cattle disease. Was Gogol attempting to become a model landowner, following through on an idea articulated in *Selected Passages*: that before writing volume two of *Dead Souls*, he had to become that about which he wished to write?

Parts of the instructions sound notes similar to the ethos of "The Russian Landowner" from *Selected Passages*: specifically, the insistence that the provincial nobleman must be present during the peasants' labor. Gogol writes to his mother and sisters, "during the planting, it is necessary to be present yourself [*samomu*], so as to see whether all has indeed been planted correctly. During the planting of trees, it is again necessary that you be present, not having neglected to have with you at all times a small kit of water, into which the root of the tree that is to be planted must be dipped, so as to ensure that the soil adheres to it."[31] Gogol, of course, could not be present "himself" at the planting. That while writing to his female relatives, he uses the masculine *samomu* highlights both his absence and a potential internalization of the maleness of the good *pomeshchik* as he was produced by Russian public discourse. As is well known, the Gogol family estate was managed by the writer's mother.

From still another perspective, Gogol's attention to such details as the necessity of bringing a "small kit of water" begins to recall the work of another writer who not only wrote about but also cast himself as the model landowner-steward of the Russian country estate. For the reader of *Ekonom,* it becomes hard not to think of Faddei Bulgarin's advice literature when one encounters Gogol's suggestion that "when planting trees that are particularly sensitive to the cold, it is necessary to dilute in water a little fresh one-day-old cow manure."[32] (On the pages of *Ekonom,* Bulgarin treated a variety of subjects related to fertilizer.) The chief and crucial difference between the two authors' texts is that while Gogol's instructions were meant for private, family use, Bulgarin wrote on similar topics for the perusal of every willing member of his paying, anonymous audience. There is plenty of evidence to suggests that neither writer was a professional agronomist with anything approaching an ability to provide a scholarly account of the subject. Still, both tried their hand at the task.

To be clear, the purpose of these chapters is neither to continue to vilify nor to rehabilitate Bulgarin and his confrères. Rather, this investigation of the multi-generic discourse that sought to give shape and structure to the identity of the Nicholas-era country nobleman shows that during the second quarter of the nineteenth century, novelistic and extra-literary (especially instructional) texts not only coexisted in the readerly practices of the provincial gentry, but also cross-pollinated in the novelistic imagination of Gogol and Bulgarin. Moreover, Gogol's creative process as well as his achievements in the composition of volume two of *Dead Souls*, both of which proved crucial for the subsequent development of the Russian novelistic tradition, may be viewed with some profit as part of a broader narrative about the continued attempts to imagine the provincial landowner as a productive citizen of the empire. Both in Gogol's *Dead Souls* and in the tradition that follows it, the concept of *becoming* looms large in the representation of the nobleman's selfhood and domestic ideology. When it comes specifically to the novelistic tradition inherited by subsequent writers, it should be noted here that in the brief description of Chichikov's childhood and youth in volume one and in the Tentetnikov visit of volume two, *Dead Souls* comes very close to displaying the sensibilities of the bildungsroman, a genre that would prove highly productive for the writer considered in the next chapter.

CHAPTER FIVE

Becoming Noble in Goncharov's Novels

Although it had an epoch-defining significance for European culture in the nineteenth century, the bildungsroman is marginal to the Russian literature of the same period, with one important exception. The entirety of Ivan Goncharov's novelistic oeuvre, which he considered a trilogy (*A Common Story*, *Oblomov*, *The Precipice*), revolves around the related forms of the bildungsroman and the *Künstlerroman*.[1] All three novels exhibit features of both of these genres, but to varying degrees and with different points of emphasis. Nowhere among the texts and authors examined in this study so far is becoming a more central preoccupation. When it comes to *Bildung* (the French *formation*, the Russian *vospitanie*) and social identity, all three of Goncharov's novels contemplate a nineteenth-century Russian iteration of the Molièrian conceptual coupling of the bourgeois and the gentleman, or the *gentilhomme*.[2] This conceptual pairing has both a thematic and a formal dimension. As each novel narrates the social formation and self-fashioning of a Russian nobleman, the Western bourgeois (sometimes in the guise of a highly enterprising, industrious, commercially minded noble) is suggested as an alternative identity. In part due to the centrality of the bildungsroman to his career, Goncharov has been regarded as one of the most Western of the major nineteenth-century Russian writers in his sensibility. A biographical dimension, namely that he was born into the merchant estate and spent the entirety of his adult life as a civil servant, a bureaucrat, has contributed to his characterization as someone who may have shared a general outlook with members of the Western bourgeoisie.[3] The narrative that follows will deal largely with the discursive fabric and compositional histories of Goncharov's novels in order to indicate various points of correspondence with the Western European realist novel. Ultimately, it will be suggested that Goncharov's noblemen inhabit a close Russian analogue of the European "bourgeois" realist novel, an affinity that is most evident in the status afforded to the domestic detail as an aesthetic category.

Goncharov's first novel, *A Common Story*, is among the few Russian texts that can be classified as a "pure" bildungsroman in the sense that, especially when considered in the context of its native literary tradition, it does not much depart from the basic generic conventions of the cultural form.[4] Its chief organizing principle seems to be that of polarities between romantic idealism and realism, the provinces and St. Petersburg, youth and maturity, passion and reason. *A Common Story* charts Alexander Aduev's transformation from a young provincial nobleman with naïve and misplaced hopes for writerly fame to a practically minded and successful denizen of the northern capital. For much of the novel, the young man and his uncle embody opposite poles of the operative contrasts upon which the novel turns. Aduev begins the bildungsroman a nobleman-dilettante, a poet whose engagement with his craft shows far more passion than grit or, for that matter, ability. The initial emphatically amateurish quality of this pursuit marks Aduev strongly as a nobleman of the old mold in both a Russian and a European context, because the insistence on remaining a dilettante in any number of fields of activity had long been an artifact of aristocratic self-fashioning. As *A Common Story* narrates Aduev's gradual loss of illusions regarding the life of the poet, it also suggests—in parallel fashion—another loss: the young man sheds his aristocratic dilettantism and becomes almost an industrialist. Valerian Pereverzev's outlandish suggestion that Goncharov's nobles were, in fact, middle class—or, the *burzhua* of Sovietese—much as it was motivated by early Marxist literary historiography, rings almost true in the case of the young protagonist of Goncharov's first novel.[5] More generally, as far-fetched as the suggestion is—and Pereverzev made similarly hard-to-sell claims about the noble characters in the works of other nineteenth-century writers—his appraisal of Goncharov's heroes not as bourgeois but as not-quite-nobles, if taken more as an invitation to a query than a statement of fact, holds the potential to yield interesting insights.

In this light, the representation of Aduev's work deserves some attention. The young man's uncle, upon learning about his interest in the arts,
offers him a "literary pursuit"—a characterization drenched in sarcasm—
to translate from German an article called "About Fertilizer."[6] Meant for
the rural domestic culture section of a journal, the article is, of course, not
at all what young Alexander has in mind when he dreams of the poet's life.
With the mention of "About Fertilizer" begins a set of allusions to agricultural advice literature that accompany the plot concerned with Aduev's
unsuccessful attempts to become a writer for much of the novel. After
the article about fertilizer, he translates another piece titled "About Potato
Syrup."[7] Aduev's work, first as a translator, then as an author of articles
on the subject of agriculture, is mentioned at least fifteen times in a relatively short text. This work signals the professionalization of his writerly
(albeit, no longer creative) pursuits. With time, the young man becomes
"an important personage" in the fictional journal, a prolific contributor
who "chooses, translates as well as reworks others' articles, [and] himself
wr[ites] various theoretical treatises on the subject of estate work" (1:234).
The editor's remark that "everything shows [. . . the work of] an educated
producer, not a craftsman" underscores the hero's gradual abandonment of
his purely literary and amateurish undertakings for the work of a specialist (1:335). That Aduev is to be compensated for his labor (one hundred
rubles a month for three print-size pages) gives more proof of the same
(1:230). Moreover, his work for the journal both punctuates and, in many
ways, is meant to enable his formation, or *Bildung*, which transpires largely
as he outgrows his youthful dreams and ambitions. This much is suggested
by the elder Aduev's initial surprise that his nephew who has been "writing
for two years [. . .] about fertilizer, about the potato crop, and other serious
subjects, where the style is strict, concise," still speaks "in a savage fashion," like a young man with misplaced aspirations for writerly fame, like
a Romantic who has arrived at the scene too late (1:245). Later, the letter
that the younger Aduev writes to his Petersburg relatives toward the end
of the novel showcases the degree to which his work with instructional
literature about estate administration has produced the projected effect.
Having announced that he has just completed an original treatise on farming, Alexander draws his readers' attention to the changes in his epistolary
style: "lines written in a calm, uncharacteristic [for the protagonist] tone"
(1:449). Gone are his romantic effusions. But what has Aduev become?

At a late point in the novel, upon his return to his ancestral estate, Aduev observes farm work to find that his advice as a Petersburg journalist was often erroneous ("how often we lied there") (1:446). He begins to take what looks to be a more authentic interest in farming, to "become immersed in the matter more deeply and attentively" (1:446). He researches estate administration now in earnest, ordering literature from the capital, seemingly primed to become a real landowner. After a year's work, he produces a treatise on farming. To a significant degree, the near-completion of Alexander's *Bildung* is conveyed via this monograph, giving rise to the expectation that the young man will become a colleague of the likes of Saburov, the Penza landowner whom Gogol read, a self-styled gentleman farmer who emphasizes the authenticity of his own experiences in order to disprove the works of urban armchair agronomists.[8] Yet no such ending is provided. Paradoxically, even though Aduev inherits his mother's estate and prepares to marry a woman in possession of considerable rural properties of her own, at the end of the novel, Alexander—turned, one imagines, an expert farmer—eschews estate-keeping for a career in the capital. And inasmuch as he emulates closely the sensibility of his uncle, Aduev's *Bildung* begins to veer toward the bourgeois end of the *bourgeois-gentilhomme* spectrum. The elder Aduev is known to not only work in state service, but also to co-own a factory that produces glass and porcelain ware. Without making too much of the Aduev family's proclivity toward the activities of a nineteenth-century *noblesse commerçante*, or trading nobility (since their taste for industry, like everything else in the novel, is satirized), let it suffice for the moment to simply point out that in *Oblomov* an analogous sort of enterprising spirit will be associated explicitly with Stolz's German bourgeois, or burgher, roots. That at the novel's end the uncle Aduev regrets his old, far too rational ways and acquires some of the traits of his nephew perhaps holds the key to understanding that the novel's chief opposing designations (romantic versus realist, rural versus urban, passionate versus rational, and so forth) easily collapse into each other, revealing a remarkable flexibility in the text's conceptual operations that also holds true for the *bourgeois-gentilhomme* coupling. In other words, it is not that the representation of the younger Aduev as a proper gentleman farmer eludes Goncharov, who, instead, produces a kind of hybrid nobleman-bourgeois. Rather, it is that the two categories remain unstable and linked, so that both the uncle and the nephew Aduev embody both ends of the spectrum, the bourgeois and the *gentilhomme*, identities that will prove key to the rest of Goncharov's trilogy as well.

Goncharov began planning *Oblomov* and *The Precipice* during the late 1840s, while a fairly active contributor to the journal *The Contemporary*, where he had published his first novel in 1847.[9] A few months later, the journal's editor, Nikolai Nekrasov, announced that "the author of *A Common Story* is preparing a *new novel* that the editors also hope to publish."[10] Notoriously slow to complete his novels, Goncharov would wait another twelve years to publish *Oblomov*. The short works that appeared in *The Contemporary* in the meantime contributed to the novelistic idiom of his most famous work. These early texts help illuminate both the thematic and formal features of *Oblomov*. Goncharov's unsigned review of a popular conduct manual by Dmitrii Sokolov, a feuilleton entitled "Letters from a Dweller of the Capital to His Friend, a Provincial Groom" ("Pis'ma stolichnogo druga k provintsial'nomu zhenikhu") and the sketch "Ivan Savich Podzhabrin" when taken together illustrate Goncharov's creative engagement with advice literature, as well as the growing centrality of home life in his works.[11] That Goncharov should take an interest in advice literature is far from unusual for a member of his generation. As the previous chapters document, such writers as Odoevsky and Gogol reviewed instructional literature and reworked it artistically.

Conversational and lighthearted in tone, Goncharov's review of Sokolov's conduct book, *A Man of the World; or, A Guide to Social Rules* (*Svetskii chelovek, ili rukovodstvo k poznaniiu pravil obshchezhitiia*) is unusually long for a bibliographic feuilleton.[12] There are potential echoes between Sokolov's book, Goncharov's review, and *Oblomov*: from the titular hero's socially inappropriate attachment to his housecoat (Sokolov advises against wearing this garment while receiving guests) to not quite knowing what to do with oneself when visiting with respectable company (Oblomov chez Ilyinskie). Sokolov's book aimed to instruct middling persons in topics related to behavior in polite society, that is, to help middling persons act like cultured nobles. While Sokolov addressed a readership of lower social standing than the Oblomov of the final redaction of the novel, the Ilya Ilyich of the early drafts of the text is quite a bit closer to the target audience of this conduct book. Goncharov "ennobled" Oblomov in the course of his revisions. The rewriting of Oblomov into a more refined character had a largely formal dimension that involved taking out mostly domestic details (for example, descriptions of furniture from Gostiny Dvor and other bourgeois attempts at luxury) that would have suggested a less aristocratic protagonist. As he revised a text he had started writing in the 1840s, Goncharov was attempting to distance himself from the Natural School, which was quickly becoming outdated and which had a higher tolerance for socially middling characters than the mature realist prose that came in its stead.

Published over a year after the review of Sokolov's manual, "Letters from a Dweller of the Capital to His Friend, a Provincial Groom" is an epistolary enterprise comprised of missives from the urban society lion (*lev*), A. Chelsky, to his provincial correspondent, Vasily Vasil'ich. The former advises the latter about participating properly in polite society. There are extended discussions about various aspects of "how to live," from home décor to gastronomy. The piece is a playful parody of the feuilleton *and* of advice literature, "a complete *theory of how to live*," which Chelsky hopes may be published for the public's edification (emphasis in the original, 1:492). Like the review of Sokolov's book, the "Letters" contain specific correspondences with Goncharov's novels, *Oblomov* chief among them. One may discern in Vasily Vasil'ich certain features of Ilya Ilyich. The woman he is to marry resembles Oblomov's love interest, Olga Ilyinskaya. The Country Groom of the feuilleton even has his own (embryonic) version of Oblomov's eventual landlady Agafya Matveevna in the "girl Agashka." The third of Goncharov's intervening works, the sketch "Ivan Savich Podzhabrin," has a protagonist who attempts to master the language and deportment of the aristocracy but fails at every step. To sum up, the works Goncharov published while composing *Oblomov* treat the acquisition of social identities, and of nobility especially, as process and performance, something learned then projected for a public's recognition. *Oblomov* will amplify some of these themes.

In broad terms, it will be suggested in the pages below that the eponymous hero of *Oblomov* is shown hovering about different and, in some ways, conflicting iterations of his social identity. The novel's preoccupation with the protagonist's compromised ability to inhabit his social estate is most apparent in the representation of his ancestral home. A brief comparison to another work will illustrate the point. Some three years prior to the serial publication of *Oblomov* (1859) in *Notes of the Fatherland*, Lev Tolstoy published his novella *A Landowner's Morning* (1856) in the same journal. Both Tolstoy's novella and Goncharov's novel document the attempts of a gentryman protagonist to manage his estate. Tolstoy's young prince Nekhliudov retires early and takes up residence at his rural property, where he intends to "devote [him]self to life in the country" and "the seven hundred souls" whose guardianship he calls a "sacred and direct responsibility" (4:123). Armed with Jacques Alexandre Bixio's multi-volume treatise on rural domestic affairs, *The Country Home of the XIX Century* (*Maison rustique du XIX siècle*), the young man spends almost the entirety of the novella in motion, visiting various parts of his property (4:125). Goncharov's *Oblomov* opens with another sort of a landowner's morning.[13] Arguably the most incurable homebody in Russian fiction, Oblomov wakes up at an apartment from which he is being evicted. A host of other domestic mishaps follows: money owed to vendors, general untidiness that manifests itself on every surface of the hero's study, and, finally, the letter from the village elder about the mismanagement of his country estate. Goncharov's text reverses the spatial organization of Tolstoy's novella. Whereas the latter takes place at Nekhliudov's rural property, strictly speaking, none of the waking action of *Oblomov* transpires at Oblomovka. The estate serves as a setting only for a rather fantastic (as opposed to realistic) narrative, "Oblomov's Dream," throughout the duration of which the "action" of the novel remains limited spatially to the couch on which the hero is sleeping. Aside from its representation in the dream, Oblomovka is only spoken about. Readers are informed about the state of affairs at the estate via letters and hearsay.

Yet all of the major characters are tied to Oblomovka. The titular hero spends much of the novel agonizing about its mismanagement. His man-servant Zakhar sees himself as an "item of decoration," a fancy fixture of the ancient noble home (4:72). Oblomov's friend Stolz, whose father was the manager at the estate of Verkhliovo, which belonged to the Oblomov family in the past, ultimately inherits some of his father's work as he takes over the management of Oblomovka completely by the end of the novel. Ilya Ilyich repeatedly imagines his love interest, Olga, as the mistress of the estate and offers to take his landlady Pshenitsyna as his housekeeper (*ekonomka*) in the country. The novel's villains, Tarantyev and Mukhoyarov, plot (initially, with success) to appropriate fraudulently the profits received from the estate. Moreover, Oblomovka as a space is systematically transposed onto two locations in St. Petersburg: Stolz refers both to

Oblomov's Gorokhovaia Street apartment and to the house on the Vyborg Side as Oblomovkas. The novel is all but fixated on a piece of property the text never represents directly.

Absent though it is from the direct representational frame of the text, Oblomovka creeps into some of the most unlikely portions of the novel, a tendency that is best revealed in a passage from Goncharov's drafts. In an attempt to describe the hero's inability to negotiate between state service and a private domestic existence, Goncharov writes, "his main station in life—his employment [in state service]—at first proved perplexing in the most unpleasant way, [. . .] his future employment seemed to him some sort of a family [business] activity, like [preserves] [pickling cucumbers], the yield of threshed grain, the pickling of cucumbers, the making of preserves, or the [transcription] transcribing into a notebook the revenues and expenses [associated with estate-keeping]" (5:83).[14] Noblemen of Oblomov's generation could choose to pursue a career in military or civil service or they could devote their time to the management of their estates. The appearance of the "pickling of cucumbers" and an estate manager's credit-debit record-keeping in the context of the world of the government official (where these things do not properly belong) points to a pathological attachment to country housekeeping that springs from his failures as a landowner. A notoriously poor steward of his property, Oblomov nevertheless approaches even service in the capital, the part of his life most removed from the country estate, as akin to rural domestic pursuits. The spatial organization of the novel (that Oblomovka is both nowhere and everywhere) reflects the titular hero's unhealthy preoccupation with his property.

If in *A Common Story* the young Aduev's work as a journalist who writes about farming accompanies him for much of the text, the hero of Goncharov's next novel spends almost the entire book purportedly thinking about the reorganization of his rural property. Oblomov stops "dreaming about the arrangement of the estate and the trip there" only in the concluding pages of the novel (4:474). Whereas in *A Common Story* the word *pomeshchik* is used only once, and even then not to describe any of the major characters, Oblomov is called a landowner a number of times as if to underscore both his inability and his successive (in their own way, exasperating) attempts to grow into this self.

Given the relative centrality of becoming, multiple generic designations may be applied to *Oblomov*—(anti-)bildungsroman and *Künstlerroman* (the latter with Oblomov as poet) chief among these. The process of becoming is rendered problematic by the titular hero's inability to act like a modern landowner. In a very famous episode, Oblomov becomes offended when his servant Zakhar compares him to "the others who are no worse" (*drugie ne khuzhe*); he becomes fixated on the idea of the "other" as he considers what another person (*drugoi*) might have done in his place (4:87). This prompts a lengthy discussion between the landowner and his serf. With great feeling, Oblomov announces that he has been working hard in order to better the lot of the serfs (a comical assertion, of course, since he has scarcely left the apartment). Most important of all, in this scene Oblomov refers to himself repeatedly as a *barin*; the narrator calls him the same (4:87–96). The word *barin* means "master," but by the nineteenth century the word has a decidedly outdated flavor in no small part because of the etymological link with the pre-Petrine boyar nobleman, the *boyarin*. Oblomov's characterization as a *barin* is not limited to this scene. In fact, the word *barin* is used well over one hundred times (as many as 170 by one count), whereas the word for "landowner" (*pomeshchik*) comes up only a dozen times. The word "nobleman" (*dvorianin*) is applied to Oblomov only once. This distribution of the words that mark Oblomov's nobility indicates his difficulties in inhabiting the modern iteration of his own social estate (*dvorianstvo*); in other words, he is a fine *barin*, but not a good landowner and even less a nobleman.[15]

There is a rather strong meta-literary dimension to the characterization of Oblomov as a not quite modern nobleman. A "carrier of a lyrical consciousness" informed, above all, by the genre of the friendly epistle, Oblomov prefers to view the country estate as a safe retreat from city life, a place devoted above all to *otium* (leisure), not activity.[16] And yet especially in the early parts of the novel, Oblomov manages to process his inactivity as the *work* of a provincial landowner. In part one, while at home at his Gorokhovaia Street apartment, the couch-bound hero gets "to work on the development of the plan for the estate" and is able to "quickly review in his mind some serious, seminal articles about quitrent, about plowing" (4:75). Next, Oblomov turns to the layout of rooms in the house he plans to build. In a matter of a few paragraphs,

Oblomov sees "himself several years later living permanently in the country after all his plans for the estate have been accomplished," and transitions swiftly to "his favorite fantasy": a life with "the small circle of friends" who "visit each other every day for dinner, for supper," and sees "nothing but sun-filled days, beaming faces, free of cares and wrinkles, round smiling faces, cheeks rosy with health, double chins, and healthy appetites," an "endless summer, unflagging good humor and high spirits, and food as delectable as the leisure to enjoy it" (4:76). This fantasy has its rather obvious generic roots in the idyll (faces free of wrinkles) and the friendly epistle (the small circle of companions). As if unable to remain rooted within one genre, within one type of discourse about noble identity, Oblomov retreats from articles about plowing and quitrent into the comforts of the idyll and the friendly epistle. Unable to find a viable hybrid between competing ways to conceive of himself as a nobleman, Oblomov remains in paralysis, attempting to become but never fully becoming a novelistic nobleman of his own historical epoch. Oblomov's reasons for refusing to return to the countryside and to participate in such local institutions as the district court elections are presented as an inherited problem. For example, the novel registers the 1809 introduction of an educational requirement for the attainment of the eighth rank of collegiate assessor from the satirized point of view of the older Oblomovs, who would rather not be forced by the state to receive additional schooling (4:139). In such moments, the representation of the older Oblomovs, Ilya Il'ich's parents, has some of its roots in the eighteenth-century nobles of satirical journalism who respond to the state-generated modernizing normative modes of behavior with an analogous indignation. Oblomov himself hovers precariously somewhere between the consummate *barin* of the pre-Petrine period and the decidedly non-aristocratic milieu of his environment in the latter parts of the novel that take place on the Vyborg Side.

The first time Oblomov's future Vyborg Side landlady and common-law wife is mentioned in part one of the novel, Tarantyev describes her as a woman who keeps a clean, orderly home. When Oblomov finally meets Pshenitsyna for the first time, her servant, Akulina, runs into the living room, holding an unruly, live, cackling rooster, asking whether this bird is the one meant for sale. Although embarrassed to be seen engaged in such an unsophisticated task, Pshenitsyna advises Akulina about the sale of poultry. Immediately thereafter, Oblomov exclaims "Housekeeping!" (4:299). But much as he may utter an admiring "house-keeping!" in response to the bird episode, Oblomov is initially set on not staying at Pshenitsyna's home. Yet he proves all but powerless in the face of good housekeeping. Especially the first stages of the romance (if one may call it that) between Oblomov and Pshenitsyna read quite like an extended rendition of the proverbial notion that the way to a man's heart is through his stomach, although, it is not only Pshenitsyna's culinary prowess that Oblomov admires. If in his affair with Olga, Oblomov's faulty housekeeping continually threatened to and finally did corrode the relationship, his second romantic dalliance is inspired and fueled by Pshenitsyna's faultless domesticity: her pies, homemade vodka infusion and coffee, how well she makes his bed and repairs his stockings. Ulti-mately, much of this prose of everyday life comes to serve as a sort of barometer for their relationship.

The first time he kisses Pshenitsyna ("lightly on the neck") reveals the degree to which Oblomov, a terrible steward of his own property, essentially lusts after a good housekeeper. First, the hero observes that "the elbows are working away with incredible agility." Oblomov begins his advances with the following remark that refers to Agafya's ample housework:

> "Always so busy!" he said, walking up to her. "What's that?"
>
> "I'm grinding cinnamon," she replied, looking down into the mortar as if it were a deep pit, pounding relentlessly with the pestle.
>
> "And what if I bother you a bit?" he asked, cupping her elbows and stop-ping her.
>
> "Let go! I still have to grind the sugar and pour out the wine for the pudding."
>
> He kept holding her by the elbows and brought his face up close to the nape of her neck. "What would you say if . . . I came to love you?"
>
> She giggled.
>
> "Would you love me back?" he persisted.
>
> "Why wouldn't I, God tells us to love everyone."
>
> "And what if I kissed you?" he whispered, lowering his head so that his breath burnt her cheek.
>
> "This isn't Holy Week," she said with another giggle.
>
> "Come now, give me a kiss!"

"Let's wait for Easter, then if Lord grants it, we can kiss," she said without surprise, not at all embarrassed, unabashed, and standing up straight and still as a horse having its collar put on. He kissed her lightly on the neck.

"Look now! If I spill the cinnamon, there'll be nothing to put in your pastries!" she responded.

"I don't care!" he said.

"How did you get another stain on your dressing gown?" she asked caringly, taking the hem of his dressing gown into her hand. "Seems like it may be oil." She sniffed the stain. "Where did you get it? Could it have dripped from the lamp?"

"I don't know how I acquired it."

"I bet you got it from the door," she said, suddenly realizing what must have happened, "yesterday they greased the hinges—they were creaking. Take it off and give it to me right away, I'll take it and wash it and tomorrow the stain will be gone."

"You're so good to me, Agafya Matveevna!" said Oblomov, lazily taking the dressing gown off his shoulders, "you know what, why don't we go and live in the country, on my estate; that would really be the place for you to keep house, it has everything: our own mushrooms, berries, preserves, poultry, cattle . . ."

[. . .] All he felt like doing was sitting on the divan and just watching her elbows. (4:384)

Here, as elsewhere in portions of the novel that take place on the Vyborg Side, Oblomov is attracted to Pshenitsyna's working body (she all but becomes *elbows*); he is attracted to the sight of good housekeeping. Just before the cited text, Pshenitsyna is shown sewing so vigorously that Oblomov jokes that she might sew her nose to her skirt. Later, they discuss dinner. The kiss is embedded in a long list of activities associated with the home. And indeed, as will be shown in a moment, even the compositional history of Pshenitsyna is replete with the stuff of good housekeeping.

E. A. Liatskii has noted that Olga appears very early in Goncharov's manuscripts for the novel.[17] The same cannot be said of Pshenitsyna, who is never directly represented in surviving published drafts.[18] This feature of the novel's compositional history may be illuminated by continuing to trace aspects of Goncharov's artistic process that are relevant for considering his representation of domestic culture. During an 1857 trip to

Marienbad, where Goncharov would write much of parts three and four of *Oblomov*, the novelist met a fairly prominent author of domestic manuals, Ignatii Radetskii, who produced a number of titles on the subject of gentry domestic culture. In a letter written while the novelist was en route to Marienbad, Goncharov recounts in some detail how he shared a stagecoach with Radetskii: "he thought to engage me, starting up conversations about trade, about politics and then suddenly, oh horrors, about literature. He is very clever and has read some things; by the way, he wrote the book *The Gastronome's Almanac*, which was censored by Elagin, who all but found much 'free spirit' in it."[19] *The Gastronomes' Almanac* instructs its reader in subjects pertaining to society dining and entertaining;[20] its target audience would include the head butler of a well-to-do household, for example. Two sentences after this passage, Goncharov muses about the way in which travel affords one the possibility to engage in introspection. He writes:

> nowhere can one become so excruciatingly immersed in oneself and sort out all sorts of trash, rubbish, with which a person becomes filled in the course of many, many years. Some female housekeepers [*inye domovodki*] begin to collect rubbish in old chests in their youth and then like to sort it out; perhaps she will find a worm-eaten little piece of fur, a discolored piece of fabric from a wedding dress, a needle-case and then suddenly, she will stumble upon some sort of an old garment, now turned black and yellow, but with a diamond.[21]

The presence of the author of domestic manuals inspires the introduction of the figure of the housekeeper and the accumulation of details pertaining to material objects. In part three of *Oblomov*, the reader may find a reworked version of the same passage: "Agafya Matveevna sat on the floor and sorted out junk in an old chest; heaps of rags, cotton, old dresses, buttons, and pieces of fur lay near her" (4:355). Thus, the representation of Agafya Matveevna issues compositionally from the encounter with the advice literature author Radetskii.

The scene about Pshenitsyna sorting through the contents of her chest is immediately followed by news that the house at Oblomovka has become uninhabitable—it has nearly fallen apart and had to be vacated. The new "Oblomovka" of the Vyborg Side is depicted in a way that suggests multiple points of contact with middling domestic advice literature. This may be illustrated by a passage read normally for the Homeric dimensions of its attention to detail. About the good rapport between Pshenitsyna and the servant Anisya, Goncharov's narrator exclaims,

> and my God, what knowledge they exchanged about housekeeping, not only in the culinary affairs, but also regarding canvas, thread, sewing, the washing of linens, dresses, the cleaning of white silk lace, and common lace, gloves, the removal of stains from various fabrics, as well as the use of various home remedies, herbs—all that, which was introduced into that certain sphere of life by the observant mind and centuries' worth of experience! (4:313–14)

On the 21st of February, 1858, Ivan Goncharov signed off as censor for a subject-specific domestic manual titled *Instructions about How to Wash, Clean, and Generally Keep Linen and Other Objects of the Feminine Wardrobe and Dress* (*Nastavlenie o tom, kak myt', chistit', i voobshche soderzhat' bel'e i drugie predmety zhenskogo garderoba i tualeta*). This tome, penned by one Glafira Shchigrovskaia (a pseudonym used by Sofia Burnasheva),[22] would be published during the same year as Goncharov's masterpiece. The instructional manual is divided into four major sections that treat the subjects of "the renewal and keeping of linens," "the cleaning and washing of various things and fabrics," "the removal of stains and the keeping of linens and other fabrics," and "miscellany." Upon a closer examination of the table of contents, it turns out that where in *Oblomov* one reads about "the washing of linens, dresses, the cleaning of white silk lace, and common lace, gloves, the removal of stains from various fabrics," Burnasheva's book contains the following chapter headings: "the washing of linens," "on dresses," "the washing of white silk lace and common lace," "the cleaning and washing of gloves," as well as a lengthy section on "the removal of stains."[23] Questions of any deliberate intertextuality aside,[24] a juxtaposition of the passage from *Oblomov* with a domestic manual to which Goncharov had direct access reveals that the discursive texture of the passage is such that the poetic (even Homeric) tenor of the description is achieved in phrases that look identical to the manual's table of contents. That such seemingly divergent sensibilities coexist on the same page is a feature of Goncharov's novelistic imagination.

If Goncharov, whose work as a censor exposed him to a rather broad segment of the period's book market, was well versed enough in advice literature to recognize Ignatii Radetskii as a fairly well-known author in that genre, he may have been familiar with a still more prolific and prominent figure in this area, Ekaterina Avdeeva.[25] In the introduction to the fourth edition of her highly popular domestic manual, *The Handbook of the Russian Experienced Housewife* (*Ruchnaia kniga russkoi opytnoi khoziaiki*), Avdeeva writes,

> I am not requiring that every lady of the house should bake and cook herself, herself go to purchase provisions (although to tell the truth, I see nothing loathsome or worthy of scorn in this), but I insist that to *know* all this, to know the price and the quality of provisions, to know what provisions are stored in her own cellar, her own basement, to know how to cook cabbage soup, bake *pirogi,* and direct the cook in her activities, is the duty of every good housewife.[26]

Pshenitsyna fits this description to a tee, even surpassing Avdeeva's minimal requirements since she both supervises and famously cooks herself. Zakhar notes that without Pshenitsyna, her servant Akulina would not be able to bake a *pirog,* given that she "does not know how to start the dough" (4:305). In adherence to Avdeeva's instructions, Pshenitsyna "thunders with orders to take out, to place, to heat up, to salt," the succession of infinitives resembling formally the language of a recipe (of which Avdeeva's books contain many), where strings of these and related verbs, either in the infinitive or imperative, are commonly found (4:313). When Oblomov dines at home, Pshenitsyna supervises his cook, tells her "whether it is time to take out the roast, whether it is necessary to add some red wine or sour cream to the sauce" (4:313). And, finally, Pshenitsyna frequently visits the market, where "she unerringly decides with one look or at most with a touch of the finger how old the chicken is, when the fish was caught, when the parsley or lettuce was harvested from the garden," thus fulfilling Avdeeva's order that a good housekeeper should be able to recognize the quality of provisions (4:313).

What does it mean that the eponymous hero of Goncharov's novel ends his days cohabitating with Pshenitsyna, a character who appears to be composed according to extra-literary discourses about model

domestic culture?[27] To begin with, the contrast between Olga and Pshenitsyna as housekeepers is amply apparent to the titular hero of the novel. For
instance, he tells Zakhar about a way of life he finds wholly objectionable
for himself and Olga: "only one woman serves the entire household. The
lady of the house herself goes to the market! But will Olga Sergeevna ever
go to the market?" (4:323). She certainly will not. Direct engagement in
domestic activity was something of a social taboo in the sorts of circles to
which Olga and, for much of the novel, Oblomov belong.[28] Thus, in one
reading, Oblomov's cohabitation with Pshenitsyna amounts to the hero's
fall from the gentry, his embourgeoisement. But if one takes the matter
in terms of the textual fabric (as opposed to the plot) of the novel, then
the gradual and systematic incorporation of a variety of middlebrow texts
renders Oblomov's fall from the gentry less dramatic in that from this perspective, both Oblomov the character and *Oblomov* the novel have a rather
more hybrid character.

Here, a closer consideration of the advice literature discussed thus far
is in order. Dmitrii Sokolov, the author of *Man of the World; or, a Guide
to Social Rules*, addresses his book to the "middle circles of society," adding that the book would be useless for the aristocratic reader. Radetskii
writes for his colleagues, literate head chefs and head butlers of reasonably
well-to-do gentry households. Burnasheva's audience consists of "rural
housewives of limited means and urban dwellers with little money." Avdeeva insists forcefully that her readership is composed of "persons of the
middling estate."[29] What, then, does it mean that *Oblomov* can be connected in a variety of ways to books that purport to have middling (almost
middle-class) addressees? The novel's discursive fabric, particularly the
preponderance of details in its representation of domesticity, holds the
answer to this question. Anne Lounsbery, who reads *Oblomov* in relation
to nineteenth-century economics, concludes that the novel's investment
in extensive descriptions ("why description is interesting and narration is
dull") has an explanation in the "politics of the hero's passivity." She suggests that "[Oblomov's] indolence is a thoroughly futile but nonetheless
satisfying (to us, not to him) form of resistance against the new (to Russia) capitalist imperatives of activity, productivity, rational mastery and so
on."[30] This line of interpretation—that, at root, Goncharov's tendency to
describe at length is a response to Russia's experience of a capitalist modernity processed as a relatively new Western import—may be extended to

include the ways in which Goncharov's trilogy as a whole deploys detailed domestic descriptions in a manner that is imbricated with the novels' processing of evolving, unstable social estates in a modernizing Russia.

"Everything can be classified as somehow prosaic," wrote Ivan Goncharov in his travelogue *The Frigate Pallas* (*Fregat Pallada*) (2:14). Alexander Herzen, who in 1857 penned a rather unflattering article called "The Uncommon Story of the Censor Gon-cha-ro from Shi-Pan-Khu," the title here referring pointedly to Goncharov's professional identity and recent travels in Asia, claimed that the author of the travelogue had gone on a journey around the world in order to describe a long series of dinners.[31] And while Herzen's critical pronouncements were likely fueled by ideological differences, it is difficult not to agree with his appraisal that *The Frigate Pallas* is a text replete with such prosy subjects as what Admiral Putiatin's secretary ate for dessert on Madeira or how he dined at the Cape of Good Hope.[32] What one may call "the prose of everyday life" figures prominently in critical responses to Goncharov's oeuvre. In his 1860 review of *Oblomov*, Alexander Miliukov regarded Goncharov as a consummate *bytopisatel'*, a writer who excels in descriptions of everyday and, especially, domestic life.[33] The author of one of the earliest monographs on the novelist, E. A. Liatskii, calls Goncharov "the great master of Russian everyday life," assessing his skill for descriptions of "lackeys' quarters, kitchens, the back stairs."[34] Iulii Aikhenval'd finds Goncharov to be most artistically successful when describing simple, "elementary" things—often objects or practices related to home life. In what has come to be one of the most often-cited pronouncements on the author of *Oblomov*, Aikhenval'd calls the novelist "a poet of the room, a bard of the household."[35] This trend was started by the novelist's contemporary, Alexander Druzhinin, who famously compared Goncharov's prose technique to Flemish genre painting, labeling it *flamandstvo*.[36]

Ruth Yeazell explores the role of Flemish genre painting in the aesthetic sensibilities and contemporary critical reception of the Western European realist novel. She notes that the prose of such novelists as Jane Austen, Honoré de Balzac, Gustave Flaubert, and George Eliot was frequently compared to Flemish genre painting by contemporary critics. Yeazell accounts for this trend in part by what she calls "the common origins" of Dutch painting and the Western European novel in "bourgeois culture."[37] She contemplates the degree to which Dutch art served as a descriptive idiom

for artists who worked to render the particulars of middle-class life. Yeazell
also writes about another kind of correspondence between Dutch genre
painting and, now, specifically, the British novel. She points out that "like
British novels after them, Dutch paintings were particularly influenced by
the ideals of household virtue and marital companionship that began to
circulate in the domestic conduct books of seventeenth-century Europe—
many of which, as it happened, first traveled to Holland from England."[38] In
Yeazell's discussion of Western European literature, three generic-cultural
registers converge: Dutch genre painting, domestic conduct books, and the
realist novel. All of them are identified as middle-class or bourgeois.

The observation that Goncharov's novels resemble their Western European counterparts has been made by a number of scholars. However, one
must be careful not to overstate this suggestion, especially in dealing with
the task of situating *Oblomov* in a socioeconomic context. The kinds of
"middle-class texts" (instructional literature) identified in this study as
material reworked in *Oblomov* have been used extensively in treatments
of the Western European novel as an important condition for the very
appearance of the genre.[39] Russia would lack a middle class until well into
the concluding decades of the nineteenth century. What remains a bit
curious (and, taken in the strictest sense, belongs in the domain of historians) is that so much of the Russian popular advice literature is addressed
explicitly to people of middling means. This is a category that does not
neatly correspond with the Western concept of the bourgeoisie. Nor would
it be prudent to insist that these writers' claims refer to a documentary
reality, an actual Russian middle-class readership. The "middling" reader
of Russian manuals may be a primarily discursive phenomenon, perhaps
the result of the genre's strong tendency to translate or otherwise borrow from Western European sources. The very fact that Russian authors
of manuals use a variety of formulations to call their readership people
of "the middling estate," "average means," "limited or modest means,"
or members of "middling circles of society" may be read as a series of
attempts to approximate a demographic category, a collective search for a
term that will describe a readership that is perhaps primarily a discursive
construct that may or may not have a clear referent.

Instructional literature about domestic affairs comes up in every one
of Goncharov's three novels. Domestic culture figures prominently in his
last novel, *The Precipice*. Originally called *The Artist*, the text examines

the relationship between art and life, especially in scenes where the young landowner Raisky contemplates various artistic projects, from sculpture to novels. Through the representation of Raisky's creative pursuits, Goncharov introduces a distinctly meta-literary dimension with ample commentary on the artistic process. Much like *A Common Story* and *Oblomov*, *The Precipice* contains many pairs of characters who are opposites of each other, including good and bad housekeepers.[40] The landowner Raisky is juxtaposed with his more practically minded neighbor, Tushin. Raisky continually reveals his ineptitude and lack of interest in running his own estate, which he leaves in the care of his grandmother, Tatiana Markovna. In contrast to Raisky, Tushin is described as an excellent landlord.

Goncharov calls Tushin a *bourgeois-gentilhomme* as he, in a very explicit allusion to Molière's M. Jourdain, "spoke in prose without knowing it" (7:735). Goncharov reverses the French play's plot: Molière's M. Jourdain is, in fact, a bourgeois, the comedic aspect of whose situation boils down precisely to the fact that he has endeavored to assume a gentlemanly lifestyle. Tushin, of course, is a nobleman. What, then, does it mean that he speaks in prose? He certainly reads prose, and it is prose of the most prosaic variety that this young landowner consumes: "works about agronomy and housekeeping in general" (7:352). The same cultural register of domestic advice literature served to mark the contrast between poetry and the prosiness of life for the young Aduev in *A Common Story* when the hero found useful employment in the translation of articles about farming. Likewise, Tushin's prose (juxtaposed as it is to Raisky's passion for artistic projects) refers to the prosaic business of running an estate.

A similar phenomenon is to be observed in another coupling of characters, another pair of good and bad housekeepers, Marfin'ka and Sofia Belovodova. Both are noblewomen, but the former has grown up in the country, immersed in domestic affairs, while the latter is a Petersburg society woman. The central hero, Raisky, contemplates what sort of novel one might write about these two women: "'Yes, they will make for a novel,' he thought, 'perhaps a real novel, but a flaccid, minor one, with aristocratic details for one woman and bourgeois ones for the other'" (7:183). The Russian for "bourgeois details" is *meshchanskie podrobnosti*. Yet throughout the novel, Goncharov's narrator is quite fond of noting that both Marfin'ka and her grandmother Tatiana Markovna are noblewomen; in fact, it is indicated emphatically that the grandmother is a *stolbovaia dvorianka*, a woman whose family belongs to the old nobility. Likely the only thing that could be "bourgeois" about Marfin'ka (and her grandmother) is that they are excellent housekeepers. Given that Raisky's thinking is concerned explicitly with the composition of an artistic text, the episode suggests that the phrase "bourgeois details" refers to the formal characteristics of a novel. The adjective "bourgeois" in Goncharov's novelistic imagination may be treated as shorthand for a representational register that is centered around and thoroughly consumed with the details of everyday, most often, domestic life. It is his Flemish genre painting. In a curious and likely unexpected way, Goncharov's novelistic imagination reveals, most notably in the function of the domestic detail as an aesthetic category, a largely formal overlap with some of the representational sensibilities of the Western European bourgeois realist novel. It should be underscored that the typically middle-class conflation of stylistic registers (Flemish genre painting and instructional literature in a realist novel) may be understood as a distinguishing feature of Goncharov's prose. In this context, the explicit marking of the bourgeois details (*meshchanskie podrobnosti*) in *The Precipice* serves to adumbrate the purportedly middle-class origins of detailed novelistic narration that foregrounds the domestic. Thus, Goncharov places all of his landowners manqués in what may be regarded as formally middle-class rhetorical vessels.

But are all of Goncharov's fictional landowners failures? Certainly, the depiction of Tushin suggests a positive hero. As was mentioned in the discussion of *Oblomov*, the representation of the consummate housekeeper Pshenitsyna accords rather strikingly with the period's leading works of advice literature about domestic affairs. In *The Precipice*, Goncharov comes close to depicting a successful agriculturalist in Tushin, who looks to be another character borrowed from advice literature; but here the task proves to be quite complicated. Initially, the contrast with Raisky, the landowner-artist who takes little interest in the management of his properties, suggests that Tushin will be an enterprising figure in the mold of a Stolz. Young and energetic, Tushin is the first and only representative of Goncharov's gallery of noblemen to engage actively and systematically in the work undertaken at his estate; one could say that of all of Goncharov's readers of agricultural literature, Tushin is the only one who puts it to good practical use. But he turns out to be very difficult to depict, and the novel is very self-conscious about this difficulty.

Once again employing Raisky as the novel's stand-in for the creative mind, the character who consistently approaches his surroundings as potential objects of artistic representation, Goncharov devotes passages of considerable length to the difficulty experienced by the artist in his attempt to apprehend and to capture Tushin fully. During his visit to the landowner, Raisky "wished to understand deeply the workings of Tushin's estate-keeping mechanism" (*vniknut' v poriadok khoziaistvennogo mekhanizma Tushina*) (7:732). Raisky "had just enough time to notice the superficial order, to see the striking results of [Tushin's] estate management, but did not have the time to understand deeply (*vniknut'*) the process by which it was accomplished" (7:732). Moreover, "Raisky's eye, given that it was not a landlord's eye [*nekhoziaiskii glaz*], was unable to appreciate fully all of the good housekeeping [*vsei khoziaistvennosti*] at Tushin's estate" (7:732). In all of these passages, it is underscored that the good landowner eludes the artist's gaze.

A similar insufficiency in the artist's perception is discernible in Goncharov's more extended description of Tushin's property as it appears to Raisky. Here, both the landowner and the estate consistently surprise Raisky. Both Tushin and his surroundings look strikingly strange in a passage that highlights the "unreal" (*nebyvalyi*) aspects of the landowner's work and life:

> The view of the forest really did strike Raisky. The forest was maintained as well as a park, where at each turn one sees the traces of movement, work, care, and science. The crew [*artel'*] looked like some sort of a brigade. The peasants [*muzhiki*] resembled landlords [*khoziaev*], and looked as if they were busy with their own work [*khoziaistvo*].
>
> [...] The sawmill seemed to Raisky to be something unreal, due to its vastness, due almost to the luxuriousness of the buildings, where comfort and refinement made it resemble an exemplary English establishment. The machines, which were made of shiny steel and metal, were exemplary creations of their kind.
>
> Tushin himself looked for a moment to be the first workman [*pervym rabotnikom*] when he became engrossed in his technology, in all the

minutiae, in the details, crawling into the machine, inspecting it, touching the wheels with his hand.

Raisky gazed with surprise, especially when they came to the factory office and when about fifty workers burst into the room with their requests, with explanations, and surrounded Tushin. (7:737)

The description of Raisky as someone who is continuously attempting to understand Tushin fully, but who fails and remains bewildered at every step, has an explicit meta-novelistic dimension. In other words, Raisky's confusion may be read here as a rather thinly veiled allusion to Goncharov's own anxieties about his depiction of Tushin.

Many years later, Goncharov would respond to the criticism that he had failed to portray Tushin more convincingly by asserting that he was writing about a representative of a new and still developing phenomenon, a man of the future and not a landowner of the familiar mold. Tushin was to be a new nobleman of the post-Emancipation period in a novel famous for its historical incongruities and its hodgepodge absorption of Russian cultural and political life from the 1840s until the late 1860s.[41] Given the heterogeneity of historical epochs entertained in *The Precipice*, it is noteworthy that while writing about his novel in the 1880s Goncharov cast a retrospective glance and alluded to Gogol's failure in volume two of *Dead Souls*, where, in Goncharov's words, the former had "attempted [...] to describe a positive type and was unsuccessful."[42] Goncharov conceived all three of his novels when Gogol was working on volume two of *Dead Souls*, during the late 1840s. In 1847, when Gogol's *Selected Passages* appeared, Goncharov was publishing *A Common Story*, whose protagonist is, in a limited sense, Gogol's colleague, inasmuch as Aduev's agricultural writings also imagine exemplary noblemen and excellent landlords. The critic M. V. Otradin reads Aduev's shifting choices of genres throughout *A Common Story* as the representation of a creative process that leads to the novel.[43] Although Otradin does not discuss the young man's composition of works about estate management, the ultimate turn to this genre likely ought to be included in his artistic evolution as one that also leads to novelistic discourse. Now, if one widens the lens somewhat to encompass Goncharov's creative process throughout the trilogy, then one may glimpse a long series of encounters with advice literature both in its compositional history and narrative texture. These encounters run parallel to the formation of Goncharov's realist idiom and they shape both the formal and the thematic preoccupations of his novels.

All three of Goncharov's novels turn upon contrasts (for example, active/passive, dreamer/realist, passion/reason) among which the one between the bourgeois and the *gentilhomme* may well be the most pervasive. The very categories of bourgeois and *gentilhomme*, which Goncharov manipulates in a number of ways in the course of his oeuvre, are perhaps above all performative and correspond primarily to various modes of representation. An episode from the novelist's final years demonstrates this point rather well. In 1887, Goncharov summered at a dacha near Narva in today's Estonia. He went there with his adopted family: Aleksandra Ivanovna Treigut, Goncharov's housekeeper and the wife of his deceased manservant, and her children. He had assumed full financial responsibility for the family following the death of the paterfamilias, Karl Treigut. In his old age, the writer lived out something quite like the plot of his most famous novel in cohabitating with his housekeeper and becoming a veritable guardian, not to say father, to her children. Goncharov appears to have enjoyed the dacha despite some discomforts in a realm of life the novelist took very seriously: the gastronomic. Thus, he reports to his friend Anatolii Koni,

> there is no market [*rynok*], everything is delivered by traveling vendors, and one must eat whatever they bring. Sometimes they bring fresh salmon, white fish, even asparagus; or sometimes, they bring dry beef, flaccid veal. Aleks<andra> Iv<anovna> grows upset and quarrels, as is her habit, with me on account of this, as of everything else.
>
> We eat a lot, but poorly. She also quarrels with me for the fact that there are no berries, that the cucumbers here are bad and so on.[44]

This state of affairs notwithstanding, Goncharov manages to remark that the "most delightful thing" about his vacation is the "desertedness [of the place], the quiet, the isolation" (*pustynnost', tishina, uedinenie*). He continues to observe facetiously that "away from crowds and acquaintances, it is as if I have been transported to a faraway village; at my vast dacha, with its three verandas, each of them facing a different direction, I feel like an absolute landowner of the old mold [*chuvstvuiu sebia sovershennym pomeshchikom à la vieille façon*]."[45] What about the setting, a dacha near Narva, inspires such commentary and such a feeling? First, the detail that "no noise and no sounds reach me except those of the shepherds [*pastush'ikh*]" suggests the pastoral.[46] Further, the emphasis on quiet, desertedness, and isolation, being away from worldly cares, coupled with the inclusion of the protracted grocery list, recall the sensibility of Oblomov's favorite generic register: that of the friendly epistle, particularly in its tendency to foreground the nobleman's well-deserved rustic *otium* and to depict it in detail. To put it bluntly, Goncharov's feeling of being a landowner of the old mold is produced rhetorically by the generic markers and the sensibility of perhaps the prime verse vehicle for the celebration of gentry private life at the turn of the century—the friendly epistle. The playful epistolary performance of the part of a *pomeshchik à la vieille façon*, then, points to the considerable degree to which for Goncharov social identities are imbricated with the cultural forms used to narrate them.

Reading and Social Identity in Aksakov's *Childhood Years of Bagrov the Grandson*

First of all we should point out that the life that we would like to present to our readers, according to the notes, whose contents pertain to the end of the previous century, in no way resembles the life of present-day landowners. Now the dissemination of learning has, in many respects, altered even life in the countryside. Landowners, of course, have now understood their relationship to the serfs much better than they did before: the joyful feeling with which they, with the exception of the most uncouth and uneducated among them, receive the tsar's supreme intention to free the serfs attests to this. Now rare are the landowners who live only by the labors of their serfs and do nothing themselves; now nobles consider it their duty to serve the state or to have some sort of useful activity outside service. With time, more and more nobles introduce improvements in agriculture, take part in industrial and trading ventures and so forth. It is the rare landowner who, while living in the countryside now, does not subscribe to journals and order good books.[1]

Such was the disclaimer that the radical critic Nikolai Dobroliubov included in his discussion of late eighteenth-century landowning life and culture in the provinces, a disquisition prompted by the appearance of Sergei Aksakov's *Childhood Years of Bagrov the Grandson* (1858), a semi-fictional account of the author's life as a young boy. Known for his tendency to read the contemporary literary scene chiefly for political content, while deliberately, indeed sometimes emphatically, paying little attention to aesthetic and formal complexity, Dobroliubov purports to take *Childhood Years* to be about the real life of real landowners, whose historicity he feels justified in exploring.[2] He does this by contextualizing Aksakov's account in relation to a non-literary text he implicitly considers comparable, Andrei Bolotov's recollections, parts of which were then being published, and Novikov's satirical journalism, which the critic likewise treats as something akin to a documentary source. Dobroliubov writes at a time when the public's expectations for the emancipation of the serfs grew precipitously. In setting up a comparison between the eighteenth-century landowner and the nobleman of his own present moment, the critic would seem to posit that education and maximally avid participation in the cultural and economic life of the empire are what distinguishes the new, enlightened nobility from the old, eighteenth-century likes of the semi-fictional Bagrov's grandfather, Stepan Mikhailovich, who cuts a boorish and despotic figure in Aksakov's 1856 *Family Chronicle.* Much as Dobroliubov may not have intended for the juxtaposition to suggest this, the contrast he establishes between the simple, impulsive, and parasitic landowner of the past and the compassionate and educated nobleman of the future proves operative in Aksakov's depiction of his protagonist's youth, especially in the young boy's gradual development of a social identity.

The novel-memoir *Childhood Years* functions much like a bildungsroman.[3] Young Sergei Bagrov's development is punctuated, to a significant extent, by milestones in his reading habits. *Childhood Years* expends an enormous amount of narrative energy on the representation of its young protagonist's manner of reading. In a text that typically takes up about three hundred pages in most editions,[4] books—reading alone, reading to family members, reciting for company, the acquisition and handling of reading materials, their availability or shortage, and naturally their contents, ideas, and their reception—are mentioned dozens of times. In a narrative about the early stages of *Bildung* rendered by Aksakov as a process conditioned by many practices related to reading, two points receive a particularly high level of attention. First, the young boy's gradual acquisition of a small private library is described systematically and in great detail. Second, the narrative places an emphasis on what even his family perceives as a set of peculiar habits, his rather extreme tendency to reread the same text or the same small set of texts repeatedly, and to experience strong emotional (almost ecstatic) states while reading. A closer look at both of these points will help explain the prominence of reading in Aksakov's account. In broad terms, Aksakov's references to reading tell a story about the constitution of selfhood, in particular about the formation of a young provincial noble-man's sense of identity in relation to the social world he inhabits.

But first, a few disclaimers are in order. To begin with, Aksakov's was a text both conceived and, to a significant degree, received as a writer's biography. For this reason, it should be highlighted from the start that the novel offers Bagrov's experiences as those of a future man of letters, a young boy who may not have been an average or typical reader. Moreover, like all of the material included in the *Childhood Years*, the narrative about Bagrov's reading has been refracted by the semi-fictional generic character of the text, which, unlike, say, Bolotov's recollections, is not an attempt at a straightforwardly autobiographical or documentary reconstruction of lived experience.[5] *Childhood Years* has a strongly novelistic (but, of course, also far from an exclusively novelistic) dimension. The account that follows foregrounds how Aksakov's narrative imagines reading as a cultural practice, perhaps at the expense of dealing with whether the novel provides a historically accurate or in any way representative portrayal. Although historicized, the findings below are primarily about cultural and discursive trends, not hard documentary evidence.

There are ways in which the novel-memoir depicts certain aspects of the Bagrovs' life as historical in a qualitative sense that has to do largely with literary genre and cultural register. Writing about a work that both Aksakov and contemporaries understood as the precursor to *Childhood Years*, his *Family Chronicle*, Andrew Durkin has pointed out the text's generic ambidexterity, the ways in which it "resists identification as auto-biography or history [...] and defies complete categorization as fiction."[6] Marcus Levitt has suggested that all attempts to locate *Family Chronicle* in a generic catalogue miss the point, at least partly, because such attempts always issue from the position of a *reader*, a member of a literate public who comes to the text with expectations that it conform to the conven-tions of one or another genre. Levitt himself offers to read *Family Chron-icle* as "an attempt to capture the vanishing world of oral culture in print," pointing—among other things—to the narrator, who casts himself as the "impartial chronicler of oral traditions," thereby situating himself firmly in a premodern and preliterate context dominated by the oral transmission of narratives.[7] *Family Chronicle* actively contemplates an encroaching modernity by alluding frequently to a veritable mythology of the premodern understood as a conceptual category, which the text applies to various facets of the eighteenth-century Russian provincial life it depicts.[8] The narrative of *Childhood Years* picks up more or less where *Family Chronicle* ended. The later text is self-conscious about literacy as an artifact of modern experience in a different, but related, way. In an oft-cited letter to Ivan Turgenev, Aksakov described *Childhood Years* as a narrative that was to begin with and, in a sense, depart from what he called the "fabled, prehistorical time" (*vremeni basnoslovnogo, doistoricheskogo*) of childhood.[9]

Whereas *Family Chronicle* deploys the frequently non-linear temporalities of myth and legend, in *Childhood Years* the Aksakovs enter identifiably historical time through a variety of self-historicizing gestures, many of them pertaining to reading. The narrative opens with young Sergei recovering from a dangerous illness. Bagrov's mother treats him according to a medical book for home use and she ultimately ascribes the child's recovery "to God's limitless mercy, and secondly, to Buchan's medical book" (1:292). She teaches her son to pray for Buchan's soul. Eventually, they acquire a handsome, decorated portrait of the physician.[10] The representation of the first major event in Sergei's life—his recovery from illness—is shown emphatically to occur in a thoroughly, one might say, hyper-literate context. It seems reasonable to call their family environment hyper-literate for their own time for many reasons, the characterization of Sergei's mother as an educated woman conversant with a remarkably broad range of the period's intellectual life chief among these.

Soon after his recovery from illness, Bagrov turns to reading. The first topic of discussion in the first chronologically coherent chapter (called "Coherent Recollections," the title here pointing to the text's increasing incorporation of linear time in contrast to the distinctly cyclical, pre- or antimodern temporality of *Family Chronicle*) is Bagrov's first childhood book: *The Mirror of Virtue and Morality for Children* (*Zerkalo dobrodeteli i blagonraviia dlia detei*). A Russian translation from German was published in Moscow in 1794. Here, as in the case of Buchan's fashionable medical book, the narrative's very linearity, its tendency toward the representation of a process akin to *Bildung*, coincides with its attention to the family's access to recently produced books. That *The Mirror of Virtue* had predictably didactic ends adds another dimension to the ways in which Sergei's formation (in the sense here of *vospitanie*) is linked quite explicitly to books that seek to shape their readers. As will be the case throughout the account, young Bagrov reads the same text—here *The Mirror of Virtue*—repeatedly and memorizes it from cover to cover.

Sergei's interest in books is multivalent and rather strikingly so. The young Bagrov's library begins to grow thanks to their Ufa neighbor Anichkov and their relation Praskof'ia Ivanovna, both of whom have long been in the habit of receiving books from the capitals. Among the first and certainly the most significant additions to Sergei's library is Russia's oldest children's periodical, *Children's Reading for the Heart and Mind*, edited by Karamzin and Petrov and published by Nikolai Novikov. Sergei's powerful attachment to *Children's Reading* goes well beyond the content, as both the young man and the narrative in which the reader encounters him all but fixate on the booklets as material objects. Much attention is paid to the handling of the journal—that issues of it can be stored properly or improperly, transported from one location to another, touched, rationed, and so forth. Among the most fruitful tendencies in the study of the history of reading is the turn to foregrounding the materiality of printed fare. There is particular merit to such an approach when dealing with the early modern period. As Robert Darnton puts it while describing the reader of the ancien régime:

> Books themselves were individuals, each copy possessing its own character. The reader [...] would finger the paper in order to gauge its weight, translucence, and elasticity. [...] He would study the design of the type, examine the spacing, check the register. [...] He would sample a book the way we might taste a glass of wine; for he looked *at* the impressions on the paper, not merely across them to their meaning. And once he had possessed himself fully of a book, in all its physicality, he would settle down to read it.[11]

Sergei's enthusiasm for his books recalls the ancien régime reader described by Darnton. The twelve issues of *Childhood Reading* occupy a very prominent position in the object world (in the anthropological sense) that young Sergei inhabits. They are among his few, and very possibly his most important, personal material possessions. Aksakov describes repeatedly and in detail the care taken by Sergei to pack up and to carry with him these volumes throughout the family's peregrinations, as they visit relations across the provincial landscape. The narrator never seems to tire of registering repeatedly such seemingly prosaic activities as the packing and the unpacking, the arranging and the rearranging of these books now recorded largely as objects, as things that travel with Sergei. In fact, it may be worth pointing out as an aside that when read with an eye to tracing this traffic in books, Aksakov's *Childhood Years* threatens to become a story about the circulation of culture across a provincial landscape.

More pointedly, Sergei's reading habits appear to dramatize obliquely the transformative, if relatively small-scale, democratization of reading that reached Russia towards the end of the eighteenth century.[12] Much as *Children's Reading* remains Sergei's most frequently enjoyed book, the young man reads rather widely. He is given the works of such authors as Alexander Sumarokov and Mikhail Kheraskov, some of which he becomes fond of reciting for company, as his reading becomes a vehicle for polite sociability. Eventually, Sergei gains temporary access to translations of various novels, which, although he does not have the time to read them in full, leave a lasting impression. These include a variety of European works, for example, Richardson's *Clarissa*, which was published in English in 1748 and in a Russian translation from French in 1791. Here it is worth noting that the novels he reads (*Clarissa*, *The Vicar of Wakefield*) are frequently discussed in the context of book history, particularly in relation to the increasing democratization of reading in the West, what Rolf Engelsing called the "Reading Revolution."[13]

Sergei's reading habits lend themselves to being situated and interpreted vis-à-vis the history of reading broadly for a few reasons. First of all, the young boy's reading calls attention to itself. Although Sergei grows passionate about nearly all of his pursuits (fishing prime among these), his reading habits remain peculiar because of the anxiety the imagined and much-feared effects of this activity engender in his mother. Sergei's happiness at the acquisition of *Childhood Reading* provides a particularly vivid example of the intensity of affect elicited by the boy's reading. The narrator recalls his mother's account of the first time the family found him reading *Childhood Reading* as follows:

My mother told me later that I was like a madman: I said nothing, I did
not understand what I was being told, and did not want to go have dinner.
They had to take away the book from me, despite my bitter tears. [...] After
dinner I again seized the book and read until evening. Naturally, my mother
put an end to such frenetic reading: she locked the keys in her cabinet and
gave them out to me one by one, and even then only at the appointed hours.
(1:298–99)

The frenetic enthusiasm, the nearly pathological extent of his engagement with the journal, recalls accounts of the so-called European reading
fever, especially in his mother's recurring concern that this excessively
engaged and copious reading will damage his health and in her resultant
rationing of the books lest they harm the child.

From another, related perspective, certain aspects of Sergei's reading
look like a peculiar reenactment in miniature and from a child's point of
view of the large-scale transformations in the European, and rather more
complicatedly Russian, history of the book and of reading. The descriptions in roughly the first two thirds of the narrative of Sergei rereading
the same small set of texts with what looks like an almost religious or
ritualistic devotion and his practice (much emphasized) of memorizing
the contents of books from cover to cover look rather similar to the early
modern phenomenon of "intensive reading." Characterized by access to
a small set of books, often of a religious or devotional nature, "intensive
reading" is thought to have been repetitive and to have resulted in mem-
orization of the material, so that reading constituted a ritual as opposed
to serving as a way to gather information. The so-called Reading Revolution was characterized by the shift from reading few books repeatedly to
access to a broader and ever-expanding book market that enabled "extensive reading." However, the period of "extensive reading" also coincided
with the rise of cultural forms that encouraged a potentially new kind of
engagement, including rereading that now enabled modes of sociocultural
identification and reflection leading to modern subject formation. And
in this context, particular cultural and generic forms, especially the eighteenth-century novel and satirical journalism, are often studied for their
discursive cultivation of social identities. Here, extensive reading turned
inward, becoming more "intensive" than it had been before, in what

Reinhard Wittmann calls the "familiar pan-European *embourgeoisement* of society, culture, and literature," a process understood to have run parallel to the development of the bourgeois public sphere.[14]

As has been suggested throughout this study, one ought not look for a genuinely Habermasian public sphere in eighteenth- and even much of nineteenth-century Russia due both to the absence of a significant bourgeoisie and a difference in the configuration between the autocracy and the institutions that enable civil society and a politically powerful public. Nor should one look for a Russian Reading Revolution that can be described as an embourgeoisement of society and culture. What remains curious is that some Russian writers—notably Novikov and Karamzin—liked to imagine a distinctly unsophisticated, common, native burgeoning audience for their works. First came Novikov's announcement in *The Painter* that his commercial success must be due primarily to his popularity with the *meshchane*, a term for which the best English translation may be townspeople. And, second, in his oft-consulted essay "About the Book Trade and the Love for Reading in Russia," Karamzin described a group of bakers who pool their money to purchase a newspaper, which only one of them can decipher and which he reads aloud to the others. Of course, accounts given by literati are not to be trusted as facts. These statements suggest more about Novikov's and Karamzin's awareness of the transformation of the European reading publics than they do about the situation in Russia. Although scholarly attempts to reconstruct reading practices in the eighteenth century remain incomplete, when it comes specifically to the audience for periodicals Gary Marker shows both Novikov's and Karamzin's assertions about a reading public that would include commoners to be difficult to support. The majority of their verifiable subscribers came from the hereditary service nobility, or, as Marker puts it, "the relatively well-educated, affluent and socially privileged elite that had produced the journalists themselves."[15] Judging by available evidence, this audience was uniquely aristocratic by the pan-European standards of the period. But it was quite diverse when it came to geographic distribution, reaching as far east as Aksakov's own Ufa. All of this suggests that while one cannot speak of the history of reading in Russia as an embourgeoisement of cultural life, to regard the ascendancy of reading as a cultural practice that aided in the formation of Russian gentry selves seems a fruitful avenue.

What emerges in Sergei's reading, then, is a twofold phenomenon. On the one hand, there is a dramatized account of a future writer's entry into modern book culture, a process that is depicted in highly affect-laden terms. On the other hand, there is Sergei's gradual acquisition of something like a consciousness of his social identity. *Childhood Years* registers some of the rather specific ways in which young Sergei's personality is being shaped by his reading. Much as the scope of Sergei's reading broadens throughout the narrative, the text that receives the greatest attention is *Childhood Reading*. Bagrov reads an incomplete set, twelve books out of a total of twenty. While working on *Childhood Years* Aksakov is known to have borrowed a full set and found it disappointing. Nevertheless, a parallel review of *Childhood Reading* and *Childhood Years* makes it possible to trace and identify with some precision which issues young Bagrov may be reading and how the material affects his sensibilities. In other words, Aksakov appears to have built parts of the text around Sergei's encounters with the journal.

Much as Bagrov claims that the journal's general treatises on good behavior were the least appealing fare, there are ways in which the specific and, in its own way, normative vision of the young nobleman in the provinces offered by *Childhood Reading* finds its way into *Childhood Years*. First and foremost, Sergei's seemingly limitless and multifaceted enthusiasm for the natural world, a topic to which the journal devoted copious attention, issues (at least in part) from his reading. Aksakov's narrator emphasizes that the young man's understanding of the elements, for example, of thunder, is profoundly affected by the journal. Further, Bagrov's ability to sometimes see peasants as fellow human beings ("I was comparing myself to the peasant boys who walk back and forth from dusk until dawn [...] and eat bread and water") for whose lot he might even feel remorse ("I began to feel guilty, ashamed") likely also comes from his reading (1:512). Finally, his interest in performing farm work has a clear precedent in *Childhood Reading*.

Sergei's curiosity about serf labor reveals the most about how he comes to understand his own social identity. Bagrov admits to having been so engaged by the sight of peasant labor that he wished to participate. When he does finally obtain his mother's permission and goes out into the fields, Sergei fails miserably, as he turns out to be unable not only to work, but

even to walk down a freshly plowed field. A peasant boy laughs at him
(1:513). On the one hand, the experience settles Sergei more firmly into
the distinction between his own social estate and that of his serfs. On
the other hand, the notion that a *stolbovoi dvorianin*—a member of an
old Russian aristocratic family—might be compelled to work the fields
with his hands has, by the late 1790s of the narrated account, something
of a pedigree in the Russian cultural imagination. As was suggested in
chapter 1, the cultural myth about the landowner who performs manual labor may be best understood as a hypertrophied version of a far
more basic and frequent call for male nobles to take a more active part
in estate life, particularly after the 1762 manifesto that gave gentrymen
the legal right to abstain from previously obligatory state service. As
was discussed in chapter 1, the aftermath of the 1762 manifesto—and
especially of Catherine's 1785 Charter to the Nobility, which endowed
the estate with something approaching inalienable rights—included
a state-propelled effort to rethink and reimagine male noble identity.
Catherine II's reign saw a broad and multifaceted attempt to produce
scenarios for productive noble life in the provinces through the dissemination of a variety of texts that offered a vision of exemplary estate life
generally and of the landowner's duties more specifically. To give perhaps
the most relevant example in the context of this discussion: as was mentioned in chapter 1, Andrei Bolotov's *Economic Magazine* was appended
to Novikov's *Moscow News* contemporaneously with *Childhood Reading*.
Of course, Bolotov's journal produced a vision of the model active landlord in a text geared toward adult readers. The most immediate source
for young Bagrov's desire to work in the fields is very likely the "Correspondence between a Father and Son about Country Life," published in
Childhood Reading in installments in the course of 1785 and discussed
in chapter 1 of this study. Bagrov's interest in nearly every aspect of the
landscape upon which the events of *Childhood Years* transpire comes
partly from these articles. To recapitulate from chapter 1, "The Correspondence" relates the development of a young nobleman who is sent
by his father from the city to the countryside where he must live with
and live like his cousins who are avidly engaged in studying their rural
surroundings, planting crops, working with their hands, and learning the
fundamentals of farming. Bagrov seems to embrace much of the enthusiastic ethos around labor and a very strong localism. These and similar

articles likely shape his worldview as he continues to contemplate his role as a young nobleman vis-à-vis his property, both his serfs and his land. Thus, Bagrov's development of a social self shows the mutual imbrication of identity formation and reading, as Sergei attempts, albeit not always successfully, to embody specific iterations of a broad Catherine-era discourse that sought to cultivate scenarios for a productive noble presence in the provinces among adults and children alike.

But the discussion above should not obscure other, equally important dimensions of the novel's representation of books and of reading, particularly the close attention to the materiality of the printed fare, the prosaic reconstruction of the reader's quotidian contact with books, and its sometimes repetitive treatment of the topic. This characteristic pervades all of Aksakov's prose, not just his treatment of reading. As has been acknowledged by nineteenth-century contemporaries and critics alike, much like Goncharov, Aksakov is a writer who describes quotidian life at great length. "We do not know what the future historian of our literature will glean from the fact that S. T. Aksakov and his friends ate freshly churned butter, radish that had just been picked from the hothouse, sour cream, farmer's cheese and so on," wrote Nikolai Dobroliubov in another polemical review of Aksakov's works.[16] The radically minded critic seeks to undermine all that is valued positively in Aksakov's comprehensive representation of a country morning. Dobroliubov finds Aksakov's impulse to document an ordinary breakfast to be almost Gogolian. He compares Aksakov to Gogol's Ivan Ivanovich, who in "The Story of How Ivan Ivanovich Quarreled with Ivan Nikiforovich" produces a formidable record of his gastronomic practices pertaining to the consumption of melons, which he appends to a melon seed collection—a discursive tendency Cathy Popkin diagnoses as both the author's and the hero's "fanatical alimentary retentiveness."[17] In Dobroliubov's biting commentary, Aksakov's measured celebration of a simple meal turns pathological. In the 1858 review with which this chapter began, Dobroliubov glimpses a kinship between Bolotov's and Aksakov's writings, precisely in both writers' very high tolerance for the detail as an aesthetic category. Not surprisingly, Dobroliubov finds this quality grating. The radical critic finds little value in the Slavophile's encyclopedic treatment of the everyday that, with its emphasis on simple, native sustenance, paid homage to a long tradition of Russian writing about gentry private life.[18]

Ultimately, the preponderance of the everyday in Aksakov's prose may
be regarded alongside Goncharov's novelistic idiom, his *flamandstvo*.
Such writing can be repetitive and exceedingly concerned with minutiae,
because it tends to afford a high degree of prominence to details. Andrew
Durkin treats Aksakov's prose as a laboratory for subsequent stages in the
Russian novelistic tradition, especially when it comes to the genre's representation of gentry households. Durkin writes about a tendency toward
what he calls a "canonization of ordinary life," which, "in keeping with the
empirical, even statistical tendency underlying realism," aided in the "affir-
mation of the coherent society of [...] the gentry family."[19] Describing the
ordinary and the everyday with an eye to the book or the radish on the
table amounts to a brand of writing that insists on documenting a gentry
private life that was, by Aksakov's time, reaching its vanishing point. To a
certain degree, such writing also anticipates Tolstoy's exploration of the
meanings that may accrue to the prosaic domesticity of a gentry nest at
mid-century and beyond.

Anna Karenina in Its Time

Correspondences between Tolstoy's novels and the works of Russia's national poet, Pushkin, have been documented amply. The best-known example—the oft-articulated suggestion that *Anna Karenina* begins where *Eugene Onegin* ended (with a heroine trapped in a passionless marriage)—confirms another critical mainstay: that the Russian canon has an uncommonly high degree of intertextual continuity. Some of the connections between Pushkin's and Tolstoy's prose lie in specific, textual links. It is known, for example, that before beginning work on *Anna Karenina* Tolstoy reread some Pushkin. In his correspondence Tolstoy conveys a new appreciation for the *Tales of Belkin*, which he reports to have been reading for the seventh time. But while the Belkin tales provided a kind of training ground and object of study ("A writer must never cease to study this treasure"), it was Pushkin's unfinished fragment "The Guests Were Arriving at the Dacha" that served as the clearest known impetus for *Anna Karenina*.[1] Reportedly, upon reading it, Tolstoy began to sketch a scene from the novel.

The many echoes between "The Guests" and Tolstoy's novel are not difficult to glimpse. Pushkin's text features an attractive married woman, Zinaida, whose appearance and behavior may well have yielded a novelistic adulteress similar to Anna had the poet continued working on the fragment. But "The Guests" has other preoccupations as well, ones consonant with the direction of Pushkin's interests in many other unfinished prose works. Much of the fragment is comprised of scenes that take place among and are concerned chiefly with the representation of the Petersburg beau monde. The version of "The Guests" that tends to be anthologized in Soviet and later editions of Pushkin's works is longer than what was published in prerevolutionary collections and what would have been available to Tolstoy, who read the 1855 Annenkov edition. This longer version includes a final scene: a conversation between two men who appear in the opening of "The Guests." (Hence the editorial decision to append this piece to the whole.) A Spaniard visiting St. Petersburg questions his native interlocutor about the Russian elites:

> "You have mentioned your aristocracy: What is the Russian aristocracy? Studying your laws, I see that in your country there is no hereditary aristocracy founded on the indivisibility of landed property. There exists, it seems, a civil equality among your nobility, and access to its ranks is not limited. What, then, is your so-called aristocracy founded on? On ancient lineage alone?"
>
> The Russian laughed.
>
> "You are mistaken," he answered. "The ancient Russian nobility, precisely because of the reasons you have mentioned, has fallen into obscurity and has formed a kind of third estate. This noble plebs of ours, to which I myself belong, considers Riurik and Monomakh its forefathers. I can tell you, for instance," continued the Russian with an air of self-satisfied unconcern, "that the roots of my family reach back into the dark, distant past; you come across the names of my forefathers on every page of our history. Yet if it entered my head to call myself an aristocrat, many people would probably laugh. As for our actual aristocrats, they can scarcely name their grandfathers. The ancient families among them trace their lineage back to the reigns of Peter and Elizabeth." (8:42)[2]

Many of Pushkin's chief political interests are evident here. The contrast between the old, now impoverished and weakened nobility and the new, wealthy and powerful elite takes center stage. Noble control and distribution of property, the Russians' eschewal of primogeniture in preference for partible inheritance, which Pushkin understood to have caused the dissolution of the formerly wealthy old noble clans, and the Petrine opening of the elite to enterprising newcomers through the Table of Ranks are the factors that together explain the current state of affairs. The very question

posed by the Spaniard, "What is the Russian aristocracy?" will look familiar to readers of this study's second chapter, in which the predominance
of similar concerns in a generically motley selection of Pushkin's works
is examined. A similar question animates much of Tolstoy's thinking in
Anna Karenina. Overt intertextual ties aside (the problem of noble identity penetrates many aspects of Pushkin's oeuvre and Tolstoy need not have
been prompted by the passage above specifically), what *Anna Karenina*
inherits not just from Pushkin but from the preceding cultural tradition
more broadly is its multivalent investment in noble identity encapsulated
in a series of questions. "What is the Russian aristocracy?" And what roles,
what privileges, and what obligations might it have in relation to the period's social world and political culture? Tolstoy's novel processes these and
related subjects.

The novel's treatment of its most prominent nobleman-protagonist
illustrates this well. Consider how Konstantin Levin understands his social
identity:

> In the eyes of [Kitty's] relatives, he had no regular, defined activity or posi-
> tion in society, whereas now that he was thirty-two years old, one of his
> friends was already a colonel and imperial aide-de-camp, another a pro-
> fessor, still another the director of a bank and the railroads or in charge of
> an office like Oblonsky; he, on the other hand (he knew very well what he
> must seem like to others), was a landowner, occupied with breeding cows,
> shooting snipe, and building things, that is, an untalented fellow who had
> amounted to nothing and was doing, in society's view, the very thing that
> good-for-nothing people do.[3]

The main source of Levin's insecurity lies in the contrast between his
peers' vocations—military and civil service positions, work in the new
"private sector" represented here by the banks and the railroads—and his
own choice to live and work as a landowner. The novel's action transpires
during the 1870s. Over one hundred years after the 1762 manifesto that
freed the nobility from obligatory state service and long after the subsequent reformulation of noble identity during Catherine II's reign, Levin
still inhabits a social world that refuses to acknowledge his identity as a
landowner as worthwhile. In its representation of noblemen (Levin, but
also Vronsky and Oblonsky, among others), Tolstoy's novel occupies a

late stage in a many-decades-long process that was taking place in various spheres of Russian public discourse, both the novelistic tradition and various brands of nonfiction. Like the texts discussed in the preceding pages of this study, *Anna Karenina*'s multifaceted investment in male noble identity means that it, too, offers a masculine domestic ideology of its own. In its exploration of male noble subjectivity, *Anna Karenina* foregrounds and emphatically celebrates the private realm of family life as an alternative to publicly oriented institutions (for example, the zemstvo, noble elections) and the political experience of selfhood that they foster. This dimension of the novel yields both formal and thematic consequences.

Much as Levin may experience self-doubt about his social position as a landowner, *Anna Karenina* is unapologetic about its, by most standards, extensive depiction of how the landowner goes about "breeding cows, shooting snipe, and building things." Levin's country housekeeping and the private domestic world of the gentry generally are given encyclopedic coverage throughout. Agriculture is a major object of representation. The sheer volume of textual space devoted to what Tolstoy repeatedly calls *khoziaistvo*, here meaning "estate management," has prompted a good deal of stimulating commentary. Gary Saul Morson, whose foregrounding of prosaics has done a great deal to explain a key Tolstoyan preoccupation with the ordinary that is at once formal and thematic, even philosophical, invites his readership to "pause for a moment on the strangeness of Tolstoy's decision to devote so much of his novel to ideas about agriculture."[4] Mindful of the ways in which "Russian novels stand out as peculiar enough for including long speeches on God, death, immortality, determinism, fatalism, moral relativism, political nihilism, and many other topics," the so-called "accursed questions," Morson asks, "Accursed questions may be tolerable, but agriculture? What possible reason could there be to include digressions on a topic so obviously unpoetic or unnovelistic, even by the prevailing standards of the Russian novel?"[5] He offers two answers: the first has to do with Tolstoy's interest in philosophical inquiry, the second amounts to a contemplation of reform as a cultural, political, and economic undertaking.[6] Morson's readings are both original and compelling in that they place Tolstoy in dialogue with the critic's own contemporary moment by considering his novel in relation to such topics as, for example, twentieth-century attempts at social or economic reform. My own study of the representation of the provincial landowner and such "unpoetic" subjects as agriculture in the Russian novel, although prompted in part by observations not unlike Morson's (why *does* Tolstoy represent so many facets of estate administration so extensively?), has shown that as peripheral as discussions of agriculture may be to most accounts of Russian literary genres, for the novel about the landowner, they prove absolutely central.

After all, what does it mean that throughout *Anna Karenina* Levin attempts to produce an original composition about farming? Tolstoy's nobleman-protagonist inhabits a novel that, like Gogol's *Dead Souls* and Goncharov's trilogy, displays an awareness of the growing discursive field devoted to estate administration and, more specifically, to contemplating the role of the landowner in the (in this case post-reform) provinces. Levin's composition about farming has at least some of its cultural as well as literary roots in the coupling of writing about agriculture and male noble identity elaborated in Goncharov's *A Common Story*. Just as in the case of Goncharov's young Aduev writing about farming provided a barometer for his gradual maturation (the young man writes about agriculture in part in order to become an adult nobleman, the novel's logic went), so for Levin the activity is likewise about becoming. However, unlike Aduev who does not farm at the novel's end, Levin's engagement with agricultural literature is directed, more pointedly, toward his pursuits as a landowner. Especially when viewed in the context of its predecessors, *Anna Karenina* contemplates actively the extent to which writing about agriculture and understanding estate administration may be potentially constitutive of male noble selfhood.

But Levin does not write about the landowner as such. Why does he focus, specifically, on the Russian peasant as a worker? And might this be related to his own forays into manual labor in the fields, the memorable "work cure" he takes by mowing alongside peasants? As this study has shown, the depiction of Levin's *Arbeitskur* may be linked to over one hundred years' worth of attempts to articulate a coherent vision of the landowner's role and status in the provinces. Richard Peace has observed that, following Gogol's prescription of a salvific brand of manual labor that has the potential to reform the wastrel nobles of volume two of *Dead Souls*, both Tolstoy and Dostoevsky include and rework the topic in their novels.[7] Peace's genealogical line may be extended at least as far back as the young noblemen-farmers who mind vegetable gardens and discuss the potato crop at great length and with good cheer in "Correspondence between a Father and Son about Country Life" (1785). And it may well be worth going back even further to include the members of the Free Economic Society who sounded anxious notes about not being capable of "wielding the plow" in 1765 only to be encouraged to pick up the farming implement during an address delivered at a meeting in 1804. What began in the texts examined in chapter 1 as an attempt to arrive at a conceptually consistent noble masculinity in the context of post-1762 anxieties about the nobleman who does not serve the state finds its fullest expression in *Anna Karenina*, as much in Levin's agricultural treatise as in his work cure. Such is the pedigree of the novel's masculine domestic ideology.

But it will not surprise students of Tolstoy's life and work that *Anna Karenina* largely rejects estate-keeping by the book. In fact, Tolstoy rarely misses an opportunity to ridicule the agricultural advice literature that had grown still more abundant by the 1870s of the novel's action and composition. Consider, for example, Levin's earnest attempt to explain the "theory of dairy farming" to Dolly (18:283). "Cows are machines that produce milk," Dolly learns, immediately becoming suspicious (18:283). The idea that Levin's own treatise about farming was to put an end to all similar treatises about agriculture and to render obsolete the very area of inquiry altogether presents only a slightly exaggerated version of the promises made by generations of both professional and hack writers of how-to books about farming. As even the limited set of examples in the previous chapters will attest and as a more systematic look at this segment of the period's book market would confirm, such exaggerated claims—that all books have been consulted and are now made unnecessary by the composition at hand—had become a veritable feature of the genre by Tolstoy's time. So what may appear to be Tolstoy's not very gentle critique of advice literature gains another dimension when one considers that the novel shows Levin to have fallen prey, for a time, to the tactics of the agricultural authors he has been reading.

The compositional origins of Levin provide still another key for understanding the novel's points of contact with advice literature. The drafts of the novel contain an early version of Levin: Ordyntsev, who is described as a man who is "at once a cattle breeder, an agronomist, a gymnast, and a strongman" (*i skotovod, i agronom, i gimnast, i silach*) and who appears near the novel's beginning, all but consumed with an upcoming cattle breeding fair (20:53). In the draft Tolstoy comes very close to producing a caricature instead of a model gentleman farmer. The inordinate interest the mature novel's (as opposed to the draft's) Levin takes in Pava's calving appears entirely unremarkable in comparison to this earlier version of his characterization. Both Ordyntsev and his special cow are said to be too good, too healthy, too productive and wholesome to be believably Russian. In being not quite believably Russian, as well as in the outsized dimensions of his abilities as an estate manager, Ordyntsev resembles Gogol's Kostanzhoglo, the not quite Russian master agronomist who appears in volume two of *Dead Souls* and whose representation was shown to issue in part from treatises about farming. While the familiar iteration of Levin does not immediately recall Gogol's landowner, other aspects of the final version of *Anna Karenina* may be juxtaposed profitably with volume two of *Dead Souls* and one of its intertexts, Bulgarin's *Vyzhigin*.

The depiction of Vronsky living the life of a country landlord after his retirement from service is worth considering in this light. Vronsky's estate has at least a triple pedigree. First, the literary (as opposed to the cultural) origins of his English farming may be found in Pushkin's short story "Lady-Peasant," which features a feud between two landowners of whom one is an incurable Anglophile. The depiction of the improvements at Vronsky's estate (the purchase of newfangled machinery, the hospital) certainly owes something to Bulgarin's Rossiianinov (the model landowner of *Vyzhigin*) and Gogol's Koshkarev, who is a parodic version of Bulgarin's perfect *pomeshchik* as described in both the picaresque novel and in his advice literature about the estate. Although depicted in a different key, Vronsky resembles Koshkarev especially, because in addition to his new and imported tools that have enabled a thorough modernization of his estate, he has been ordering all manner of books about agriculture. But it is Anna who has developed a real expertise in the field. Vronsky turns to her for agricultural advice because, by novel's end, Anna is reading everything (including agronomic treatises) and writing a composition (a children's book) of her own, positively giddy with the period's robust book culture.

That Tolstoy's novel engages heartily with Russia's growing public sphere has become a critical, if perhaps insufficiently explored, commonplace. *Anna Karenina* announces the modernity of its media environment from the start: Oblonsky reads the centrist liberal newspaper *The Voice* (*Golos*) in the novel's opening pages, and most of the major characters are shown participating in one way or in another in the now quite mature institutions of print culture. A particularly telling series of episodes takes place in part 7 (19:265–74). Levin is in Moscow and, as always, feels overwhelmed by the both familiar and strange life he leads in the city. By necessity, he engages in many gentlemanly pursuits. Thus, he spends a good deal of time at the English Club. He is invited to hear a presentation at the agricultural society. Here it deserves to be noted that given that Anna has been reading Vronsky's books about farming, Levin's decision to skip the agricultural society meeting and go with Oblonsky to meet Anna instead does not turn upon a great contrast. Rather, the moment marks the preponderance of agricultural concerns in the novel: by part 7 even its ever-alluring adulteress has become an expert agronomist! In this same part of the novel, Levin catches himself repeating something he has heard someone else say; next, he realizes that the phrase comes from a Krylov fable that has been quoted in a recent newspaper feuilleton. Exhausted and inundated by Moscow life, Levin has come to parrot the press. For Oblonsky as for Levin, the press threatens to replace genuine reflection and authentic communication altogether; of course, only one of them finds this disturbing. Still, the novel registers that the public sphere enabled by the circulation of texts has become, by Tolstoy's 1870s, an instrument of coercion into a kind of mental passivity that Tolstoy criticizes throughout.

Another institution meant to foster participation in the empire's politics and public culture, the noble elections, proves sorely disappointing. Tolstoy devotes a handful of chapters to this topic. Perhaps the point of view expressed by the reactionary landowner whom Levin had met at Sviiazhsky's and whom he encounters again at this point in the text, that the noble elections are an outdated institution and have outlived their utility, best conveys the novel's treatment of them. While the other men go about scheming to elect a man of their faction with great excitement and at great length, Levin cannot understand the matter that so occupies his peers, try though he might. Conversely, the retired officer turned mildly caricaturish landowner Vronsky turns out to be an excellent country squire in every respect, including his willing and successful participation in the local gentry elections. Levin remains unable to cast an informed and deliberate vote, much as he is called upon to (and does) vote repeatedly. Inasmuch as Levin's is the viewpoint most aggressively championed by the novel, *Anna Karenina* presents an altogether less than optimistic image of the noble elections as an avenue for the nobility's meaningful participation in the empire's political life.

This study opened with a discussion of Tolstoy's university journal entries related to the assignment that the young count compare Catherine II's *Instruction* to Montesquieu's *The Spirit of the Laws*. The novelist's youthful musings about the nobility as a corporate body that may act as a check on the autocracy's unrestricted power find a somewhat different form in *Anna Karenina*. In the beginning of his career, Tolstoy had planned to write a novel that would comment on the relationship between the hereditary, landowning nobility and the state. This was to be his *Novel of the Russian Landowner*. In *Anna Karenina* the chief landowner-protagonist ultimately becomes disillusioned with and abandons the various avenues for a participatory, communal experience of a corporate noble identity, whether it be in relation to the autocratic state or a public more generally construed. Throughout the operations of the novel's conceptual vocabulary, this rejection of public life is expressed in such moments as when Levin finds disappointing both the English Club and the prospect of an agricultural society meeting where he might continue to think about his treatise about farming, where he might even come to discuss it with others. Instead, as the novel approaches its end, Levin leaves town for the provinces again and turns inward. The novel closes at Levin's estate, while all matters of state (for which the South Slavic question supplies an emblem) recede to a decidedly secondary importance. Instead, the reader is invited to look once again and to look closely at the small happenings of the insular world of the Levin household; this world is insular in the sense that all readers of Tolstoy know the railroad that will bring the estate into contact with the greater world to be famously bad. If, like Pushkin's 1829 novelistic fragment, *Anna Karenina* asks, "What is the Russian aristocracy?" then the answer appears to come in the novel's final image of the gentry nest, radically closed in upon itself. This moment encapsulates the novel's robust rejection of the public, state-oriented institutions of modern Russia in favor of the private, domestic world of the gentry into which retreats a nobleman whose representation has a long pedigree in the Russian cultural imagination.

Notes

Introduction

1. Throughout this study I provide the Russian titles in parentheses at the first mention of a given work, except when dealing with very well-known texts such as, for example, Gogol's *Dead Souls*.

2. Lev Tolstoi, *Polnoe sobranie sochinenii*, ed. V. G. Chertkov et al. (Moscow: Khudozhestvennaia literatura, 1928–1958), 46:4. All subsequent references to this edition of Tolstoy's works will be marked parenthetically in the body of the text with volume and page number.

3. The majority of the writers examined in this study (Pushkin, Bulgarin, Gogol) produced works that represented or responded to the social worlds of their time period; however, these writers were *not* realists. For this reason, I reserve my treatment of realism largely for Goncharov.

4. I will be using the Russian word *soslovie* translated as "social estate" throughout this study even though the concept of "*soslovie*" as estate did not appear until the early nineteenth century. For example, in 1785 Catherine II used the word *obshchestvo* (society) to refer to corporate bodies. The word *sostoianie* retained meanings close to those of *soslovie* for the duration of this study. I prefer *soslovie*, because it has long been the accepted term among historians of the imperial period both in Russia and in the West.

5. I take the origins of the novelistic tradition to be fundamentally varied and multiple. For an account of the popular or middlebrow novel, see David Gasperetti, *The Rise of the Russian Novel: Carnival, Stylization, and Mockery of the West* (DeKalb: Northern Illinois University Press, 1998).

6. There existed a rich variety of novelistic texts in the eighteenth century. These texts fall outside the scope of this study, because they tended not to represent their contemporary moment with verisimilitude. Andrew Kahn has indicated the ways in which a broad-ranging scholarly desire to see realism as the endpoint of a literary evolution toward mature novelistic forms has resulted in considerable lacunae in our understanding of Russian prose fiction during the eighteenth century. In an essay devoted primarily but not exclusively to Vasilii Trediakovskii's 1730 translation of Paul Tallemant's *Le voyage de l'isle d'amour* (1663), Kahn explains that the romances that flourished between the 1770s and 1790s (as well as the republished *Ezda v ostrov liubvi*) comprised a register of culture that, although it had no overt ties to Russian social or political reality, served an important function for the nobility who were an enthusiastic audience for works that celebrated such mainstays of European noble self-fashioning as chivalry, virtue, and honor. Andrew Kahn, "The Rise of the Russian Novel and the Problem of Romance," in *Remapping the Rise of the European Novel*, ed. Jenny Mander (Oxford: Voltaire Foundation, 2007), 185–98.

7. Boris Eikhenbaum, "Iz studencheskikh let L. N. Tolstogo," in *O proze. Sbornik statei*, ed. I. Iampol'skii (Leningrad: Khudozhestvennaia literatura, 1969), 96–97.

8. The full title was *The Trading Nobility as Opposed to the Military Nobility; or, Two Discussions about Whether the Nobility's Entry into the Merchantry Contributes to the Well-Being of the State* (*Torguiushchee dvorianstvo protivupolozhennoe dvorianstvu voennomu, ili dva rassuzhdeniia o tom, sluzhit li to k blagopoluchiiu gosudarstva, chtoby dvorianstvo vstupalo v kupechestvo?*).

9. For a discussion of the European debate in relation to the French nobility and political culture, see John Shovlin, *The Political Economy of Virtue: Luxury, Patriotism, and the Origins of the French Revolution* (Ithaca, NY: Cornell University Press, 2006), 49–79.

10. It should be noted that the historical evidence suggests that among the members of the nobility there were many active entrepreneurs. See Edgar Melton, "Enlightened Seigniorialism and Its Dilemmas in Serf Russia, 1750–1830," *Journal of Modern History* 62, no. 4 (December 1990): 675–708.

11. Tolstoy's travels and military service during the 1850s are not of immediate relevance to the discussion above.

12. For a somewhat longer discussion of *A Landowner's Morning*, see chapter 5.

13. See, for example, the following diary entry: "It is decidedly shameful for me to work on such foolish things as my stories when I have such a wondrous thing as the *Landowner's novel*" (46:135). Tolstoy also makes clear that he had initially endeavored to write a novel about the impossibility of living a virtuous life as a serf owner.

14. The translation comes from Kathryn B. Feuer, *Tolstoy and the Genesis of War and Peace*, ed. Robin Feuer Miller and Donna Tussing Orwin (Ithaca, NY: Cornell University Press, 1996), 25. As Feuer points out, the "R" of the manuscript could stand for Russia or, conceivably, something else (Rousseau?).

15. In her study of Tolstoy as a diarist, Irina Paperno explains that in the early journals "Tolstoy was actually working not on a history but on a utopia of himself: his own personal *Instruction*," thus suggesting a link between Tolstoy's study of Catherine's *Instruction* and his turn to intense self-examination and self-improvement. Irina Paperno, *"Who, What Am I?" Tolstoy Struggles to Narrate the Self* (Ithaca, NY: Cornell University Press, 2014), 10.

16. Boris Eikhenbaum, *Molodoi Tolstoi* (St. Petersburg: Izdatel'stvo Z. I. Grzhebina, 1922), 16. Eikhenbaum then establishes the considerable extent to which the musings of an eighteen-year-old diarist recently transplanted from village to provincial town offer a meaningful glimpse of the mature novelist and thinker who would continue to have a distinct preference for eighteenth-century French and English literature.

17. Joseph Bradley, *Voluntary Associations in Tsarist Russia: Science, Patriotism, and Civil Society* (Cambridge, MA: Harvard University Press, 2009); Elise Kimerling Wirtschafter, *The Play of Ideas in Russian Enlightenment Theater* (DeKalb: Northern Illinois University Press, 2003); Mary Cavender, *Nests of the Gentry: Family, Estate, and Local Loyalties in Provincial Russia* (Newark: University of Delaware Press, 2007). For more on this topic, see chapter 1.

18. The temptation to apply a straightforwardly Habermasian framework to imperial Russia must, on the whole, be resisted. Jürgen Habermas, *The Structural Transformation of the Public Sphere: An Inquiry into a Category of Bourgeois Society*, trans. Thomas Burger and Frederick Lawrence (Cambridge, MA: MIT Press, 1989).

19. And it bears noting that the contrast between the Russian press's vitality in the 1760s and 1770s and the situation in England and France, for example, is quite a bit less

stark than it would become in the decades to come. For a study of eighteenth-century Russian print culture, see Gary Marker, *Publishing, Printing, and the Origins of the Intellectual Life in Russia, 1700–1800* (Princeton, NJ: Princeton University Press, 1985).

20. The potentially despotic dimension of the autocratic polity ought not be overstated. Valerie Kivelson has shown that the seventeenth-century Muscovite gentry could act with a considerable degree of autonomy from the state. Valerie Kivelson, *Autocracy in the Provinces: The Muscovite Gentry and Political Culture in the Seventeenth Century* (Stanford, CA: Stanford University Press, 1996). For a reconsideration of eighteenth-century modes of governance as a "political dialogue" between the autocrat and a cultural elite, see Cynthia Hyla Whittaker, *Russian Monarchy: Eighteenth-Century Rulers and Writers in Political Dialogue* (DeKalb: Northern Illinois University Press, 2003). Whittaker suggests that the Russian autocracy owes its relative longevity to the degree to which governing through a scenario of dialogue could both compel and implicate the participants.

21. For a seminal treatment of Russian literature and culture in the first half of the nineteenth century that takes literary sociology as its methodological lens, see William Mills Todd III, *Fiction and Society in the Age of Pushkin: Ideology, Institutions, and Narrative* (Cambridge, MA: Harvard University Press, 1986).

22. Ian Watt, *The Rise of the Novel: Studies in Defoe, Richardson, and Fielding* (Berkeley: University of California Press, 1957).

23. Of especial import to my own study is Michael McKeon, *The Origins of the English Novel, 1600–1740* (Baltimore, MD: Johns Hopkins University Press, 1987).

24. William Mills Todd III has written about the inadvisability of turning to such terms as "middle class" and "bourgeois" in relation to the rise of the novel in nineteenth-century Russia. William Mills Todd III, "The Ruse of the Russian Novel," in *The Novel*, ed. Franco Moretti (Princeton, NJ: Princeton University Press, 2006), 1:404.

25. Recent historical scholarship on social estates in imperial Russia has shown that estate designations as such were rather more porous than specialists have tended to imagine. This means that a good deal of movement between estates took place; the estates themselves, as Alison K. Smith shows, retained their significance at multiple levels of society from the federal to the very local. Alison K. Smith, *For the Common Good and Their Own Well-Being: Social Estates in Imperial Russia* (Oxford: Oxford University Press, 2014).

26. Gregory Freeze, "The *Soslovie* (Estate) Paradigm and Russian Social History," *American Historical Review* 91, no. 1 (February 1986): 11–36.

27. A useful example would be Adrian Jones, "A Russian Bourgeois's Arctic Enlightenment," *The Historical Review* 48, no. 3 (September 2005): 623–40.

28. Both here and in the pages below my discussion has benefited from E. N. Marasinova, *Vlast' i lichnost': Ocherki russkoi istorii XVIII veka* (Moscow: Nauka, 2008), especially 9–75.

29. Isabel de Madariaga, "The Eighteenth-Century Origin of Russian Civil Rights," in *Politics and Culture in Eighteenth-Century Russia* (London: Routledge, 2014), 78–94.

30. Valerie Kivelson, "Kinship Politics/Autocratic Politics: A Reconsideration of Eighteenth-Century Political Culture," in *Imperial Russia: New Histories for the Empire*, ed. Jane Burbank and David L. Ransel (Bloomington: Indiana University Press, 1998), 7. Kivelson gives a highly nuanced account of the period's political culture that explains both the origins and the failure of the attempt to limit the autocrat's powers.

31. Ibid.

32. This is not to say that the nobility's acquisition of rights was the result of an effort or even a desire shared by the estate as a whole. In the words of Robert E. Jones, in the middle to late eighteenth century, there would have been "few issues on which the nobility spoke with one voice or with anything resembling a consensus." He also points out that this high degree of heterogeneity within the estate appears normal in a European context; unusual is the lack of precise divisions within the nobility. See his *Emancipation of the Russian Nobility, 1762–1785* (Princeton, NJ: Princeton University Press, 1973), 17.

33. My translation comes from Whittaker, *Russian Monarchy*, 115.

34. Robert E. Jones, *Provincial Development in Russia: Catherine II and Jacob Sievers* (New Brunswick, NJ: Rutgers University Press, 1984), 162–63.

35. David Griffiths and George Munro, eds., *Catherine II's Charters of 1785 to the Nobility and the Towns* (Bakersfield, CA: Charles Schlacks Jr., 1991), liii.

36. De Madariaga cautiously compares it to the Virginia Bill of Rights of 1776. De Madariaga, "The Eighteenth-Century Origin," 84–85.

37. For an incisive treatment of how the duel functioned as an unofficial, almost surrogate means for nobles to secure inviolability of person, see Irina Reyfman, *Ritualized Violence Russian Style: The Duel in Russian Culture and Literature* (Stanford, CA: Stanford University Press, 1999).

38. Richard Pipes, "Private Property Comes to Russia: The Reign of Catherine II," in *Property and Freedom* (New York: Alfred A. Knopf, 1999), 432.

39. Brenda Meehan-Waters, "The Development and the Limits of Security of Noble Status, Person, and Property in Eighteenth-Century Russia," in *Russia and the West in the Eighteenth Century*, ed. Anthony Glenn Cross (Newtonville, MA: Oriental Research Partners, 1983), 300.

40. For a discussion of Catherinean Russia as a *Rechtsstaat* and a *Ständestaat*, a polity defined by the rule of law and by the operation of specific social estates, respectively, see Whittaker, *Russian Monarchy*, 104–10. I should add that another way in which the 1785 Charters made for an uneven arrangement was in the complete omission of the peasantry. Catherine II had prepared a Charter to the Peasantry, but it was never promulgated.

41. Iurii Lotman, *Besedy o russkoi kul'ture: Byt i traditsii russkogo dvorianstva (XVIII–nachalo XIX veka)* (St. Petersburg: Iskusstvo-SPB, 1994), 19.

42. Richard Wortman, *Scenarios of Power: Myth and Ceremony in Russian Monarchy from Peter the Great to the Abdication of Nicholas II* (Princeton, NJ: Princeton University Press, 2006), 9.

43. The modern Russian word for landowner, or *pomeshchik*, comes from *pomeshchennyi*. Lotman contrasts the *pomeshchennyi* with the *votchinnik*, to whom land was granted for a relatively more permanent sort of ownership. However, this land too could be taken away if the owner fell into disfavor. For a discussion of the extent to which noblemen *had* to serve to maintain control over either kind of property, a *pomest'e* or a *votchina*, especially following Peter I's 1714 ukase that made them identical, see Marasinova, *Vlast' i lichnost'*, 25–26. For a discussion of the Russian iteration of "propertied individualism" in the context of the relations between the Russian monarch and her or his subjects, see Ekaterina Pravilova, *A Public Empire: Property and the Quest for the Common Good in Imperial Russia* (Princeton, NJ: Princeton University Press, 2014).

44. The emperor "enforced a requirement of lifetime service for the landowning classes" in the course of a series of transformations that "helped to consolidate and

strengthen the service state structure that had taken form in the previous two centuries." Wortman, *Scenarios of Power*, 27.

45. Additionally, the terms were not stable in Russian eighteenth- and nineteenth-century usage to begin with.

46. It should be noted that at least initially, the introduction of the Table of Ranks did little to open the upper echelons of the elite to newcomers. Brenda Meehan-Waters has shown the longevity of specific noble families at the top of the social hierarchy during the Muscovite period and into the 1730s. See her *Autocracy and Aristocracy: Russian Service Elite of 1730* (Rutgers, NJ: Rutgers University Press, 1982).

47. In his influential study *The Origins of the Russian Intelligentsia*, Marc Raeff argued that state service remained a significant source of identity for the Russian nobility, "the normal path to status, greater prosperity and full participation in the cultural life of Russia." Marc Raeff, *The Origins of the Russian Intelligentsia: The Eighteenth-Century Nobility* (New York: Harcourt Brace, 1966), 113. Michael Confino, in his critical response to this book, took issue with Raeff's methodology, and perhaps most important of all, made the point repeatedly that a great deal remains understudied when it comes to the diversity of gentry life and sensibilities in the second half of the eighteenth century. Michael Confino, "Histoire et psychologie: À propos de la noblesse russe au XVIIIe siècle," *Annales, Economies, Sociétés, Civilisations* 22, no. 6 (1967): 1163–1205. See especially pages 1193–99 for Confino's discussion of the economic diversity within the noble estate and the implication that Raeff's findings would apply to a rather small elite (Confino puts it at 3 percent, or the "high nobility," or *haute noblesse*). Although the full scope of the 1762 manifesto's effects remains unknown, Carol Leonard's findings shed some light on the matter of the gentry's retreat to the countryside following the measure. Leonard provides a detailed numerical account of nobles residing in specific provinces in order to show that both immediately after Peter III's manifesto and in the aftermath of Catherine II's provincial reforms during the 1770s, "more and more [nobles] lived on their estates after a brief period in service." Leonard's research suggests that the gentry not only lived in the country, but also participated quite willingly in local institutions of self-government such as the noble assemblies that Catherine encouraged by 1785. Carol Leonard, *Reform and Regicide: The Reign of Peter III in Russia* (Bloomington: Indiana University Press, 1993), 65, 54–72.

48. In addition to the titles above, see Jones, *Emancipation*, as well as Paul Dukes, *Catherine the Great and the Russian Nobility: A Study Based on the Materials of the Legislative Commission of 1767* (Cambridge: Cambridge University Press, 1967). Dukes ascribes a rather high level of agency to the noble elite in prompting Catherine's legislative activities well after the Commission; Jones's nobility is not as politically active and organized. Marasinova provides an insightful overview of the rich diversity of interpretations the 1762 manifesto has received. See Marasinova, *Vlast' i lichnost'*, 49.

49. *Polnoe sobranie zakonov Rossiiskoi imperii s 1649 goda* (St. Petersburg: V Tipografii II Otdeleniia Sobstvennoi E. I. V. Kantseliarii, 1830), 15:915.

50. Vasilii Kliuchevskii, *Kurs russkoi istorii: Sochineniia v deviati tomakh* (Moscow: Mysl', 1990), 5:146–69; see especially 146–48.

51. A. P. Sumarokov, *Izbrannye proizvedeniia: Biblioteka poeta* (Leningrad: Sovetskii pisatel', 1957), 189–91.

52. Ibid.

53. Michelle Lamarche Marrese, *A Woman's Kingdom: Noblewomen and the Control of Property in Russia, 1700–1861* (Ithaca, NY: Cornell University Press, 2002).

54. Katherine Pickering Antonova, *An Ordinary Marriage: The World of a Gentry Family in Provincial Russia* (Oxford: Oxford University Press, 2012).

55. Although there were some notable exceptions, typically, women took the ranks of their husbands.

56. I am mindful, of course, of the considerable presence of the *pomeshchitsa*, or female landowner, in nineteenth-century fiction, in the works of such writers as Ivan Turgenev, Mikhail Saltykov-Shchedrin, and Anton Chekhov. To examine the representation of the noblewoman-landowner would require a separate study.

57. A *Künstlerroman* is a sub-genre of the bildungsroman that foregrounds an artist's development.

Chapter 1

1. Rostopchin was responding to Dmitrii Poltoratskii, a member of the Moscow Society of Agriculture and a major proponent of English farming and the iron plow in particular. For more on the influence of English farming in Russia, see Anthony Glenn Cross, *"By the Banks of the Thames": Russians in Eighteenth-Century Britain* (Newtonville, MA: Oriental Research Partners, 1980), 57–92.

2. Fedor Rostopchin, "Plug i sokha," in *Mysli vslukh na krasnom kryl'tse*, ed. O. A. Platonov (Moscow: Institut russkoi tsivilizatsii, 2014), 98.

3. For a perceptive survey of Russian conservative thought during Alexander I's reign see Alexander Martin, *Romantics, Reformers, Reactionaries: Russian Conservative Thought and Politics in the Reign of Alexander I* (DeKalb: Northern Illinois University Press, 1997).

4. Dashkova produced a response to Rostopchin titled "An Opinion about the Plow and the Wooden Plow" ("Mnenie o pluge i sokhe") and published in 1807. For a detailed discussion of Rostopchin's authorship of the first pamphlet as well as some examples of its misattribution, see N. S. Tikhonravov, *Graf F. B. Rastopchin i literatura v 1812 godu* (St. Petersburg: Tipografiia Koroleva, 1854), 27–29. See also Rostopchin, *Mysli vslukh*, 618.

5. Marrese, *A Woman's Kingdom*.

6. It should be made clear that the claim here is *not* about the exclusivity of male noblemen in Russian public discourse. I am grateful to Christine Ruane for pointing out that some agricultural advice *was* aimed at women.

7. For a discussion of the reforms in the context of the cultural life of the provincial gentry, see John Randolph, *The House in the Garden: The Bakunin Family and the Romance of Russian Idealism* (Ithaca, NY: Cornell University Press, 2007), 19–47.

8. Michael Warner, *Publics and Counterpublics* (New York: Zone Books, 2005), 94–95, 114.

9. Incidentally, this aspect of noble identity in its broadest outlines is in *no* way unique to Russia. For a comparative survey of the European nobilities, see the two-volume collection of essays edited by H. M. Scott, *The European Nobilities in the Seventeenth and Eighteenth Centuries* (New York: Longman, 1995).

10. For a seminal work on the topic, see Michael Confino, *Domaines et seigneurs en Russie vers la fin du XVIIIe siècle* (Paris: Institut d'Études Slaves, 1963).

11. Stepan Dzhunkovskii, "Rech' o pol'ze i neobkhodimosti opytnogo uprazhneniia v zemledelii i domostroitel'stve, dlia dvorian i vsekh vladel'tsev sobstvennykh imenii, chitannaia v torzhestvennom sobranii Vol'nogo Ekonomicheskogo Obshchestva 1804 goda

dekabria 3go," *Trudy Vol'nogo Ekonomicheskogo Obshchestva k pooshchreniiu v Rossii zem-ledeliia i domostroitel'stva* 57 (1805): 20–21.

12. Iurii Lotman, "Poetika bytovogo povedeniia v russkoi kul'ture XVIII veka" and "Teatr i teatral'nost' v stroe kul'tury nachala XIX veka," in *Izbrannye stat'i v trekh tomakh*, vol. 1, *Stat'i po semiotike i topologii kul'tury* (Tallinn: Aleksandra, 1992), 248–86.

13. Bradley also points out that "in the 1750s and 1760s a few government officials, such as Nikita Panin, began to realize the benefits of improvements in Russian agriculture and estate management." Bradley, *Voluntary Associations*, 46.

14. Ibid., 47. For a discussion of Lomonosov's plans, and especially the link between the newspaper (the *Internal Russian Gazette* [*Vnutrennie rossiiskie vedomosti*]) and the organization he envisioned, see A. V. Zapadov, *Russkaia zhurnalistika XVIII veka* (Moscow: Nauka, 1964), 42–45.

15. "Preduvedomlenie," *Trudy Vol'nogo Ekonomicheskogo Obshchestva* 1 (1765): pagination unclear.

16. In thinking about the shape of public culture in the second half of the eighteenth century, the author has found particularly useful the concept of the prepolitical public sphere as elaborated by Wirtschafter, *Play of Ideas*.

17. Bradley, *Voluntary Associations*, 48–49, 83.

18. Colum Leckey, *Patrons of Enlightenment: The Free Economic Society in Eighteenth-Century Russia* (Newark: University of Delaware Press, 2011), 183.

19. Confino, *Domaines et seigneurs*, 19–38, 106–83.

20. As Bradley puts it, in both Russian and European (notably, English) agricultural societies, "perhaps above all" the chief motivating factor among the membership was the "desire for the 'company and fellowship of like-minded men.'" He goes on to call these societies "bastions of masculinity and privilege." Bradley, *Voluntary Associations*, 52.

21. It should be noted that throughout his study, Leckey emphasizes the extent to which differences in status and rank structured relations among the membership, making for a less than egalitarian system.

22. Gary Marker, "The Creation of Journals and the Profession of Letters in the Eighteenth Century," in *Literary Journals in Imperial Russia*, ed. Deborah Martinsen (Cambridge: Cambridge University Press, 1997), 11–37.

23. W. Gareth Jones, *Nikolay Novikov: Enlightener of Russia* (Cambridge: Cambridge University Press, 1984), 21–22.

24. Treating the implications of this period in the context of Russian social and political developments, Andrzej Walicki maintains that Catherine's project sought to form public opinion and to "stimulate social initiatives that could be exploited in support of the policies of the government." Andrzej Walicki, *A History of Russian Thought from the Enlightenment to Marxism* (Stanford, CA: Stanford University Press, 1979), 15.

25. Novikov was working with the part of the Legislative Commission that dealt with the so-called "middle estate." W. Gareth Jones notes that Novikov "must have sharpened his political wits and social observation in such an assembly." Jones, *Nikolay Novikov*, 17.

26. N. I. Novikov, *Satiricheskie zhurnaly N. I. Novikova* (Moscow: Izdatel'stvo Akademii nauk SSSR, 1951), 46–47. The common Soviet interpretation of this line as well as the journal's epigraph ("They work, while you eat [the fruits of] their labor" [*Oni rabotaiut, a vy ikh trud edite*]), taken from Sumarokov, casts Novikov as the first Russian intellectual to question the utility of the gentry, to suggest cautiously that the estate as a whole may be parasitic and useless. However, Jones argues convincingly that the line and the

journal's title were meant as homage to Sumarokov, the title especially referring to the latter's periodical, *Busy Bee*. In contrast to the ideologically inflected Soviet interpretations, Jones shows rather more soberly that Novikov sought primarily to establish continuity in Russian periodical production, and that he worked to frame the enterprise as a coherent tradition. Jones, *Nikolay Novikov*, 20–21.

27. Novikov, *Satiricheskie zhurnaly*, 47.

28. V. I. Glukhov, "Obraz Oblomova i ego literaturnaia predistoriia," in *I. A. Goncharov: Materialy mezhdunarodnoi konferentsii, posviashchennoi 185-letiiu so dnia rozhdeniia I. A. Goncharova*, ed. M. B. Zhdanova, A. V. Lobkareva, and I. V. Smirnov (Ul'ianovsk: Pechatnyi dvor, 1998), 103–11.

29. Dobroserd is from an old Novgorodian noble clan. "Country" here refers to the fact that all territories other than Moscow and St. Petersburg can be classified as provincial. Incidentally, it may well be that Novikov places his virtuous nobles in Novgorod in order to activate associations with the political culture of the Novgorod Republic. To explore this possibility in detail falls outside the scope of this study.

30. Novikov, *Satiricheskie zhurnaly*, 65.

31. Ibid., 66.

32. For a reading of Pushkin's *Dubrovskii*, see the next chapter.

33. Ibid., 334.

34. Ibid., 334–35. There is a similarity here to the sentiments expressed by Prostakova in Denis Fonvizin's comedy *The Minor*; and indeed, it has long been suggested that Fonvizin might have authored the Falalei letters.

35. Ibid., 394.

36. Andrei Bolotov, *Zhizn' i prikliucheniia Andreia Bolotova, opisannye samim im dlia svoikh potomkov* (St. Petersburg: V. Golovin, 1870–1873), 2:616. Bolotov's *Life and Adventures* did not become available to the reading public until the 1870s. By contrast, his agricultural advice enjoyed considerable popularity among landowners both male and female. Avgusta Butkovskaia recalls that as late as in the 1820s, Bolotov's *Economic Magazine* was a necessary resource for any landowner interested in agricultural improvements. Butkovskaia, "Rasskazy babushki," *Istoricheskii vestnik* 18 (1884): 594–631. For a seminal study of Bolotov, see Thomas Newlin, *The Voice in the Garden: Andrei Bolotov and the Anxieties of Russian Pastoral* (Evanston, IL: Northwestern University Press, 2001).

37. In fact, Bolotov did reenter service following his retirement; he oversaw lands belonging to the Crown. However, this left him with plenty of time to cultivate his private pursuits. For a discussion of Bolotov as royal gardener, see Andreas Schönle, *The Ruler in the Garden: Politics and Landscape Design in Imperial Russia* (New York: Peter Lang, 2007), 116–63.

38. Bolotov, *Zhizn' i prikliucheniia*, 2:754–55.

39. Bolotov produced a *great* deal of writing in multiple genres, both literary and not. He was particularly successful as a published writer of agricultural and broadly domestic advice.

40. *Sel'skii zhitel'* 1 (1778): pagination unclear.

41. Ibid.

42. Ibid.

43. The full title of the first of Bolotov's two domestic advice periodicals, *The Rural Resident, an Economic Publication Serving to Benefit Village Residents* (*Sel'skii zhitel'*,

ekonomicheskoe v pol'zu derevenskikh zhitelei sluzhashchee izdanie), emphasized the provincial character of its target audience by alluding to the countryside twice.

44. *Sel'skii zhitel'* 2 (1778): pagination unclear.

45. In *Life and Adventures*, Bolotov writes that "since the main goal of the publication was to engage the readership in real correspondence with [him]," in order to compel his audience by example, "in the second issue and the next ones [Bolotov] placed a few letters [he] had composed, pretending that [he] had received them, so as to encourage readers [to correspond with him], offering even various kinds of examples of letters [they might send in]." He imagined that with this "permissible ploy" (*pozvolitel'noiu ulovkoi*), he could, taking the European journals as examples, render his own publication more lively and interesting. Bolotov, *Zhizn' i prikliucheniia*, 2:766.

46. This is certainly in agreement with Newlin's findings about the more general features of Bolotov's personality and writings. Newlin, *The Voice in the Garden*, 55. For example, while discussing Bolotov's poetry, Newlin calls him "the most relentlessly and massively *apostrophic* poet in all of Russian literature," pointing out another manifestation of this gentryman's often frustrated and frustrating need for an addressee (136). Newlin explains Bolotov's tendency to address his works to a "Dear Friend" as the product of his "fear of a hostile readership," adding that "[Bolotov] may actually have believed, on a subconscious level, that he could preempt any sort of negative reaction by positing his readers' friendliness from the very onset" (90).

47. In his *Life and Adventures*, Bolotov recounts meeting with Novikov in 1779 and agreeing on the terms according to which he would produce an addition to *Moscow News* under the title of *Economic Magazine*, a periodical venture in which he would continue the work begun in *The Rural Resident*. Year after year, the *Moscow News* would print announcements about the continuation of Bolotov's enterprise, noting that it was performing its function well, bringing significant benefits to rural landowners.

48. *Ekonomicheskii magazin* 1 (1779): pagination unclear.

49. It is likely that these four contributors were *not* invented, fictive personae, but Bolotov's real collaborators who wrote under pseudonyms. In his recollections he explains that eventually his activities as a journalist brought him into close contact with other provincial noblemen.

50. Eventually Bolotov dropped the epistolary format and primarily presented his readers with excerpts from a variety of publications (many of them foreign) on subjects relevant to life at an estate. It should be pointed out that his *Life and Adventures* is also written in the form of letters to a "dear friend," which is to say that the practice of writing to a dear friend and, by extension, his sense of isolation and his attempts to remedy it through the printed word remained quite prominent throughout his career. Bolotov worked on his memoir from 1789 to 1816.

51. Bolotov's periodicals also contained information that was addressed to women. This study deliberately foregrounds the ways in which the journal imagined noblemen.

52. Novikov himself edited *Children's Reading* upon its founding in 1785, eventually passing it on to Karamzin and Aleksandr Petrov in subsequent years. For a treatment of Karamzin as a journalist, see Anthony Glenn Cross, "Karamzin's 'Moskovskii Zhurnal': Voice of a Writer, Broadsheet of a Movement," *Cahiers du monde russe et soviétique* 28, no. 2 (April–June 1987): 121–26. See also Jones, *Nikolay Novikov*, 198–99.

53. N. I. Novikov, *Izbrannye pedagogicheskie sochineniia* (Moscow: Gosudarstvennoe uchebno-pedagogicheskoe izdatel'stvo ministerstva prosveshcheniia RSFSR, 1959), 217.

54. Ibid., 224. In the father's view, his son's manual labor might develop skills that prove useful in other, for example, academic pursuits. Yet farm work must still be the route by which the young nobleman matures.

55. Lotman writes that the editor wished to "foster public opinion." He also underscores the uniqueness of Karamzin's announcement that he was going to publish a private periodical devoted, in part, to matters of politics. Iurii Lotman, *Sotvorenie Karamzina* (Moscow: Kniga, 1987), 280.

56. Nikolai Karamzin, "Pis'mo k izdateliu," *Vestnik Evropy* 1 (January 1802): 3.

57. Karamzin had made use of the language of friendship and the discursive scenario of epistolary exchange in his *Letters of a Russian Traveler*. Moreover, the travelogue itself has been interpreted as "the traveller's multiple performances—as guide, thinker, historian and connoisseur," which "give the broadest picture of what the individual in the age of Enlightenment can be and become." Andrew Kahn, "Karamzin's Discourses of Enlightenment," in *Letters of a Russian Traveler*, by Nikolai Karamzin, trans. Andrew Kahn (Oxford: Voltaire Foundation, 2003), 550.

58. Karamzin, "Pis'mo k izdateliu," 5.

59. Ibid., 7–8.

60. In his article "About the Book Trade and the Love for Reading in Russia" ("O knizhnoi torgovle i liubvi ko chteniiu v Rossii," 1802), Karamzin would report that rural landowners are amassing excellent small libraries.

61. N. M. Karamzin, *Izbrannye sochineniia v dvukh tomakh* (Moscow: Khudozhestvennaia literatura, 1964), 275–76.

62. Ibid.

63. Ibid.

64. Anthony Cross in his survey of the *Messenger of Europe* calls Karamzin "an apologist for the Russian gentry," and finds that Eremeev's "Letter from a Rural Resident" is Karamzin's "most open defense of serfdom." Anthony Glenn Cross, *N. M. Karamzin: A Study of His Literary Career, 1783–1803* (Carbondale: Southern Illinois University Press, 1971), 206–7.

65. Karamzin, *Izbrannye sochineniia*, 288.

66. Ibid.

67. Ibid., 295.

68. Ibid.

69. Specifically, that Luka abolishes drinking in his territories (except on very special occasions) and becomes good friends with his local priest all but prefigures what Gogol would write some forty-five years later in his prescriptive essay "The Russian Landowner." Eremeev's interest in peasant health and in the minutiae of estate life in general will be replayed by the younger prince Nekhliudov of Tolstoy's *A Landowner's Morning*. Karamzin's text articulates quite clearly the parameters within which many aspects of male noble identity will be treated in the subsequent prose tradition.

70. Here it would be useful to recall Rostopchin's Sila Andreevich Bogatyrev, the fictive landowner whose folksy, nationalist (sometimes xenophobic) musings proved highly popular with the public. The pamphlet *Thoughts Aloud on the Red Staircase* sold seven thousand copies in 1807, at a time when many successful periodicals measured their audiences by the hundreds and twelve hundred was considered a good print run.

71. Martin, *Romantics*, 68.

72. Quoted in ibid., 67.

73. In fact, Rostopchin's language in the epigraph quoted in the beginning of this chapter lends itself to multiple interpretations that may well amplify the reading suggested here. The line "I serve with the Wooden Plow"—*sluzhu s sokhoi*—may contain a pun on the additional meaning of *sokha* as a unit of land measurement that determined the taxation obligations due from a given piece of land. If Rostopchin is punning on such uses of the word *sokha* as, for example, "*byti v sokhakh*," meaning to owe a service obligation based on the amount of land one worked, then his rhetoric alludes still more explicitly to the waning of noble obligations in the face of which his lyric subject takes up the wooden plow, yoking himself to the state, as it were. See *Slovar' russkogo iazyka XI–XVII vv.*, s.v. *sokha*.

74. Habermas, *Structural Transformation*, 48.

Chapter 2

1. A. S. Pushkin, *Polnoe sobranie sochinenii v shestnadtsati tomakh*, ed. D. D. Blagoi et al. (Moscow: Izdatel'stvo AN SSSR, 1937–1959), 12:206. All subsequent references to this edition of Pushkin's works will be marked in the body of the text with volume, followed by page number.

2. For a recent summary of approaches to Pushkin's unfinished prose and a discussion of the relative preponderance of poetry in studies that foreground questions of social status in Pushkin's works, see Irina Reyfman, *How Russia Learned to Write: Literature and the Imperial Table of Ranks* (Madison: University of Wisconsin Press, 2016), 72–73.

3. The treatment of the novel as a vehicle for articulating a multiperspectival worldview will sound familiar to students of Bakhtin, especially his "Discourse in the Novel." The ensuing discussion of the relationship between the novel and social class, and the ways in which the novel has the capacity to "mediate—to represent as well as contain—the revolutionary clash between status and class orientations and the attendant crisis of status inconsistency" owes a good deal to Michael McKeon's work on the rise of the English novel. McKeon, *Origins*, 173.

4. The *variagi* is a term for largely Scandinavian (likely Russified Viking) populations in Old Rus, circa the ninth century and beyond.

5. Peasants in Old Rus; they were free, but connected to princely holdings.

6. *Udels* were feudal principalities.

7. The term *mestnichestvo* refers to the ways in which service positions (and, ultimately, power) were distributed among the pre-Petrine polity's upper classes according to clan and family status. It was effectively abolished by Peter I's introduction of the Table of Ranks.

8. Boris Eikhenbaum's essay about Alexander Pushkin's "route" to prose ("Put' Pushkina k proze," 1923) begins with the following statement: "Russian literature of the eighteenth century was mainly busy with the organization of poetry." Treating the poet as an heir to the aesthetic sensibilities—especially, the literary language—of the "long" eighteenth century, Eikhenbaum attributes Pushkin's turn to prose partly to the need to develop what was then still a relatively unwieldy prose idiom. Eikhenbaum,

O proze, o poezii (Leningrad: Khudozhestvennaia literatura, 1986), 29–44. Elsewhere, Eikhenbaum examines the increasing professionalization of Russian letters and the concomitant rise of journalism as factors that precipitated Pushkin's turn to prose. See Boris Eikhenbaum, "Literaturnyi byt," in *O literature* (Moscow: Sovetskii pisatel', 1987), 428–36.

9. In particular, the following titles should be mentioned. Nancy Armstrong, *Desire and Domestic Fiction: A Political History of the Novel* (New York: Oxford University Press, 1990); Armstrong, *How Novels Think: The Limits of Individualism from 1719–1900* (New York: Columbia University Press, 2006); Toni Bowers, *The Politics of Motherhood: British Writing and Culture, 1680–1760* (Cambridge: Cambridge University Press, 1996); and certainly Michael McKeon's *The Origins of the English Novel, 1600–1740*. All three critics consider the interplay between English eighteenth-century politics and the novel as a generic form that contemplates various social estates and identities; i.e., the domestic middle-class woman (Armstrong), the Augustan mother (Bowers), the aristocracy and the middle class (McKeon).

10. For a foundational study of the interplay between literature and real-life behavior in a specific segment of Russian society of roughly this time, see Lotman's essay "Dekabrist v povsednevnoi zhizni," in his *Besedy o russkoi kul'ture*, 331–85. On the degree to which Pushkin's writerly behavior was informed by literary models drawn from the French tradition, see Larisa Vol'pert, *Pushkin v roli Pushkina: Tvorcheskaia igra po modeliam frantsuzskoi literatury* (Moscow: Iazyki russkoi kul'tury, 1998). Vol'pert identifies Benjamin Constant's *Adolphe* (which young Liza reads in *Roman v pis'makh*) as one of the texts to which Pushkin turns.

11. Pushkin followed a similar plot pattern in his representation of Tatiana Larina's mother in *Eugene Onegin*.

12. Until 1809 the court service title of *kammerjunker* conferred the ninth rank in the Table of Ranks. After 1809 *kammerjunker* became an honorary title that did not correspond to a specific rank.

13. The reference here is to Denis Fonvizin's *The Minor* (*Nedorosl'*, written in 1781, performed in 1782, and published in 1783).

14. For an insightful discussion of the meta-literary concerns in "The History of the Village of Goriukhino," see David M. Bethea and Sergei Davydov, "The [Hi]story of the Village of Gorjuxino: In Praise of Puškin's Folly," *Slavic and East European Journal* 28, no. 3 (Autumn 1984): 291–309.

15. Alexander Pushkin, *Alexander Pushkin: Complete Prose Fiction*, trans. Paul Debreczeny (Stanford, CA: Stanford University Press, 1983), 128–30.

16. In her survey of the provincial periodical press, its contributors, and its public, Susan Smith-Peter has shown that nobles were frequently encouraged to act as local correspondents and subscribers. However, Smith-Peter also shows that in fact the gentry in no way constituted a majority among those who engaged in the burgeoning media environment. By the second quarter of the nineteenth century, although the nobility were encouraged to take part in local writing, it was the merchantry and the clergy who were especially well-represented among the sociologically diverse public Smith-Peter documents. Susan Smith-Peter, "The Russian Provincial Newspaper and Its Public, 1788–1864," *Carl Beck Papers in Russian and East European Studies*, no. 1908 (October 2008): 16.

17. Boris Tomashevskii, *Pushkin*, vol. 2, *Materialy k monografii* (Moscow: Aka-demiia nauk SSSR IRLI [Pushkinskii Dom], 1961), 146.

18. Sam Driver, *Pushkin: Literature and Social Ideas* (New York: Columbia University Press, 1989), 51.

19. Reyfman points to various details in the text that suggest that the nobility of the Troekurov family is of recent origin. Reyfman, *How Russia Learned to Write*, 80.

20. The *Räuberroman* genre (literally, a robber-novel, or a novel about brigandry) gained popularity in German letters towards the end of the eighteenth century, after the appearance of Friedrich Schiller's play *Die Räuber* in 1781.

21. Pushkin is believed to have used an authentic court document. This may have given rise to some (but not all) of the inconsistencies in the novel's temporal structures. These will be discussed below.

22. Kistenevka was also the name of a Pushkin family property, one that the poet inherited in 1830. While the potential biographical dimensions of *Dubrovskii* fall outside the scope of this study, it should be noted that Pushkin liked to imagine his own clan as the opposite of the upstart Troekurovs, who are said to have benefited from the 1762 coup. For an incisive discussion of Pushkin's likely dubious claims about his family's shifting fortunes and his ancestors' "allegedly independent behavior at several historical turning points in the seventeenth and eighteenth centuries," see Reyfman, *How Russia Learned to Write*, 74. See also Mark Al'tshuller, *Mezhdu dvukh tsarei: Pushkin v 1824–1836 gg.* (St. Petersburg: Akademicheskii proekt, 2003).

23. The former association with simply "oak" surfaces in young Vladimir's affair with Masha Troekurova. They use an oak tree as a sort of forest mailbox. The same device is used in Pushkin's *Tales of Belkin*, in the short story "Lady-Peasant" (Baryshnia-Krest'ianka).

24. Costlow writes, "In turning toward the great world of the forest, Russian writers and artists engage with [...] the complex moral and social geography of a society in which two cultures are mapped on one ground; the traditions of folk culture—both idealized and occasionally mocked or excoriated; the brutal legacies of property and class as they have fundamentally wounded humans' relationships to each other and to the natural world; religious and symbolic identities (both European and Russian) mapped onto space; the forest as locus of historical—often repressed—memory; the search for grounding—for *home*—in a culture that had come to be defined in terms of *homelessness*." Jane Costlow, *Heart-Pine Russia: Walking and Writing the Nineteenth-Century Forest* (Ithaca, NY: Cornell University Press, 2014), 38.

25. By "conservative" here is meant a way of thinking that would have been opposed to the modernizing activities that, since the beginning of the imperial period in Russia, were associated with the state and the monarch.

26. "We, who are of as good noble birth as you and the emperor ... etc."

27. "You are a true member of your family; all of the Romanovs are revolutionaries and egalitarians."

28. "Thank you, now here's a reputation that I really needed."

29. As Sergei Davydov puts it, for Pushkin "the independent ancient nobility was the only class possessing the will to lead and the only one capable of restraining the excesses of autocracy. But to achieve that, it was necessary to restore its political and material status." Sergei Davydov, "The Evolution of Pushkin's Political Thought," in *The Pushkin Handbook*, ed. David M. Bethea (Madison: University of Wisconsin Press, 2005), 309.

Chapter 3

1. Faddei Bulgarin, "Pis'ma na Kavkaz. 2. (Prodolzhenie)," *Syn otechestva* 2 (1825): 313.

2. Petr Viazemskii, "Zhukovskii—Pushkin—o novoi Piitike Basen," *Moskovskii telegraf* 1, no. 4 (January 1825): 353.

3. For the literary dimension of the disagreement, see M. I. Gillel'son, *P. A. Viazemskii: Zhizn' i tvorchestvo* (Leningrad: Nauka, 1969), 136. The discussion above has benefited from this source.

4. Aristocracy here did not necessarily refer to the writers' backgrounds, although the old nobility were certainly represented. Rather, to paraphrase these men's sensibility, it was an aristocracy of talent, not of birth. The classic interpretive work on this period remains Todd, *Fiction and Society*.

5. A. I. Reitblat, "Pushkin kak Bulgarin: K voprosu o politicheskikh vzgliadakh i zhurnalistskoi deiatel'nosti F. V. Bulgarina i A. S. Pushkina," *Novoe literaturnoe obozrenie* 115 (2012): 170–98. Reitblat's overview of the period's spectrum of political positions is likewise highly illuminating. He suggests, essentially, that Bulgarin and Pushkin held political views of far greater proximity than is usually assumed to have been the case.

6. See, for example, Faddei Bulgarin, "Podarki na Novyi god. (Pis'mo k Izdateliu.)," *Severnaia pchela*, January 13, 1825; and Bulgarin, "Provintsial v obshchestve bol'shogo sveta. (Pokhozhdenie vtoroe). Pis'mo k sosedu iz stolitsy," *Severnaia pchela*, January 24, 1825.

7. A. I. Reitblat, *Kak Pushkin vyshel v genii: Istoriko-sotsiologicheskie ocherki o knizhnoi kul'ture Pushkinskoi epokhi* (Moscow: Novoe literaturnoe obozrenie, 2001), 128–56, especially 144.

8. The first major study of Russian advice literature is Catriona Kelly's *Refining Russia: Advice Literature, Polite Culture, and Gender from Catherine to Yeltsin* (New York: Oxford University Press, 2001).

9. Quoted in Alison K. Smith, *Recipes for Russia: Food and Nationhood under the Tsars* (DeKalb: Northern Illinois University Press, 2008), 125.

10. In his reminiscences published serially in the *Russian Herald* (*Russkii vestnik*) and a handful of other periodicals, Burnashev intimates that both he, during the early years of his career, and some of his colleagues had scant knowledge of agriculture. See, for example, V. P. Burnashev, "Vospominaniia peterburgskogo starozhila: Vospominaniia ob epizodakh iz moei chastnoi i sluzhebnoi deiatel'nosti," *Russkii vestnik* 12 (1872): 670–704. For a discussion of Burnashev's reminiscences, see A. I. Reitblat, ed., "Anekdotika. Letopisets slukhov. (Nepublikovannye vospominaniia V. P. Burnasheva)," *Novoe literaturnoe obozrenie* 4 (1993): 162–77. In addition to publishing some of Burnashev's previously unpublished recollections, Reitblat advances a reasonable argument regarding the utility of Burnashev's memoirs. Although Burnashev has long been considered a suspect source of information, Reitblat goes some way toward rehabilitating him as he points out that Burnashev's factual mistakes are likely the product of mis-remembering; thus, while Burnashev may err and mix up well-known dates and information, there is little to suggest deliberate misinformation.

11. Throughout this study the author's understanding of what constitutes a middlebrow cultural register and of the possible positions taken by writers within a field of

cultural production comes largely from Pierre Bourdieu's works on the subject. It seems reasonable to propose that by the second quarter of the nineteenth century, Russia's book market was sufficiently well developed to include a sizable segment comprised of middle-brow fare, a designation particularly applicable (for the purposes of this study) to advice literature, which it would be difficult to categorize as belonging either to a high or low register. Pierre Bourdieu, *Distinction: A Social Critique of the Judgement of Taste*, trans. Richard Nice (London: Routledge, 1984); and Bourdieu, *The Rules of Art: Genesis and Structure of the Literary Field*, trans. Susan Emanuel (Stanford, CA: Stanford University Press, 1996).

12. For a treatment of Russian transpositions of *Gil Blas*, see Ronald LeBlanc, *The Russianization of "Gil Blas": A Study in Literary Appropriation* (Columbus, OH: Slavica, 1986). Grits, Trenin, and Nikitin call it "the 'first Russian novel.'" T. Grits, V. Trenin, and M. Nikitin, *Slovesnost' i kommertsiia: Knizhnaia lavka A. F. Smirdina*, ed. V. B. Shklovskii and B. M. Eikhenbaum (1929, repr., Moscow: AGRAF, 2001), 182.

13. This point grows especially salient in LeBlanc's juxtaposition of Bulgarin's text with Vasilii Narezhnyi's *Russian Gil Blas* (*Rossiiskii Zhil' Blaz*), a much more sophisticated text that was banned before it could be published in its entirety.

14. Faddei Bulgarin, *Sochineniia* (Moscow: Sovremennik, 1990), 197–98.

15. Ibid., 198.

16. Ibid., 205. Incidentally, as is indicated in the novel, the number five hundred refers to the male serfs, since only male serfs were counted.

17. Ibid., 365.

18. A. I. Reitblat, "Gogol' i Bulgarin: K istorii literaturnykh vzaimootnoshenii," in *Gogol': Materialy i issledovaniia*, ed. Iu. V. Mann (Moscow: Nasledie, 1995), 91.

19. V. P. Burnashev, "Bulgarin i Pesotskii, izdateli ezhenedel'nogo zhurnala 'Ekonom' v sorokovykh godakh," *Birzhevye vedomosti* 284 (1872): 257.

20. While the majority of *Ekonom* contained advice aimed at the rural nobleman, the information about such subjects as recipes and interior decoration was meant for an audience comprised of both men and women.

21. Faddei Bulgarin, "K chitateliam Ekonoma," *Ekonom* 10 (1841): 84.

22. Smith, *Recipes for Russia*, 170–72.

23. See *Ekonom* 56 (1842): 25–27; *Ekonom* 57 (1842): 33–35; *Ekonom* 59 (1842): 49–51; *Ekonom* 66 (1842): 105–6; *Ekonom* 70 (1842): 137–39. It should be noted that inasmuch as serfdom had been abolished in the province of Estonia (Estliandia) in 1816, it stands to reason that Bulgarin's Karlovo was hardly typical in the context of imperial Russia.

24. A. I. Reitblat, *Vidok Figliarin: Pis'ma i agenturnye zapiski F. V. Bulgarina v III otdelenie* (Moscow: Novoe literaturnoe obozrenie, 1998), 21.

25. For Reitblat's ongoing republication of Grech's letters to Bulgarin, see *Novoe literaturnoe obozrenie* 40 (1999): 94–112; 42 (2000): 264–317; 89 (2008): 93–112. The letter about the bad harvest is part of the first set. Nikolai Grech to Faddei Bulgarin, St. Petersburg, August 31, 1832, in *Novoe literaturnoe obozrenie* 40 (1999): 99.

26. Faddei Bulgarin, "Prakticheskii domashnii kurs sel'skogo khoziaistva, dlia nachinaiushchikh khoziainichat'," *Ekonom* 57 (1842): 33.

27. Anon., "Ekonom: Khoziaistvennaia obshchepoleznaia biblioteka, izdavaemaia I. Pesotskim, pod redaktsieiu F. Bulgarina," *Otechestvennye zapiski* 14 (February 1841): 73, sec. "Russkaia literatura."

28. *Notes of the Fatherland* published articles signed by anonymous provincial gentrymen in other contexts as well. For example, A. P. Zabolotskii-Desiatovskii's critical response to a piece by Aleksei Khomiakov in the *Muscovite* (*Moskvitianin*) was published anonymously, signed by a "Russian Landowner." See "Zamechaniia na stat'iu g. Khomiakova v #6 'Moskvitianina' na 1842 god," *Otechestvennye zapiski* 25 (November 1842): 1–12, sec. "Domovodstvo."

29. Melissa Frazier, *Romantic Encounters: Writers, Readers, and the Library for Reading* (Stanford, CA: Stanford University Press, 2007), 182.

30. Of course, this was not the first time Pushkin wrote as a provincial: his alter ego Feofilakt Kosichkin's articles about Faddei Bulgarin came earlier.

31. George Gutsche, "Pushkin and Belinsky: The Role of the Offended Provincial," in *New Perspectives on Nineteenth-Century Russian Prose*, ed. G. J. Gutsche and L. G. Leighton (Columbus, OH: Slavica, 1982), 48–49.

32. Senkovskii's article "Pervoe pis'mo tverskikh pomeshchikov Baronu Brambeusu" is quoted in Frazier's *Romantic Encounters*, 181.

33. Ibid.

34. Mary Cavender, *Nests of the Gentry: Family, Estate, and Local Loyalties in Provincial Russia* (Newark: University of Delaware Press, 2007), 179.

35. Having checked the reviewers' accusations on this last count, the author is able to confirm that (to take one year) in 1844 *Ekonom* reprinted, on average, roughly two articles per month from the *Transactions of the Free Economic Society* without attribution of the source.

36. Faddei Bulgarin, "Zametki na prevratnoe suzhdenie Otechestvennykh zapisok ob Ekonome, obshchepoleznoi, khoziaistvennoi biblioteke, pomeshchennoe vo vtorom nomere Otechestvennykh zapisok na 1841 god, str. 71–76," *Severnaia pchela*, February 19, 1841.

37. Faddei Bulgarin, "Zhurnal'naia vsiakaia vsiachina," *Severnaia pchela*, December 9, 1844. Bulgarin continued to advertise *Ekonom* on the last page of the *Northern Bee* after 1844. Bulgarin did not speak again on behalf of *Ekonom* until he resumed its editorship (about which more below). In his notes to the Third Section written after 1844, he persisted in urging that *Notes of the Fatherland* be shut down, because the journal spread dangerous, revolutionary ideas among the readership. See his note to the Third Section entitled "Sotsialism, kommunism i panteism v Rossii v poslednee 25-letie," in Reitblat, *Vidok Figliarin*, 490–505. See also Reitblat's accompanying commentary about the ineffectiveness of Bulgarin's attempts to have Kraevskii's journal shut down.

38. The original title is *Prakticheskoe polnoe korovovodstvo*. The ironically suggested titles are "*Polnoe bykovodstvo, Polnoe volovodstvo, Polnoe telenkovodstvo, Polnoe telkovodstvo* i t.d. k raznogo roda vodstvam." See Anon., "Zamechaniia o tom, kak izdaetsia 'Ekonom,' khoziaistvennaia obshchepoleznaia biblioteka," *Otechestvennye zapiski* 38 (January 1845): 31, sec. "Smes."

39. For an argument regarding this earlier iteration of Puf as a parody of Bulgarin, see Alison K. Smith, "National Cuisine and Nationalist Politics: V. F. Odoevsky and Dr. Puf, 1844–1845," *Kritika* 10, no. 2 (Spring 2009): 242.

40. [Vladimir Odoevskii], "Domostroitel'stvo i domovodstvo: Vecher pervyi," *Otechestvennye zapiski* 44 (February 1846): 13–28, sec. "Domovodstvo."

41. Ibid., 12.

42. Ibid.

43. Ibid.

44. Ibid., 13.

45. Ibid.

46. Ibid.

47. According to Burnashev's own rather colorful account, in 1849 the journal's publisher, Ivan Petrovich Pesotskii (the author's memory fails him here: Pesotskii died in 1848; thereafter *Ekonom* was published by Iulii Iungmeister), summoned Bulgarin from his estate of Karlovo, asking him to resume his duties as the editor of the journal he had founded. The two quarreled in short order; the publisher "beat up Bulgarin so badly that Faddei spent six weeks recovering." See Reitblat's publication "Anekdotika," 172–74, for the full piece, which includes a similar anecdote about how another publisher, Ivan Lisenkov, gave Bulgarin a thorough beating with a chair. Regarding the Pesotskii affair, Reitblat reasonably suggests that while one such fight very likely took place between Bulgarin and the publisher as early as May 15, 1843, he judges that it is possible that the two quarreled multiple times, though certainly not in 1849.

48. Faddei Bulgarin, "Fel'eton Ekonoma," *Ekonom* 1 (1850): 1.

49. Ibid.

50. Ibid., 2.

51. Ibid.

52. Ibid. To some degree, Bulgarin claims to conceive of the reader as a kind of consumer or even the proverbial customer, who is always right. See, for example, Bulgarin's formulation from "Writers and Readers" (1838), where he writes that "it is not the writer, but the *reader*, who rules, legislates and judges in literature." He continues: "verdicts uttered by the reader [...] strike the haughty writer in the most sensitive place—the pocket!" Faddei Bulgarin, *Durnye vremena: Ocherki russkikh nravov* (St. Petersburg: Azbuka-Klassika, 2007), 309.

53. Antonova, *An Ordinary Marriage*, see especially 202–27. See also Tatiana Golovina, "Golos iz publiki (Chitatel' i sovremennik o Pushkine i o Bulgarine)," *Novoe literaturnoe obozrenie* 40 (1999): 13–14.

54. Antonova, *An Ordinary Marriage*, 214.

Chapter 4

1. Emphases added. N. V. Gogol to M. I. Gogol, St. Petersburg, July 24, 1829. Quoted in Vladimir Nabokov, *Nikolai Gogol* (New York: New Directions, 1961), 15–16. Nabokov's translation is used here for reasons discussed in the pages that follow. All subsequent references to Gogol's texts will be from Nikolai Gogol', *Polnoe sobranie sochinenii*, 14 vols. (Moscow: Izdatel'stvo Akademii nauk SSSR, 1937–1952); documentation will be provided parenthetically within the body of the text with volume followed by page number. The Russian original of this letter can be found in 10:146.

2. Nabokov, *Gogol*, 19.

3. Ibid., 21–22.

4. Furthermore, Nabokov's choice of the word "manor" puns on "manner," which may preserve some of the ambiguity in Gogol's "*v svoikh provintsiiakh*."

5. Smith, *Recipes for Russia*, 123.

6. Anne Lounsbery, *Thin Culture, High Art: Gogol, Hawthorne, and Authorship in Nineteenth-Century Russia and America* (Cambridge, MA: Harvard University Press, 2007), 133.

7. Reitblat, "Gogol' i Bulgarin," 82–98.

8. The reading advanced here has benefited from Konstantine Klioutchkine, "The Rise of *Crime and Punishment* from the Air of the Media," *Slavic Review* 61, no. 1 (Spring 2002): 88–108.

9. Iurii Mann writes that Gogol set out to write a novel approaching the picaresque in its form. See Iurii Mann, *V poiskakh zhivoi dushi: Mertvye dushi—pisatel', kritika, chitatel'* (Moscow: Kniga, 1984), 12. Simon Karlinsky judges that "the structure of *Dead Souls* utilizes and puts to its own purposes the familiar and widespread genre of the traditional picaresque novel," thus also placing it in dialogue with the *Gil Blas* trend in Russian novelistic production. See Simon Karlinsky, *The Sexual Labyrinth of Nikolai Gogol* (Chicago, IL: University of Chicago Press, 1992), 225.

10. A difficulty in the sense that Gogol was attempting to produce edifying works; the biographical dimension of this will be treated in a limited way at the end of this chapter.

11. Angle brackets in original.

12. Kelly, *Refining Russia*, 124. Incidentally, the suggestion here is *not* that Tentetnikov is *reading* the actual *Selected Passages*; rather, Tentetnikov appears as a kind of trial run at the perfect *pomeshchik* as Gogol was writing him during these years.

13. Gilman Alkire, who has catalogued an impressive number of correspondences between Bulgarin's novel and several of Gogol's works, calls "the ideal landowner" Kostanzhoglo "the clearest single borrowing from *Vyzhigin*." Gilman Alkire, "Gogol and Bulgarin's *Ivan Vyzhigin*," *Slavic Review* 28, no. 2 (1969): 293.

14. Here, it will help to have the Russian original:

> Knigi po vsem chastiam: Po chasti lesovodstva, skotovodstva, svinovodstva, sadovodstva, tysiachi vsiakikh zhurnalov, rukovodstv i mnozhestvo zhurnalov, predstavliavshikh samye pozdneishie razvitiia i usovershenstvovaniia i po konnozavodstvu i estestvennym naukam. Byli i takie nazvan'ia: "Svinovodstvo, kak nauka."

15. Valerian Pereverzev, *Gogol, Dostoevsky, Issledovaniia* (Moscow: Sovetskii pisatel', 1982), 161.

16. Robert Maguire, *Exploring Gogol* (Stanford, CA: Stanford University Press, 1994), 331.

17. The male pronoun is used here advisedly, because the imagined reader of *agricultural* articles published in *Ekonom* is frequently presumed to be male.

18. The phrase is from Edyta Bojanowska, *Nikolai Gogol: Between Ukrainian and Russian Nationalism* (Cambridge, MA: Harvard University Press, 2007), 318. She likens this exercise to his earlier interest in Ukrainian culture.

19. Long considered to have been plagiarized, this book has since been convincingly reattributed to Bulgarin. See Malle Salupere, "Bulgarin kak istorik. (K voprosu ob avtorstve *Rossii*)," *Novoe literaturnoe obozrenie* 40 (1999): 142–58.

20. Unlike the anonymous provincial reviewers of *Ekonom*, Saburov signed his articles with his name.

21. I. V. Saburov, "Zapiski penzenskogo zemledel'tsa o teorii i praktike sel'skogo khoziaistva. Chast' tret'ia i posledniaia," *Otechestvennye zapiski* 26 (January 1843): 1–2, sec. "Domovodstvo."

22. Ibid., 2.

23. I. V. Saburov, "Zapiski penzenskogo zemledel'tsa o teorii i praktike sel'skogo khoziaistva. Chast' pervaia. Okonchanie." *Otechestvennye zapiski* 21 (March 1842): 7, sec. "Domovodstvo."

24. I. V. Saburov, "Zapiski penzenskogo zemledel'tsa o teorii i praktike sel'skogo khoziaistva," *Otechestvennye zapiski* 20 (January 1842): 9–10, sec. "Domovodstvo."

25. Donald Fanger, *The Creation of Nikolai Gogol* (Cambridge, MA: Belknap Press of Harvard University Press, 1979), 208.

26. For a good overview of the process, see an 1843 review of the first volume of Burnashev's encyclopedia. "Opyt terminologicheskogo slovaria sel'skogo khoziaistva, fabrichnosti, promyslov i byta narodnogo. Sostavil V. Burnashev. Tom pervyi. A- N. Sanktpeterburg. 1843. V tip. K. Zhernakova. V 8-iu d.l. xii i 487 str.," *Otechestvennye zapiski* 31 (1843): 44–46, sec. "Bibliograficheskaia khronika."

27. Had Gogol published the nonfiction he worked on (a dictionary and a children's geography book, for example), he would have become Burnashev's colleague, as the latter, in addition to a plethora of advice books both original and translated, the *Attempt,* and various ethnographic books on Russia, also wrote children's literature (for instance, a guide to St. Petersburg suitable for young readers).

28. The author is grateful to Thomas Newlin for pointing out that Gogol's description of soil types (quoted above) appears to be at odds with an accurate, scientific understanding of black soil. When it comes to agriculture, the available evidence suggests that Gogol did not know his subject well.

29. Susanne Fusso, *Designing Dead Souls: An Anatomy of Disorder in Gogol* (Stanford, CA: Stanford University Press, 1993), 120.

30. The section titled "Subsequent Works" contains a list of detailed explanations for other labor that might be performed, time permitting: for example, Gogol gives specific measurements for the trench that is to be dug for the planting of still more acorns. These notes are published in P. O. Kulish, ed., *Zapiski o zhizni Nikolaia Vasil'evicha Gogolia, sostavlennye iz vospominanii ego druzei i znakomykh i iz ego sobstvennykh pisem v dvukh tomakh* (St. Petersburg: V tipografii Aleksandra Iakobsona, 1856), 2:278–81.

31. Ibid.

32. Ibid., 281.

Chapter 5

1. In "Forms of Time and of the Chronotope in the Novel," Mikhail Bakhtin singles out Goncharov as a Russian analogue to such major producers of bildungsromans as Stendhal, Honoré de Balzac, and Gustave Flaubert. See M. M. Bakhtin, *The Dialogic Imagination: Four Essays*, ed. Michael Holquist, trans. Caryl Emerson and Michael Holquist (Austin: University of Texas Press, 1981), 234.

2. The conceptual pairing comes from Molière's 1670 play *Le Bourgeois gentilhomme*.

3. Catriona Kelly counts Goncharov among a group she describes as "educated people who were similar to the Western bourgeoisie in its more conventional manifestations." See Kelly, *Refining Russia*, 110.

4. See Elena Krasnoshchekova, *Roman vospitaniia: Bildungsroman na russkoi pochve; Karamzin, Pushkin, Goncharov, Tolstoy, Dostoevskii* (St. Petersburg: Pushkinskii fond, 2008), 125–264. Krasnoshchekova discusses Goncharov's entire trilogy in terms of its various reworkings of the bildungsroman as a genre; she finds that *A Common Story* displays features of this genre in the most systematic and prominent way. On the bildungsroman in Russian culture and on ways in which some canonical Russian novels absorb (but also fundamentally subvert) the form, see Lina Steiner, *For Humanity's Sake: The Bildungsroman in Russian Culture* (Toronto, ON: University of Toronto Press, 2011).

5. Valerian Pereverzev, *U istokov russkogo realizma* (Moscow: Sovremennik, 1989), 455–663.

6. I. A. Goncharov, *Polnoe sobranie sochinenii i pisem v 20 tomakh* (St. Petersburg: Nauka, 1997–), 1:225, 1:229. Unless marked otherwise, all subsequent quotations from Goncharov will come from this edition of his works and will be documented parenthetically in the text with volume, followed by page number.

7. N. G. Evstratov has pointed out that both titles were taken by Goncharov from the rural domestic culture section of the *Journal of the Ministry of State Properties* (*Zhurnal Ministerstva gosudarstvennykh imushchestv*), a publication with which the novelist was familiar. See N. G. Evstratov, "Goncharov na putiakh k romanu (K kharakteristike rannego tvorchestva)," in *Uchenye zapiski Ural'skogo pedagogicheskogo instituta* 2, no. 6 (1955): 171–215.

8. See the discussion in chapter 4.

9. Incidentally, the decision to include *The Precipice* in this study is prompted by the fact that it is as much an 1840s text as a work of the 1860s.

10. Quoted in Goncharov, *Polnoe sobranie*, 6:13.

11. For more on the attribution and discussion of these short pieces and their ties to all three of Goncharov's novels, see Iulii Oksman, "Neizvestnye fel'etony I. A. Goncharova," in *Fel'etony sorokovykh godov: Zhurnal'naia i gazetnaia proza I. A. Goncharova, F. M. Dostoevskogo, I. S. Turgeneva* (Moscow: Akademiia, 1930), 15–38; as well as A. G. Tseitlin, *I. A. Goncharov* (Moscow: Izdatel'stvo Akademii nauk SSSR, 1950); and A. D. Alekseev, *Letopis' zhizni i tvorchestva Goncharova* (Leningrad: Izdatel'stvo Akademii nauk SSSR, 1960).

12. This appraisal is made in the critical commentary to the review. See Goncharov, *Polnoe sobranie*, 1:798.

13. The earliest drafts of this scene are dated at the late 1840s. To be clear, this is not a study of influences.

14. Brackets mark text crossed out by the author.

15. The argument here is prompted, in part, by Anne Lounsbery's insightful reading of the main trends in Tolstoy's use of words that indicate social estates in *A Landowner's Morning*. She points out, for example, that the absence of the word *dvorianin* "tells us something about the way Tolstoy would have preferred to define nobility: that is, not primarily as a relationship to state power, but as a relationship among people." See her "On Cultivating One's Own Garden with Other People's Labor: Serfdom in 'A Landowner's Morning,'" in *Before They Were Titans: Essays on the Early Works of Dostoevsky and Tolstoy*, ed. Elizabeth Cheresh Allen (Boston, MA: Academic Studies Press, 2015), 277.

16. E. I. Liapushkina, "Idillicheskie motivy v russkoi lirike nachala XIX veka i roman I. A. Goncharova 'Oblomov,'" in *Ot Pushkina do Belogo: Problemy poetiki russkogo realizma*

XIX–nachala XX veka, ed. V. M. Markovich (St. Petersburg: Izdatel'stvo S.-Peterburgskogo Universiteta, 1992), 102–17.

17. E. A. Liatskii, *Roman i zhizn': Razvitie tvorcheskoi lichnosti I. A. Goncharova* (Prague: Izdatel'stvo Plamia, 1925), 245–46.

18. There is one exception since one may count the appearance of the "girl Agashka" in the feuilleton as a draft for her later, novelistic representation.

19. When citing materials that are not yet available as part of the edition of Goncharov's complete works that is being published currently an earlier edition is used. Goncharov to I. I. L'khovskii, Warsaw, June 25/13, 1857, in I. A. Goncharov, *Sobranie sochinenii v vos'mi tomakh* (Moscow: Gosudarstvennoe izdatel'stvo khudozhestvennoi literatury, 1952–1955), 8:276. This edition of Goncharov's works gives the dates of his letters using both the Julian and Gregorian calendars.

20. Goncharov gives a slightly inaccurate title with the singular *gastronoma* instead of the plural *gastronomov*. The full, if awkward, title of this work is, *The Gastronomes' almanac, containing thirty complete dinners, with supplementary notes in Russian and French, rules of setting the table, serving at table, the order of wine, that is, which wine is to be served with which meal, and a practical manual for the kitchen* (*Al'manakh Gastronomov, zakliuchaiushchii v sebe tridtsat' polnykh obedov, oznachennykh zapiskami russkimi i frantsuzskimi, pravila dlia nakrytiia stola, sluzheniia za onym, poriadok vin, t.e. kakoe imenno, za kotorym kushan'em podaetsa i prakticheskoe rukovodstvo dlia kukhni*) (St. Petersburg, 1852).

21. Goncharov, *Sobranie sochinenii*, 8:277.

22. Sofia was the sister of Vladimir Burnashev, the prolific author of advice literature who was discussed in the previous chapters.

23. [Sofiia Burnasheva], *Nastavlenie o tom, kak myt', chistit', i voobshche soderzhat' bel'e i drugie predmety zhenskogo garderoba i tualeta: Sochinenie Glafiry Mikh. Shchigrovskoi* (St. Petersburg, 1859), pagination unclear.

24. It would, of course, be quite absurd to suggest that Goncharov alludes to Burnasheva's manual. But it may interest the reader to know that Burnasheva's book was reviewed in the 1859 issue of *Notes of the Fatherland* where the first two volumes of Goncharov's novel appeared. The reviewer, writing in the tongue-in-cheek style characteristic of the bibliographic feuilleton (especially one about a middlebrow book on a prosaic subject), though offering a largely positive evaluation, noted that the author had perhaps been too quick to call her book an original composition given that much of the material was borrowed from a French source, *Manuel complet du blanchiment et du blanchissage* (Paris, 1834). Such "borrowings" were not uncommon in this part of the Russian book market. Goncharov himself (along with V. Beketov) censored this issue of Kraevskii's journal. See N. Alek., "Nastavlenie o tom, kak myt', chistit', i voobshche soderzhat' bel'e i drugie predmety zhenskogo garderoba i tualeta. Sochinenie (?) [*sic*] Glafiry Mikh. Shchigrovskoi. Spb. 1859," *Otechestvennye zapiski* 122 (1859): 52–54, sec. "Russkaia literatura."

25. Ekaterina Avdeeva, née Polevaia, was the sister of Nikolai and Ksenofont Polevoi. She published a variety of works including prose fiction and ethnographic accounts, collections of songs and children's folktales, but became famous as a writer on housekeeping. Between 1841 and 1877, *The Handbook of the Russian Experienced Housewife* saw eleven editions, as well as countless forgeries.

26. Emphases in the original. Ekaterina Avdeeva, *Ruchnaia kniga russkoi opytnoi khoziaiki: Sostavlennaia iz sorokoletnikh opytov i nabliudenii dobroi khoziaiki russkoi K. Avdeevoi* (St. Petersburg: V tipografii voenno-uchebnykh zavedenii, 1844), iii.

27. It should be noted that Pshenitsyna's characterization also owes a great deal to the folkloric register. Late in the text, while in a kind of half-dreaming state, Oblomov realizes that Pshenitsyna *is* Militrisa Kirbit'evna, the folktale character associated with abundance, about whom he dreamt in part one of the novel (4:479–80).

28. For an example of Goncharov's awareness of the incongruity between being part of educated, polite society and direct participation in domestic affairs, see the novelist's 1855 letter to Elizaveta Tolstaia:

> Before supper, I quarreled with Evgenia Petrovna [. . .] Evgenia Petrovna asked me "what she was thinking about." "About supper, whether the roast has been overcooked," I answered, because the table was being set then. "What am I, some sort of cook [*kukharka, chto li*]?" "A good hostess [*gostepriimnaia khoziaika*]," I replied and immediately apologized and kissed her hand.

Goncharov to Elizaveta Tolstaia, St. Petersburg, October 22, 1855, in Goncharov, *Sobranie sochinenii*, 8:274.

29. Dmitrii Sokolov, *Svetskii chelovek, ili rukovodstvo k poznaniiu pravil obshche-zhitiia* (St. Petersburg: Tip. Sankt-Peterburgskogo gubernskogo pravleniia, 1847), 12; Burnasheva, *Nastavlenie*, iv; Avdeeva, *Ruchnaia kniga*, ii.

30. Anne Lounsbery, "The World on the Back of a Fish: Mobility, Immobility, and Economics in *Oblomov*," *Russian Review* 70 (January 2011): 64.

31. Goncharov's assumption of the post of censor (in March 1856) was greeted with a good deal of skepticism by some of his more radically minded contemporaries. For Herzen's remark, see "Neobyknovennaia istoriia tsenzora Gon-cha-ro iz Shi-Pan-Khu," in A. I. Gertsen, *Sobranie sochinenii v tridtsati tomakh* (Moscow: Izdatel'stvo Akademii nauk SSSR, 1954–1966), 13:104.

32. Goncharov was appointed to serve as secretary during Admiral Putiatin's voyage in 1852. For a detailed treatment of the travelogue's composition and publication, see Goncharov, *Polnoe sobranie*, 2:391–830.

33. A. P. Miliukov, "Russkaia apatiia i nemetskaia deiatel'nost'," in *Roman Goncharova "Oblomov" v russkoi kritike,* ed. M. V. Otradin (Leningrad: Izdatel'stvo Leningradskogo universiteta, 1991), 125–43.

34. Liatskii, *Roman i zhizn'*, 109.

35. Iulii Aikhenval'd, *Siluety russkikh pisatelei* (Berlin: Slovo, 1923), 134.

36. Writing in 1992, Petr Bukharkin noted that the word *flamandstvo* had since become "almost a term" and a fixture of Goncharov studies. P. E. Bukharkin, "Obraz mira v slove iavlennyi," in Markovich, *Ot Pushkina do Belogo*, 123. Goncharov's *flamandstvo* is to be distinguished from the much darker Russian *ten'erstvo* that tended to take on coarser objects of representation. See Ronald LeBlanc, "Teniers, Flemish Art, and the Natural School Debate," *Slavic Review* 50, no. 3 (Autumn 1991): 576–89.

37. Ruth Bernard Yeazell, *Art of the Everyday: Dutch Painting and the Realist Novel* (Princeton, NJ: Princeton University Press, 2008), 15.

38. Ibid., 16.

39. Nancy Armstrong's side-by-side readings of eighteenth-century English novels and domestic and conduct manuals come to mind. Armstrong, *Desire and Domestic Fiction*.

40. For a detailed treatment of Goncharov's creative methods and his artistic proclivity toward the representation of opposites, see Milton Ehre's seminal study, *Oblomov*

and His Creator: The Life and Art of Ivan Goncharov (Princeton, NJ: Princeton University Press, 1973), 83–98, 154–233.

41. Goncharov, *Sobranie sochinenii*, 8:93.

42. Ibid., 8:102.

43. M. V. Otradin, *Proza I. A. Goncharova v literaturnom kontekste* (St. Petersburg: Izdatel'stvo Peterburgskogo Universiteta, 1994), 69.

44. Angle brackets in original. Goncharov to Anatolii Koni, Narva-Joesuu, June 26, 1887, in O. A. Demikhovskaia and E. K. Demikhovskaia, eds., *I. A. Goncharov v krugu sovremennikov: Neizdannaia perepiska* (Pskov: Izdatel'stvo Pskovksogo oblastnogo instituta povysheniia kvalifikatsii rabotnikov obrazovaniia, 1997), 134.

45. Ibid.

46. Ibid.

Chapter 6

1. Nikolai Dobroliubov, *Sobranie sochinenii v deviati tomakh*, ed. B. I. Bursov et al. (Moscow: Gosudarstvennoe izdatel'stvo khudozhestvennoi literatury, 1961–1964), 2: 297–98.

2. Generally, radical literary critics seldom wrote about the period's social order without at least a slight ironic inflection. Throughout the review article Dobroliubov sounds caustic notes from time to time so that little, save perhaps some aspects of the effusions regarding the better future awaiting Russia, is to be taken straightforwardly.

3. The work's emphasis on youth as a dynamic process of self-formation and particularly its depiction of a kind of socialization that involves an attempt at a compromise between the protagonist's individuality and the social world he inhabits make it possible to treat the text as a bildungsroman. For a treatment of the relationship between socialization and *Bildung*, see Franco Moretti, *The Way of the World: The Bildungsroman in European Culture* (London: Verso, 1987). In the context of Moretti's typology of the bildungsroman, it should be pointed out that *Childhood Years* is probably closest in sensibility to the English tradition, not least because it shares the lot of several English works of the genre (notably *Jane Eyre* and *David Copperfield*) in being categorized as a text suitable for young adults due to its purportedly edifying properties.

4. For example, the 1955 edition of Aksakov's collected works used throughout this chapter allots about three hundred pages to it. By one admittedly rather meticulous count, reading, books, and closely related topics are mentioned about one hundred times in these three hundred pages.

5. Incidentally, this is not to suggest that the formal aspects of Bolotov's recollections are devoid of interest. Their composition as a set of letters characterized by a recurring scenario of a special brand of addressivity to an audience at once broad and intimate introduces a degree of complexity that is treated briefly in chapter 1.

6. Andrew Durkin, *Sergei Aksakov and Russian Pastoral* (New Brunswick, NJ: Rutgers University Press, 1983), 99.

7. Marcus C. Levitt, "Aksakov's *Family Chronicle* and the Oral Tradition," *Slavic and East European Journal* 32, no. 2 (Summer 1988): 198.

8. One may also discuss folk motifs and Slavic oral culture in relation to this nexus of issues. To do so falls outside the boundaries of this study.

9. Quoted in S. T. Aksakov, *Sobranie sochinenii*, ed. S. Mashinskii et al. (Moscow: Gosudarstvennoe izdatel'stvo khudozhestvennoi literatury, 1955–1956), 1:623. All

subsequent references to this edition will be given in the body of the text with volume followed by page number.

10. First published in 1769, William Buchan's *Domestic Medicine* became available in translation and was very popular in Russia (and elsewhere in the world) during the late eighteenth and early nineteenth centuries.

11. Robert Darnton, *The Great Cat Massacre and Other Episodes in French Cultural History* (New York: Basic Books, 1984), 224.

12. For a recent multifocal collection of essays on the history of reading in Russia during the second half of the eighteenth century, see Aleksandr Samarin, *Tipografshchiki i knigochety: Ocherki po istorii knigi v Rossii vtoroi poloviny XVIII veka* (Moscow: Pashkov dom, 2013).

13. Rolf Engelsing, "Die Perioden der Lesergeschichte in Der Neuzeit: Das statische Ausmass und die Soziokulturelle Bedeutung der Lektüre," *Archiv für Geschichte des Buchwesens* 10 (1969): 944–1002. Engelsing's concept of the Reading Revolution has engendered a lively area of research and, as a result, has been revised considerably. In this study, the term is used as shorthand for the manifold consequences that increasing access to printed fare brought in the course of the long eighteenth century. The purpose here is not to document a Russian Reading Revolution, but rather to employ this concept as an interpretive tool in relation to Aksakov's text.

14. Reinhard Wittmann, "Was There a Reading Revolution at the End of the Eighteenth Century," in Cavallo and Chartier, *A History of Reading in the West*, 287.

15. Gary Marker, "The Creation of Journals," 24. See also Gary Marker, "Novikov's Readers," *Modern Language Review* 77, no. 4 (October 1982): 894–905. The recent work by Aleksandr Samarin adds a great deal to the picture suggested by Marker. Samarin considers a sizable sample of subscriber records to, again, find that the majority of the purchasers for whom records survive came from the nobility. See Samarin, *Tipografshchiki i knigochety*, 52–80.

16. Dobroliubov was referring specifically to Aksakov's *Literary and Theatrical Memoirs* here. Dobroliubov, *Sobranie sochinenii*, 4: 174.

17. Cathy Popkin, *The Pragmatics of Insignificance* (Stanford, CA: Stanford University Press, 1993), 186.

18. Much of this writing used poetic forms. For example, there is the long tradition of Russian translations and adaptations of Horace's Second Epode. Horace's poem begins by celebrating country life and the speaker's purported return to till his paternal fields. Horace's lyric subject, Alfius the usurer, abandons the pastoral fantasy by poem's end. Stephen Baehr has noted that "so important was this epode and its *locus amoenus* commonplaces to the conception of a rural paradise in Russian literature of the second half of the eighteenth century that its ironic last lines, which call this paradise into doubt as a daydream of an urban usurer, were sometimes omitted in translation." Stephen Lessing Baehr, *The Paradise Myth in Eighteenth-Century Russia* (Stanford, CA: Stanford University Press, 1991), 69. In free adaptations of the poem, these last lines tended to be omitted. N. N. Popovskii was the first to translate Horace's Second Epode. His 1751 translation was published in 1757 alongside Vasilii Trediakovskii's more creative verse transposition and prose treatise "On the Irreproachability and Pleasure of Country Life" ("O besporochnosti i priiatnosti derevenskiia zhizni"). Popovskii's translation kept Horace's concluding lines, Trediakovskii's transposition omitted them. A range of poetic adaptations by Derzhavin, Pushkin, and others followed. Derzhavin's "To Eugene. Life at Zvanka" may be the best

known of such texts. Of particular relevance to the above discussion of Aksakov is the emphasis in such poetry on everyday life, including its most prosaic aspects.

19. Durkin, *Sergei Aksakov*, 244.

Conclusion

1. Quoted in Boris Eikhenbaum, *Tolstoi v semidesiatye gody* (Leningrad: Khudozhestvennaia literatura, 1974), 155.

2. Pushkin, *Complete Prose Works*, 46.

3. Lev Tolstoi, *Anna Karenina*, trans. Richard Pevear and Larisa Volokhonsky (New York: Penguin Books, 2000), 22. The translation has been altered. The author is grateful to Cathy Popkin for her suggestions on this front. For the Russian original, see Tolstoi, *Polnoe sobranie*, 18:26.

4. For an explication of the connections between the formal and ethical dimensions of prosaics, see Gary Saul Morson and Caryl Emerson, *Mikhail Bakhtin: Creation of a Prosaics* (Stanford, CA: Stanford University Press, 1990); Gary Saul Morson, *Hidden in Plain View: Narrative and Creative Potentials in "War and Peace"* (Stanford, CA: Stanford University Press, 1987), especially 221, 126–28; Gary Saul Morson, *"Anna Karenina" in Our Time: Seeing More Wisely* (New Haven, CT: Yale University Press, 2007), 149.

5. Morson, *"Anna Karenina" in Our Time*, 150.

6. Morson writes: "Tolstoy uses Levin's evolving ideas about agricultural reform as exemplary in two ways. First, they show the process of honestly thinking through a difficult question with no pat answers." The second way has to do with "the applicability of Levin's ideas not only to agricultural improvement but also, and much more broadly, to all modernization and reform." Morson, *"Anna Karenina" in Our Time*, 150.

7. Richard Peace, *The Enigma of Gogol: An Examination of the Writings of N. V. Gogol and Their Place in the Russian Literary Tradition* (Cambridge: Cambridge University Press, 1981), 249. Peace has in mind the episode in volume two of *Dead Souls* when Kostanzhoglo suggests that the landowner Khlobuev take up a spade and work his own land. See Gogol', *Polnoe sobranie*, 7:81.

Bibliography

Aikhenval'd, Iulii. *Siluety russkikh pisatelei*. Berlin: Slovo, 1923.

Aksakov, S. T. *Sobranie sochinenii*. Edited by S. Mashinskii et al. 4 vols. Moscow: Gosudarstvennoe izdatel'stvo khudozhestvennoi literatury, 1955–1956.

Alek., N. "Nastavlenie o tom, kak myt', chistit', i voobshche soderzhat' bel'e i drugie predmety zhenskogo garderoba i tualeta. Sochinenie (?) Glafiry Mikh. Shchigrovskoi. Spb., 1859." *Otechestvennye zapiski* 122 (1859): 52–54, sec. "Russkaia literatura."

Alekseev, A. D. *Letopis' zhizni i tvorchestva I. A. Goncharova*. Leningrad: Izdatel'stvo Akademii nauk SSSR, 1960.

Alkire, Gilman. "Gogol and Bulgarin's *Ivan Vyzhigin*." *Slavic Review* 28, no. 2 (1969): 289–96.

Al'tshuller, Mark. *Mezhdu dvukh tsarei: Pushkin v 1824–1836 gg.* St. Petersburg: Akademicheskii proekt, 2003.

Antonova, Katherine Pickering. *An Ordinary Marriage: The World of a Gentry Family in Provincial Russia*. Oxford: Oxford University Press, 2012.

Armstrong, Nancy. *Desire and Domestic Fiction: A Political History of the Novel*. New York: Oxford University Press, 1990.

———. *How Novels Think: The Limits of Individualism from 1719–1900*. New York: Columbia University Press, 2006.

Avdeeva, Ekaterina. *Ruchnaia kniga russkoi opytnoi khoziaiki: Sostavlennaia iz sorokoletnikh opytov i nabliudenii dobroi khoziaiki russkoi K. Avdeevoi*. St. Petersburg: V tipografii voenno-uchebnykh zavedenii, 1844.

Baehr, Stephen Lessing. *The Paradise Myth in Eighteenth-Century Russia*. Stanford, CA: Stanford University Press, 1991.

Bakhtin, M. M. "Forms of Time and of the Chronotope in the Novel" (1937–1938). In *The Dialogic Imagination: Four Essays*, edited by Michael Holquist, translated by Caryl Emerson and Michael Holquist, 84–242. Austin: University of Texas Press, 1981.

Bethea, David M. and Sergei Davydov. "The [Hi]story of the Village of Gorjuxino: In Praise of Puškin's Folly." *Slavic and East European Journal* 28, no. 3 (Autumn 1984): 291–309.

Bojanowska, Edyta. *Nikolai Gogol: Between Ukrainian and Russian Nationalism*. Cambridge, MA: Harvard University Press, 2007.

Bolotov, Andrei, ed. Untitled. *Ekonomicheskii magazin* 1 (1779): pagination unclear.

———. Untitled. *Selskii zhitel'* 1 (1778): pagination unclear.

———, ed. Untitled. *Selskii zhitel'* 2 (1778): pagination unclear.

———. *Zhizn' i prikliucheniia Andreia Bolotova, opisannye samim im dlia svoikh potomkov.* 4 vols. St. Petersburg: V. Golovin, 1870–1873.

Bourdieu, Pierre. *Distinction: A Social Critique of the Judgement of Taste*. Translated by Richard Nice. London: Routledge, 1984.

———. *The Rules of Art: Genesis and Structure of the Literary Field.* Translated by Susan Emanuel. Stanford, CA: Stanford University Press, 1996.

Bowers, Toni. *The Politics of Motherhood: British Writing and Culture, 1680–1760.* Cambridge: Cambridge University Press, 1996.

Bradley, Joseph. *Voluntary Associations in Tsarist Russia: Science, Patriotism, and Civil Society.* Cambridge, MA: Harvard University Press, 2009.

Bukharin, P. E. "Obraz mira v slove iavlennyi." In *Ot Pushkina do Belogo: Problemy poetiki russkogo realizma XIX–nachala XX veka.* Edited by V. M. Markovich, 118–135. St. Petersburg: Izdatel'stvo S-Peterburgskogo universiteta, 1992.

Bulgarin, Faddei. *Durnye vremena: Ocherki russkikh nravov.* St. Petersburg: Azbuka-Klassika, 2007.

———. "Fel'eton Ekonoma." *Ekonom* 1 (1850): 1–2.

———. "K chitateliam Ekonoma." *Ekonom* 10 (1841): 84.

———. "Pis'ma na Kavkaz. 2. (Prodolzhenie)." *Syn otechestva* 2 (1825): 302–21.

———. "Podarki na Novyi god. (Pis'mo k Izdateliu.)." *Severnaia pchela*, January 13, 1825.

———. "Prakticheskii domashnii kurs sel'skogo khoziaistva, dlia nachinaiushchikh khoziainichat'." *Ekonom* 56 (1841): 25–27; *Ekonom* 57 (1842) 33–35; *Ekonom* 59 (1842): 49–51; *Ekonom* 66 (1842): 105–6; *Ekonom* 70 (1842): 137–39.

———. "Provintsial v obshchestve bol'shogo sveta. (Pokhozhdenie vtoroe). Pis'mo k sosedu iz stolitsy." *Severnaia pchela*, January 24, 1825.

———. *Sochineniia.* Moscow: Sovremennik, 1990.

———. "Zametki na prevratnoe suzhdenie Otechestvennykh zapisok ob Ekonome, obshchepoleznoi, khoziaistvennoi biblioteke, pomeshchennoe vo vtorom nomere Otechestvennykh zapisok na 1841 god, str. 71–76." *Severnaia pchela*, February 19, 1841.

———. "Zhurnal'naia vsiakaia vsiachina." *Severnaia pchela*, December 9, 1844.

Burnashev, V. P. "Bulgarin i Pesotskii, izdateli ezhenedel'nogo zhurnala 'Ekonom' v sorokovykh godakh." *Birzhevye vedomosti* 284 (1872): 255–57.

———. "Vospominaniia peterburgskogo starozhila: Vospominaniia ob epizodakh iz moei chastnoi i sluzhebnoi deiatel'nosti." *Russkii vestnik* 12 (1872): 670–704.

[Burnasheva, Sofiia]. *Nastavlenie o tom, kak myt', chistit', i voobshche soderzhat' bel'e i drugie predmety zhenskogo garderoba i tualeta.* Sochinenie Glafiry Mikh. Shchigrovskoi. St. Petersburg, 1859.

Butkovskaia, Avgusta. "Rasskazy babushki." *Istoricheskii vestnik* 18 (1884): 594–631.

Cavallo, Guglielmo, and Roger Chartier, eds. *A History of Reading in the West.* Translated by Lydia G. Cochrane. Studies in Print Culture and the History of the Book. Amherst: University of Massachusetts Press, 1999.

Cavender, Mary. *Nests of the Gentry: Family, Estate, and Local Loyalties in Provincial Russia.* Newark: University of Delaware Press, 2007.

Confino, Michael. *Domaines et seigneurs en Russie vers la fin du XVIIIe siècle.* Paris: Institut d'Études Slaves, 1963.

———. "Histoire et psychologie: À propos de la noblesse russe au XVIIIe siècle." *Annales, Economies, Sociétés, Civilisations* 22, no. 6 (1967): 1163–1205.

Costlow, Jane. *Heart-Pine Russia: Walking and Writing the Nineteenth-Century Forest.* Ithaca, NY: Cornell University Press, 2013.

Cross, Anthony Glenn. *"By the Banks of the Thames": Russians in Eighteenth-Century Britain.* Newtonville, MA: Oriental Research Partners, 1980.

———. "Karamzin's 'Moskovskii Zhurnal': Voice of a Writer, Broadsheet of a Movement." *Cahiers du monde russe et soviétique* 28, no. 2, (April–June 1987): 121–26.

———. *N. M. Karamzin: A Study of His Literary Career, 1783–1803.* Carbondale: Southern Illinois University Press, 1971.

Darnton, Robert. *The Great Cat Massacre and Other Episodes in French Cultural History.* New York: Basic Books, 1984.

Davydov, Sergei. "The Evolution of Pushkin's Political Thought." In *The Pushkin Handbook,* edited by David M. Bethea, 283–320. Madison: University of Wisconsin Press, 2005.

de Madariaga, Isabel. "The eighteenth-century origin of Russian civil rights." In *Politics and Culture in Eighteenth-Century Russia,* 78–94. London: Longman, 2014.

Demikhovskaia, O. A., and E. K. Demikhovskaia, eds. *I. A. Goncharov v krugu sovremennikov: Neizdannaia perepiska.* Pskov: Izdatel'stvo Pskovskogo oblastnogo instituta povysheniia kvalifikatsii rabotnikov obrazovaniia, 1997.

Dobroliubov, Nikolai. *Sobranie sochinenii v deviati tomakh.* Edited by B. I. Bursov et al. 9 vols. Moscow: Gosudarstvennoe izdatel'stvo khudozhestvennoi literatury, 1961–1964.

Driver, Sam. *Pushkin: Literature and Social Ideas.* New York: Columbia University Press, 1989.

Dukes, Paul. *Catherine the Great and the Russian Nobility: A Study Based on the Materials of the Legislative Commission of 1767.* Cambridge: Cambridge University Press, 1967.

Durkin, Andrew. *Sergei Aksakov and Russian Pastoral.* New Brunswick, NJ: Rutgers University Press, 1983.

Dzhunkovksii, Stepan. "Rech' o pol'ze i neobkhodimosti opytnogo uprazhneniia v zemledelii i domostroitel'stve, dlia dvorian i vsekh vladel'tsev sobstvennykh imenii, chitannaia v torzhestvennom sobranii Vol'nogo Ekonomicheskogo Obshchestva 1804 goda dekabria 3go." *Trudy Vol'nogo Ekonomicheskogo Obshchestva k pooshchreniiu v Rossii zemledeliia i domostroitel'stva* 57 (1805): 1–23.

Ehre, Milton. *Oblomov and His Creator: The Life and Art of Ivan Goncharov.* Princeton, NJ: Princeton University Press, 1973.

Eikhenbaum, Boris. *Molodoi Tolstoi.* St. Petersburg: Izdatel'stvo Z. I. Grzhebina, 1922.

———. *O literature.* Moscow: Sovetskii pisatel', 1987.

———. *O proze, o poezii.* Leningrad: Khudozhestvennaia literatura, 1986.

———. *O proze. Sbornik statei.* Edited by I. Iampol'skii. Leningrad: Khudozhestvennaia literatura, 1969.

———. *Tolstoi v semidesiatye gody.* Leningrad: Khudozhestvennaia literatura, 1974.

"Ekonom. khoziaistvennaia obshchepoleznaia biblioteka, izdavaemaia I. Pesotskim, pod redaktsieiu F. Bulgarina." *Otechestvennye zapiski* 14 (February 1841): 71–76, sec. "Russkaia literatura."

Engelsing, Rolf. "Die Perioden der Lesergeschichte in Der Neuzeit: Das statische Ausmass und die Soziokulturelle Bedeutung der Lektüre." *Archiv für Geschichte des Buchwesens* 10 (1969): 944–1002.

Evstratov, N. G. "Goncharov na putiakh k romanu (K kharakteristike rannego tvorchestva)." *Uchenye zapiski Ural'skogo pedagogicheskogo instituta* 2, no. 6 (1955): 171–215.

Fanger, Donald. *The Creation of Nikolai Gogol.* Cambridge, MA: Belknap Press of Harvard University Press, 1979.

Feuer, Kathryn B. *Tolstoy and the Genesis of War and Peace.* Edited by Robin Feuer Miller and Donna Tussing Orwin. Ithaca, NY: Cornell University Press, 1996.

Frazier, Melissa. *Romantic Encounters: Writers, Readers, and the Library for Reading*. Stanford, CA: Stanford University Press, 2007.

Freeze, Gregory. "The *Soslovie* (Estate) Paradigm and Russian Social History." *The American Historical Review* 91, no. 1 (February 1986): 11–36.

Fusso, Susanne. *Designing Dead Souls: An Anatomy of Disorder in Gogol*. Stanford, CA: Stanford University Press, 1993.

Gasperetti, David. *The Rise of the Russian Novel: Carnival, Stylization, and Mockery of the West*. DeKalb: Northern Illinois University Press, 1998.

Gertsen, A. I. *Sobranie sochinenii v tridtsati tomakh*. 30 vols. Moscow: Izdatel'stvo Akademii nauk SSSR, 1954–1966.

Gillel'son, M. I. *P. A. Viazemskii: Zhizn' i tvorchestvo*. Leningrad: Nauka, 1969.

Glukhov, V. I. "Obraz Oblomova i ego literaturnaia predistoriia." In *I. A. Goncharov: Materialy mezhdunarodnoi konferentsii, posviashchennoi 185-letiiu so dnia rozhdeniia I. A. Goncharova*, edited by M. B. Zhdanova, A. V. Lobkareva, and I. V. Smirnova, 103–11. Ul'ianovsk: Pechatnyi dvor, 1998.

Gogol', Nikolai. *Polnoe sobranie sochinenii*. 14 vols. Moscow: Akademiia nauk SSSR, 1937–1952.

Golovina, Tatiana. "Golos iz publiki (Chitatel' i sovremennik o Pushkine i o Bulgarine)." *Novoe literaturnoe obozrenie* 40 (1999): 11–16.

Goncharov, I. A. *Polnoe sobranie sochinenii i pisem v 20 tomakh*. 20 vols. St. Petersburg: Nauka, 1997–.

———. *Sobranie sochinenii*. 8 vols. Moscow: Gosudarstvennoe izdatel'stvo khudozhestvennoi literatury, 1952–1955.

Griffiths, David, and George Munro, eds. *Catherine II's Charters of 1785 to the Nobility and the Towns*. Bakersfield, CA: Charles Schlacks Jr., 1991.

Grits, T., V. Trenin, and M. Nikitin. *Slovesnost' i kommertsiia: Knizhnaia lavka A. F. Smirdina*. Edited by V. B. Shklovskii and B. M. Eikhenbaum. Moscow: AGRAF, 2001. First published 1929 by Federatsiia.

Gutsche, George. "Pushkin and Belinsky: The Role of the Offended Provincial." In *New Perspectives on Nineteenth-Century Russian Prose*, edited by G. J. Gutsche and L. G. Leighton, 41–59. Columbus, OH: Slavica, 1982.

Habermas, Jürgen. *The Structural Transformation of the Public Sphere: An Inquiry into a Category of Bourgeois Society*. Translated by Thomas Burger and Frederick Lawrence. Cambridge, MA: MIT Press, 1989.

Jones, Adrian. "A Russian Bourgeois's Arctic Enlightenment." *Historical Review* 48, no. 3 (September 2005): 623–40.

Jones, Robert E. *The Emancipation of the Russian Nobility, 1762–1785*. Princeton, NJ: Princeton University Press, 1973.

———. *Provincial Development in Russia: Catherine II and Jacob Sievers*. New Brunswick, NJ: Rutgers University Press, 1984.

Jones, W. Gareth. *Nikolay Novikov: Enlightener of Russia*. Cambridge: Cambridge University Press, 1984.

Kahn, Andrew. "Karamzin's Discourses of Enlightenment." In *Letters of a Russian Traveler*, by Nikolai Karamzin, 459–582. Translated and with a study by Andrew Kahn. Oxford: Voltaire Foundation, 2003.

———. "The Rise of the Russian Novel and the Problem of Romance." In *Remapping the Rise of the European Novel*, edited by Jenny Mander, 185–98. Oxford: Voltaire Foundation, 2007.

Karamzin, N. M. *Izbrannye sochineniia v dvukh tomakh.* Moscow: Khudozhestvennaia literatura, 1964.

———. "Pis'mo k izdateliu." *Vestnik Evropy* 1 (January 1802): 3–8.

———. "Priiatnye vidy, nadezhdy i zhelaniia nyneshnego vremeni." *Vestnik Evropy* 12 (June 1802): 314–31.

Karlinsky, Simon. *The Sexual Labyrinth of Nikolai Gogol.* Chicago: University of Chicago Press, 1992.

Kelly, Catriona. *Refining Russia: Advice Literature, Polite Culture, and Gender from Catherine to Yeltsin.* New York: Oxford University Press, 2001.

Kivelson, Valerie. *Autocracy in the Provinces: The Muscovite Gentry and Political Culture in the Seventeenth Century.* Stanford, CA: Stanford University Press, 1996.

———. "Kinship Politics/Autocratic Politics: A Reconsideration of Eighteenth-Century Political Culture." In *Imperial Russia: New Histories for the Empire,* edited by Jane Burbank and David L. Ransel, 5–31. Bloomington: Indiana University Press, 1998.

Klioutchkine, Konstantine. "The Rise of *Crime and Punishment* from the Air of the Media." *Slavic Review* 61, no. 1 (Spring 2002): 88–108.

Kliuchevskii, Vasilii. *Kurs russkoi istorii: Sochineniia v deviati tomakh.* 9 vols. Moscow: Mysl', 1987–1990.

Krasnoshchekova, Elena. *Ivan Aleksandrovich Goncharov: Mir tvorchestva.* St. Petersburg: Pushkinskii fond, 1997.

———. *Roman vospitaniia: Bildungsroman na russkoi pochve; Karamzin, Pushkin, Goncharov, Tolstoy, Dostoevsky.* St. Petersburg: Pushkinskii fond, 2008.

Kulish, P. O., ed. *Zapiski o zhizni Nikolaia Vasil'evicha Gogolia, sostavlennye iz vospominanii ego druzei i znakomykh i iz ego sobstvennykh pisem v dvukh tomakh.* 2 vols. St. Petersburg: V tipografii Aleksandra Iakobsona, 1856.

LeBlanc, Ronald. *The Russianization of Gil Blas: A Study in Literary Appropriation.* Columbus, OH: Slavica, 1986.

———. "Teniers, Flemish Art, and the Natural School Debate." *Slavic Review* 50, no. 3 (Autumn 1991): 576–89.

Leckey, Colum. *Patrons of Enlightenment: The Free Economic Society in Eighteenth-Century Russia.* Newark: University of Delaware Press, 2011.

Leonard, Carol. *Reform and Regicide: The Reign of Peter III in Russia.* Bloomington: Indiana University Press, 1993.

Levitt, Marcus. "Aksakov's *Family Chronicle* and the Oral Tradition." *Slavic and East European Journal* 32, no. 2 (Summer 1988): 198–212.

Liapushkina, E. I. "Idillicheskie motivy v russkoi lirike nachala XIX veka i roman I. A. Goncharova 'Oblomov.'" In *Ot Pushkina do Belogo: Problemy poetiki russkogo realizma XIX–nachala XX veka,* edited by V. M. Markovitch, 102–17. St. Petersburg: Izdatel'stvo S.-Peterburgskogo Universiteta, 1992.

Liatskii, E. A. *Roman i zhizn': Razvitie tvorcheskoi lichnosti I. A. Goncharova.* Prague: Izdatel'stvo Plamia, 1925.

Lotman, Iurii. *Besedy o russkoi kul'ture: Byt i traditsii russkogo dvorianstva (XVIII–nachalo XIX veka).* St. Petersburg: Iskusstvo-SPB, 1994.

———. *Izbrannye stat'i v trekh tomakh.* Vol. 1, *Stat'i po semiotike i topologii kul'tury.* Tallinn: Aleksandra, 1992.

———. *Sotvorenie Karamzina.* Moscow: Kniga, 1987.

Lounsbery, Anne. "On Cultivating One's Own Garden with Other People's Labor: Serfdom in 'A Landowner's Morning.'" In *Before They Were Titans: Essays on the Early Works* of Dostoevsky and Tolstoy, edited and with an introduction by Elizabeth Cheresh Allen, 267–98. Boston, MA: Academic Studies Press, 2015.

——. *Thin Culture, High Art: Gogol, Hawthorne, and Authorship in Nineteenth-Century Russia and America.* Cambridge, MA: Harvard University Press, 2007.

——. "The World on the Back of a Fish: Mobility, Immobility, and Economics in *Oblomov.*" *Russian Review* 70 (January 2011): 43–64.

Maguire, Robert. *Exploring Gogol.* Stanford, CA: Stanford University Press, 1994.

Mann, Iurii. *V poiskakh zhivoi dushi: Mertvye dushi—pisatel', kritika, chitatel'.* Moscow: Kniga, 1984.

Marasinova, E. N. *Vlast' i lichnost': Ocherki russkoi istorii XVIII veka.* Moscow: Nauka, 2008.

Marker, Gary. "The Creation of Journals and the Profession of Letters in the Eighteenth Century." In *Literary Journals in Imperial Russia,* edited by Deborah Martinsen, 11–37. Cambridge: Cambridge University Press, 1997.

——. "Novikov's Readers." *Modern Language Review* 77, no. 4 (October 1982): 894–905.

——. *Publishing, Printing, and the Origins of the Intellectual Life in Russia, 1700–1800.* Princeton, NJ: Princeton University Press, 1985.

Marrese, Michelle Lamarche. *A Woman's Kingdom: Noblewomen and the Control of Property in Russia, 1700–1861.* Ithaca, NY: Cornell University Press, 2002.

Martin, Alexander. *Romantics, Reformers, Reactionaries: Russian Conservative Thought and Politics in the Reign of Alexander I.* DeKalb: Northern Illinois University Press, 1997.

McKeon, Michael. *The Origins of the English Novel, 1600–1740.* Baltimore, MD: The Johns Hopkins University Press, 1987.

Meehan-Waters, Brenda. *Autocracy and Aristocracy: The Russian Service Elite of 1730.* Rutgers, NJ: Rutgers University Press, 1982.

——. "The Development and the Limits of Security of Noble Status, Person, and Property in Eighteenth-Century Russia." In *Russia and the West in the Eighteenth Century,* edited by Anthony Glenn Cross, 294–305. Newtonville, MA: Oriental Research Partners, 1983.

Melton, Edgar. "Enlightened Seigniorialism and Its Dilemmas in Serf Russia, 1750–1830." *Journal of Modern History* 62, no. 4 (December 1990): 676–708.

Miliukov, A. P. "Russkaia apatiia i nemetskaia deiatel'nost'." In *Roman Goncharova "Oblomov" v russkoi kritike,* edited by M.V. Otradin, 125–143. Leningrad: Izdatel'stvo Leningradskogo universiteta, 1991.

Moretti, Franco. *The Way of the World: The Bildungsroman in European Culture.* London: Verso, 1987.

Morson, Gary Saul. *"Anna Karenina" in Our Time: Seeing More Wisely.* New Haven, CT: Yale University Press, 2007.

——. *Hidden in Plain View: Narrative and Creative Potentials in "War and Peace."* Stanford, CA: Stanford University Press, 1987.

Morson, Gary Saul, and Caryl Emerson. *Mikhail Bakhtin: Creation of a Prosaics.* Stanford, CA: Stanford University Press, 1990.

Nabokov, Vladimir. *Nikolai Gogol.* New York: New Directions, 1961.

Newlin, Thomas. *The Voice in the Garden: Andrei Bolotov and the Anxieties of Russian Pastoral, 1738–1833.* Evanston, IL: Northwestern University Press, 2001.

Novikov, Nikolai. *Izbrannye pedagogicheskie sochineniia.* Moscow: Gosudarstvennoe uchebno-pedagogicheskoe izdatel'stvo ministerstva prosveshcheniia RSFSR, 1959.

———. *Satiricheskie zhurnaly N. I. Novikova*. Moscow: Izdatel'stvo Akademii nauk SSSR, 1951.

[Odoevskii, Vladimir]. "Domostroitel'stvo i domovodstvo." *Otechestvennye zapiski* 44 (January 1846): 12–16, sec. "Domovodstvo."

———. "Domostroitel'stvo i domovodstvo: Vecher pervyi." *Otechestvennye zapiski* 44 (February 1846): 13–28, sec. "Domovodstvo."

———. "Domostroitel'stvo i domovodstvo: Vecher tretii." *Otechestvennye zapiski* 45 (March 1846): 23–28, sec. "Domovodstvo."

———. "Domovodstvo." *Otechestvennye zapiski* 46 (May 1846): 17–24, sec. "Domovodstvo."

———. "Domovodstvo: Vecher chetvertyi." *Otechestvennye zapiski* 46 (June 1846): 41–44, sec. "Domovodstvo."

Oksman, Iulii. *Fel'etony sorokovykh godov: Zhurnal'naia i gazetnaia proza I. A. Goncharova, F. M. Dostoevskogo, I. S. Turgeneva*. Moscow: Akademiia, 1930.

"Opyt terminologicheskogo slovaria sel'skogo khoziaistva, fabrichnosti, promyslov i byta narodnogo. Sostavil V. Burnashev. Tom pervyi. A-N. Sanktpeterburg. 1843. V tip. K. Zhernakova. V 8-iu d.l. xii i 487 str." *Otechestvennye zapiski* 31 (December, 1843): 44–46, sec. "Bibliograficheskaia khronika."

Otradin, M. V. *Proza I. A. Goncharova v literaturnom kontekste*. St. Petersburg: Izdatel'stvo Peterburgskogo universiteta, 1994.

Paperno, Irina. *"Who, What Am I?" Tolstoy Struggles to Narrate the Self*. Ithaca, NY: Cornell University Press, 2014.

Peace, Richard. *The Enigma of Gogol: An Examination of the Writings of N. V. Gogol and Their Place in the Russian Literary Tradition*. Cambridge: Cambridge University Press, 1981.

Pereverzev, Valerian. *Gogol, Dostoevskii, Issledovaniia*. Moscow: Sovetskii pisatel', 1982.

———. *U istokov russkogo realizma*. Moscow: Sovremennik, 1989.

Pipes, Richard. "Private Property Comes to Russia: The Reign of Catherine II." In *Property and Freedom*, 431–42. New York: Alfred A. Knopf, 1999.

"Pis'mo k redaktoru Otechestvennykh zapisok o mudrovaniiakh 'Ekonoma' v kartofel'nom dele." *Otechestvennye zapiski* 15 (March 1841): 28–32, sec. "Bibliograficheskaia khronika."

Polnoe sobranie zakonov Rossiiskoi Imperii s 1649 goda. Vol. 15. St. Petersburg: V Tipografii II Otdeleniia Sobstvennoi E. I. V. Kantseliarii, 1830.

Popkin, Cathy. *The Pragmatics of Insignificance: Chekhov, Zoshchenko, Gogol*. Stanford, CA: Stanford University Press, 1993.

Pravilova, Ekaterina. *A Public Empire: Property and the Quest for the Common Good in Imperial Russia*. Princeton, NJ: Princeton University Press, 2014.

"Preduvedomlenie." *Trudy Vol'nogo Ekonomicheskogo Obshchestva* 1 (1765): pagination unclear.

Pushkin, Alexander. *Alexander Pushkin: Complete Prose Fiction*. Translated by Paul Debreczeny. Stanford, CA: Stanford University Press, 1983.

———. *Polnoe sobranie sochinenii v shestnadtsati tomakh*. Edited by D. D. Blagoi et al. 16 vols. Moscow: Izdatel'stvo AN SSSR, 1937–1959.

Radetskii, Ignatii. *Al'manakh Gastronomov, zakliuchaiushii v sebe tridtsat' polnykh obedov, oznachennykh zapiskami russkimi i frantsuzskimi, pravila dlia nakrytiia stola, sluzheniia za onym, poriadok vin, t.e. kakoe imenno, za kotorym kushan'em podaetsa i prakticheskoe rukovodstvo dlia kukhni*. St. Petersburg, 1852.

Raeff, Marc. *The Origins of the Russian Intelligentsia: The Eighteenth-Century Nobility.* New York: Harcourt Brace, 1966.

Randolph, John. *The House in the Garden: The Bakunin Family and the Romance of Russian Idealism.* Ithaca, NY: Cornell University Press, 2007.

Reitblat, A. I. "Anekdotika. Letopisets slukhov. (Nepublikovannye vospominaniia V. P. Burnasheva)." *Novoe literaturnoe obozrenie* 4 (1993): 162–77.

———. "Gogol' i Bulgarin: K istorii literaturnykh vzaimootnoshenii." In *Gogol: Materialy i issledovaniia*, edited by Iu. V. Mann, 82–98. Moscow: Nasledie, 1995.

———. *Kak Pushkin vyshel v genii: Istoriko-sotsiologicheskie ocherki o knizhnoi kul'ture pushkinskoi epokhi.* Moscow: Novoe literaturnoe obozrenie, 2001.

———, ed. "Pis'ma N. A. Grecha k F. V. Bulgarinu." *Novoe literaturnoe obozrenie* 40 (1999): 94–112; *Novoe literaturnoe obozrenie* 42 (2000): 264–317; *Novoe literaturnoe obozrenie* 89 (2008): 93–112.

———. "Pushkin kak Bulgarin: K voprosu o politicheskikh vzgliadakh i zhurnalistskoi deiatel'nosti F. V. Bulgarina i A. S. Pushkina." *Novoe literaturnoe obozrenie* 115 (2012): 170–98.

———. *Vidok Figliarin: Pis'ma i agenturnye zapiski F. V. Bulgarina v III otdelenie.* Moscow: Novoe literaturnoe obozrenie, 1998.

Reyfman, Irina. *How Russia Learned to Write: Literature and the Imperial Table of Ranks.* Madison: University of Wisconsin Press, 2016.

———. *Ritualized Violence Russian Style: The Duel in Russian Culture and Literature.* Stanford, CA: Stanford University Press, 1999.

Rostopchin, Fedor. *Mysli vslukh na krasnom kryl'tse.* Edited by O. A. Platonov. Moscow: Institut russkoi tsivilizatsii, 2014.

Saburov, I. V. "Zapiski penzenskogo zemledel'tsa o teorii i praktike sel'skogo khoziaistva." *Otechestvennye zapiski* 20 (January 1842): 1–24, sec. "Domovodstvo."

———. "Zapiski penzenskogo zemledel'tsa o teorii i praktike sel'skogo khoziaistva. Chast' pervaia. Okonchanie." *Otechestvennye zapiski* 21 (March 1842): 1–18, sec. "Domovodstvo."

———. "Zapiski penzenskogo zemledel'tsa o teorii i praktike sel'skogo khoziaistva. Chast' tret'ia i posledniaia." *Otechestvennye zapiski* 26 (January 1843): 1–24, sec. "Domovodstvo."

Salupere, Malle. "Bulgarin kak istorik. (K voprosu ob avtorstve *Rossii*)." *Novoe literaturnoe obozrenie* 40 (1999): 142–58.

Samarin, Aleksandr. *Tipografshchiki i knigochety: Ocherki po istorii knigi v Rossii vtoroi poloviny XVIII veka.* Moscow: Pashkov dom, 2013.

Schönle, Andreas. *The Ruler in the Garden: Politics and Landscape Design in Imperial Russia.* New York: Peter Lang, 2007.

Scott, H. M., ed. *The European Nobilities in the Seventeenth and Eighteenth Centuries.* New York: Longman, 1995.

Shovlin, John. *The Political Economy of Virtue: Luxury, Patriotism, and the Origins of the French Revolution.* Ithaca, NY: Cornell University Press, 2006.

Slovar' russkogo iazyka XI–XVII vv. Moscow: Nauka, 1976.

Smith, Alison K. *For the Common Good and Their Own Well-Being: Social Estates in Imperial Russia.* Oxford: Oxford University Press, 2014.

———. "National Cuisine and Nationalist Politics: V. F. Odoevsky and Dr. Puf, 1844–1845." *Kritika* 10, no. 2 (Spring 2009): 239–60.

———. *Recipes for Russia: Food and Nationhood under the Tsars.* DeKalb: Northern Illinois University Press, 2008.

Smith-Peter, Susan. "The Russian Provincial Newspaper and Its Public, 1788–1864." *The Carl Beck Papers in Russian and East European Studies*, no. 1908 (October 2008): 1–64.

Sokolov, Dmitrii. *Svetskii chelovek, ili rukovodstvo k poznaniiu pravil obshchezhitiia.* St. Petersburg: Tip. Sankt-Peterburgskogo gubernskogo pravleniia, 1847.

Steiner, Lina. *For Humanity's Sake: The Bildungsroman in Russian Culture.* Toronto, ON: University of Toronto Press, 2011.

Sumarokov, A. P. *Izbrannye proizvedeniia: Biblioteka poeta.* Leningrad: Sovetskii pisatel', 1957.

Tikhonravov, N. S. *Graf F. B. Rastopchin i literatura v 1812 godu.* St. Petersburg: Tipografiia Koroleva, 1854.

Todd, William Mills III. *Fiction and Society in the Age of Pushkin: Ideology, Institutions, and Narrative.* Cambridge, MA: Harvard University Press, 1986.

———. "The Ruse of the Russian Novel." In *The Novel*, edited by Franco Moretti, 401–29. Princeton, NJ: Princeton University Press, 2006.

Tolstoi, Lev. *Anna Karenina.* Translated by Richard Pevear and Larisa Volokhonsky. New York: Penguin Books, 2000.

———. *Polnoe sobranie sochinenii.* Edited by V. G. Chertkov et al. 90 vols. Moscow: Khudozhestvennaia literatura, 1928–1958.

Tomashevskii, Boris. *Pushkin.* Vol. 2, *Materialy k monografii.* Moscow: Akademiia nauk SSSR IRLI (Pushkinskii Dom), 1961.

Tseitlin, A. G. *I. A. Goncharov.* Moscow: Izdatel'stvo Akademii nauk SSSR, 1950.

Viazemskii, Petr. "Zhukovskii—Pushkin—o novoi Piitike Basen." *Moskovskii telegraf* 1, no. 4 (January 1825): 346–53.

Vol'pert, Larisa. *Pushkin v roli Pushkina: Tvorcheskaia igra po modeliam frantsuzskoi literatury.* Moscow: Iazyki russkoi kul'tury, 1998.

Walicki, Andrzej. *A History of Russian Thought: From the Enlightenment to Marxism.* Translated by Hilda Andrews-Rusiecka. Stanford, CA: Stanford University Press, 1979.

Warner, Michael. *Publics and Counterpublics.* New York: Zone Books, 2005.

Watt, Ian. *The Rise of the Novel: Studies in Defoe, Richardson, and Fielding.* Berkeley: University of California Press, 1957.

Whittaker, Cynthia Hyla. *Russian Monarchy: Eighteenth-Century Rulers and Writers in Political Dialogue.* DeKalb: Northern Illinois University Press, 2003.

Wirtschafter, Elise Kimerling. *The Play of Ideas in Russian Enlightenment Theater.* DeKalb: Northern Illinois University Press, 2003.

Wortman, Richard. *Scenarios of Power: Myth and Ceremony in Russian Monarchy from Peter the Great to the Abdication of Nicholas II.* Princeton, NJ: Princeton University Press, 2006.

Yeazell, Ruth Bernard. *Art of the Everyday: Dutch Painting and the Realist Novel.* Princeton, NJ: Princeton University Press, 2008.

[Zabolotskii-Desiatovskii, A. P.] "Zamechaniia na stat'iu g. Khomiakova v #6 'Moskvitianina' na 1842 god." *Otechestvennye zapiski* 25 (November 1842): 1–12, sec. "Domovodstvo."

"Zamechaniia o tom, kak izdaetsia 'Ekonom, khoziaistvennaia obshchepoleznaia biblioteka.'" *Otechestvennye zapiski* 38 (January 1845): 25–32, sec. "Smes'."

Zapadov, A. V. *Russkaia zhurnalistika XVIII veka.* Moscow: Nauka, 1964.

Index

A